Introducing Interdisciplinary Modules in Higher Education

This interdisciplinary book uses key examples and specific case studies from the 'Trailblazers' of Anglia Ruskin University, UK, to address the successes and challenges experienced during the creation, development, and running of breadth modules. It's been carefully written to support anyone looking to implement this innovative method into their own university setting.

With content informed by the United Nations Sustainable Development Goals, and using active learning pedagogies, interdisciplinary student teams work together to develop sustainable solutions, allowing for the growth of skills vital for enhancing student employability. The chapters are grounded in theory, making the discussions transferable to a wide readership interested in interdisciplinary approaches at the higher education level. The theoretical underpinnings of the discussions in each chapter will open up questions relating to contemporary issues such as diversity and representation, poverty and sustainability, artificial intelligence, and social justice.

This is a must-read text for anyone seeking to implement similar breadth modules at their institutions, or considering how to develop strategies that address whole institution questions such as sustainability and employability.

Simon Pratt-Adams is the Director of the Centre for Innovation in Higher Education and Associate Professor in Academic Development at Anglia Ruskin University, UK.

Mark Warnes is the Senior Research Fellow for the Centre for Innovation in Higher Education at Anglia Ruskin University, UK.

Elaine Brown is the Institutional Lead for Ruskin Modules at Anglia Ruskin University, UK.

This book is an exceptionally welcome and timely publication. Recognition of the importance of interdisciplinary approaches and practices is gaining traction across the globe, but there is still much to do in leading students to appreciate and engage with interdisciplinary perspectives. The leadership in this area at Anglia Ruskin University, outlined and described in this compilation, is essential reading for anyone involved in conceiving, designing, and implementing interdisciplinary programmes in Higher Education.

Ida Kemp, *Chair, Interdisciplinary Learning and Teaching Conferences, UK*

Expressed in a practical and research-informed manner, the case studies in this book are honest about barriers and practical needs when developing something so unusual in higher education as interdisciplinary modules focusing on co-operation, knowledge creation, sustainability, and employability, when usually students work in discipline-focused silos. This book showcases the development, actioning, and achievement of the Ruskin Modules, which offer new ways of looking at cooperative interdisciplinary knowledge creation and transformation beyond University study into future employment and social practice.

Gina Wisker, *Senior Lecturer, International Centre for Higher Education Management, University of Bath, UK*

Introducing Interdisciplinary Modules in Higher Education

Enhancing Sustainability and Student Employability

Edited by Simon Pratt-Adams, Mark Warnes, and Elaine Brown

LONDON AND NEW YORK

Cover image: v_alex via Getty Images

First published 2025
by Routledge
4 Park Square, Milton Park, Abingdon, Oxon OX14 4RN

and by Routledge
605 Third Avenue, New York, NY 10158

Routledge is an imprint of the Taylor & Francis Group, an informa business

British Library Cataloguing-in-Publication Data
A catalogue record for this book is available from the British Library

ISBN: 978-1-032-75572-4 (hbk)
ISBN: 978-1-032-75569-4 (pbk)
ISBN: 978-1-003-47459-3 (ebk)

DOI: 10.4324/9781003474593

Typeset in Galliard
by KnowledgeWorks Global Ltd.

Contents

Figures and tables

Figures

Tables

Contributors

Editors:

Simon Pratt-Adams

Dr Simon Pratt-Adams is the Director of the Centre for Innovation in Higher Education and Associate Professor in Academic Development. His research interests include Transformational Learning, Pedagogic Research, Urban Education, and Primary Education. Simon is a Principal Fellow of the Higher Education Academy.

Mark Warnes

Dr Mark Warnes is the Senior Research Fellow for the Centre for Innovation in Higher Education. His research interests include Pedagogic Research, Teaching Excellence, Reward and Recognition, and Assessment and Feedback. Mark is a Fellow of the Higher Education Academy and an Associate Teaching Fellow.

Elaine Brown

Elaine Brown is the Institutional Lead for Ruskin Modules and was responsible for leading their design and implementation. Elaine's research interests include the transformational impacts of interdisciplinary learning and teaching. Elaine co-chaired the 2023 Interdisciplinary Learning and Teaching Conference and chairs the Interdisciplinary Learning and Teaching Network. Elaine was awarded the Vice Chancellor's Award for Outstanding Leadership (Excellent Education) and is a University Teaching Fellow.

Chapter Authors:

Beatriz Acevedo

Dr Beatriz Acevedo is an artist, writer, and educator working as Associate Professor in Creative Education, a Principal Fellow of the Higher Education Academy, and a National Teaching Fellow (Advance HE, 2022). She is interested in the theme of beauty and education, in relation to creativity, sustainability, virtues, and civic education.

Roxana Anghel

Dr Roxana Anghel is a Senior Research Fellow and a Senior Lecturer in Social Work. Her pedagogical and research interests include environmental justice and community mobilisation, criticality in HE, sustainability in social work, and research for action and change. Roxana is a Fellow of the Higher Education Academy.

Linda Brown

Dr Linda Brown is the Academic Lead: Inclusive Learning Communities and Partnerships at ARU. She works collaboratively with students and colleagues to promote equality, accessibility, and inclusion. She is a Senior Fellow of the Higher Education Academy. Her research interests include curriculum design, inclusive practice, and student partnerships.

Julia Carr

Julia Carr is Senior Lecturer in Education, ARU's Community Organising Lead, and Co-Chair of the Civic Action Group overseeing development of ARU's Civic role. She is a Fellow of the Higher Education Academy and is interested in teaching and researching about social change making, community organising, and neurodiversity.

Deborah Caws

Deborah Caws is a Senior Lecturer Practitioner in Education. Her interests are in the way teachers across education sectors develop professional knowledge, and how opportunities for professional learning can enhance teaching practice. She is also a Senior Fellow of the Higher Education Academy.

Neil Dixon

Neil Dixon is an Academic Developer (Digital Learning) at ARU. He supports staff in using technology to improve student learning. He is the module leader for the interdisciplinary Ruskin module, *Is Technology Changing Us?* Neil has experience in instructional design and teaching and previously worked as a learning technologist and librarian.

George Evangelinos

Dr George Evangelinos is a Senior Learning Technologist for the Faculty of Health, Medicine and Social Care and a University Teaching Fellow. His research interests include learning analytics, learning design, digital transformation, digital literacy, and the use of Artificial Intelligence in higher education.

Himara Govinnage

Himara Govinnage is a BEng (Hons) Civil Engineering graduate who pursues infrastructure development and sustainable solutions. Her research interests include structural design and complex problem-solving skills. She actively applies theoretical knowledge to real-world challenges and aims to contribute positively to advancing the built environment.

Isobel Gowers

Dr Isobel Gowers is the Academic Lead: Active Inclusive Learning. Her research interests include active learning, interdisciplinary learning, and digital pedagogies. She is a Senior Fellow of the Higher Education Academy and a Fellow of the Staff and Educational Developers Association.

Elsa Lee

Dr Elsa Lee is a Senior Lecturer in Education. Her work centres on the intersection of education, environmental justice, place, and curriculum. Elsa has led externally funded research projects investigating these issues and this informs her teaching on undergraduate Education degrees, and her doctoral supervision. Elsa convenes the Environmental Sustainability Education Research network and is the executive editor of the National Association of Environmental Education (NAEE) journal.

Jess Maddocks

Jess Maddocks is a Community Organiser with Citizens UK and has worked on many local and national campaigns across the south of England. She is heavily involved with supporting schools, colleges, and universities to embed community organising in institutions to benefit their students, staff, and local communities.

Andrew Middleton

Professor Andrew Middleton is Professor of Active Learning at Anglia Ruskin University and a National Teaching Fellow. His research focuses on spaces for learning in higher education and the relationship of spatial affordances to academic, student, and graduate identities. He is currently researching and developing the concept of spatial fluency.

John Parkin

John Parkin is a Senior Lecturer Practitioner in Education. His research interests include continuous professional development, playful learning, and encouraging more men to become primary school teachers. John is a Senior Fellow of the Higher Education Academy.

Uwe Matthias Richter

Dr Uwe Matthias Richter is the Associate Professor: Digital Innovative Pedagogy at the Centre for Innovation in Higher Education. His research interests include pedagogical research, digital pedagogic innovation, technology-enhanced, online, and distance learning, and work-based learning. Uwe Matthias is a Senior Fellow of the Higher Education Academy and a University Teaching Fellow.

Victoria Tait

Victoria Tait is an Academic Developer with the Institute for Academic Development (IAD) at the University of Edinburgh. She has a background in sustainability education and, prior to joining the IAD, worked as a Lecturer

Practitioner in Education for Sustainability at ARU and led the embedding of sustainability in the Ruskin Modules.

Michael Wilby

Dr Michael Wilby is Associate Professor of Philosophy at ARU. His primary research interests revolve around the concept of 'common ground' and how it manifests in interpersonal perception, belief, and action.

Foreword

As Deputy Vice-Chancellor (Education) at Anglia Ruskin University (ARU), it gives me great pleasure to write the foreword for this book.

Written at a time of significant transformation in higher education, this book shows how Ruskin Modules challenge a traditional university curriculum design that has long focused on discipline-based subjects. Our innovative work has been recognised in the form of higher education awards and accolades. In 2023, Times Higher Education named ARU University of the Year, and the Office for Students rated ARU as Gold in the Teaching Excellence Framework, and both awards specifically mention Ruskin Modules in the citations. Similarly, ARU was awarded the Next Generation Learning and Skills prize at the Green Gown Awards 2023 recognising the Ruskin Module emphasis on education for sustainability.

Ruskin Modules bring together groups of students from disparate disciplines to interact, work collaboratively, and design shared solutions to 'wicked problems'. By promoting peer learning and the co-creation of knowledge, Ruskin Modules provide an innovative approach to curriculum design that encourages problem-solving, critical thinking, and an awareness of global challenges, all of which equip students with essential skills for the workplace.

As interdisciplinary breadth modules with a curriculum incorporating sustainability and focused on graduate employability, Ruskin Modules clearly place demands on both teachers and students to think, teach, and learn in different ways. I am proud to say that ARU has shown that interdisciplinary learning is effective. This book showcases the implementation of interdisciplinary learning modules with large cohorts of students since its introduction in the 2020/21 academic year.

Our institutional approach to the development and delivery of Ruskin Modules, from the very start, has been inspired by our commitment to partnership working. We developed Ruskin Modules over a period of two years through a process involving students, academics, professional services staff, and both staff and student unions from across the ARU community. Delivered online, compulsory (at Level 5), credit-bearing Ruskin Modules enable students across ARU's campuses to work together to develop innovative thinking and problem-solving skills that the jobs of the future demand. While there may not be a magic formula for interdisciplinary learning, Ruskin Modules are a unique take on the subject, and this book captures ARU's journey.

Ruskin Module leaders are collectively known as 'Trailblazers', some of whom, keen to explore their modules further, formed the Ruskin Module Research Community and are the authors of the case studies in Part II of the book. The editors worked with the authors to help them describe, in their own voices, their experiences of designing and delivering Ruskin Modules. The book offers an edited collection of case studies which disseminates the wealth of scholarship and practice in interdisciplinary learning that ARU has pioneered for several years. Each chapter is rigorously researched, theorised, and structured to clearly grasp a specific element of Ruskin Modules. The extensive literature base in each chapter helps to understand at multiple levels.

The 16 case study authors are drawn from a variety of subject backgrounds and discipline areas and include academic and professional services colleagues, a student, and a community organiser. What they have in common is a desire to improve student engagement, experience, outcomes, and employability through approaches to learning and teaching that work in practice and are sustainable over time and across contexts. The editors have a deep knowledge of educational theories and methods and experience managing and researching Ruskin Modules. The editors and authors have all been extensively involved in working on Ruskin Modules, either as course or module leaders or in the continual evaluation of the impact of Ruskin Modules on student satisfaction and performance. As Deputy Vice-Chancellor, I have seen first-hand how this experience is implemented through ARU's commitment to enhancing teaching and learning. Furthermore, I am delighted that ARU's Centre for Innovation in Higher Education has led the production of this text during this crucial period of the development of pedagogical research across ARU.

This book makes an authoritative and constructive contribution to the field of interdisciplinary learning in higher education, which corresponds closely with students' needs, helping them to build confidence, tackle challenges during their studies, and prepare them for future careers.

This book will be of interest and a significant resource for all interested in interdisciplinary and sustainable learning and teaching. Ruskin Modules are a truly innovative, unique, and worthwhile element to studying at university. By providing valuable insights and practical guidance, I am sure that the examples in this book will inspire all those working in higher education who want to develop and implement interdisciplinarity breadth modules.

Professor Aletta Norval

Preface

This book is about interdisciplinary breadth modules at Anglia Ruskin University (ARU). Introduced in the 2020/21 academic year, Ruskin Modules (RM) are compulsory for all Level 5 (i.e., second year) undergraduate students and are based on three pillars of Interdisciplinarity, Sustainability, and Employability.

RMs are consciously interdisciplinary and unrelated to any academic subject or discipline. RMs draw focus from the United Nations Sustainable Development Goals, and module leaders embed sustainability in content, delivery, and assessment. Students learn soft skills, such as problem-solving and teamwork, required by employers beyond subject knowledge. The result is that students from all faculties and schools bring their disciplinary knowledge to the RM where it is synthesised to produce novel solutions to 'wicked problems'.

Part I of this book opens with an introduction to the core concepts of interdisciplinarity and transformative education and a detailed history of the creation of RMs. Part II contains case studies by module leaders of their experiences of designing and delivering their RMs. These case studies were written after the first delivery of RMs, and each chapter is a personal account and consequently written in the authors' own voice. Some case studies are personal reflections, while others are academic accounts, but all are authentic descriptions of the journey of discovery taken by each RM leader.

Each chapter of the book can be read in isolation, and subsequently we make no apologies for the repetition of terms, definitions, references, and explanations of acronyms, as this is inevitable if chapters are read out of sequence.

The editors all work in Anglia Learning & Teaching (AL&T), the learning, teaching, and assessment development unit at Anglia Ruskin University. Simon is the Director of the Centre for Innovation in Higher Education (CIHE), whose mission includes development of innovative interdisciplinary pedagogies. Mark is the Senior Research Fellow for AL&T and CIHE and managed the review process for this book. Elaine is the Institutional Lead for Ruskin Modules and was responsible for overseeing their design and implementation.

Acknowledgements

We would like to thank Professor Aletta Norval (Deputy Vice Chancellor, Education) for introducing Ruskin Modules and for driving their implementation, and for providing the Foreword to this book.

We would also like to thank all the Ruskin Module leaders for their hard work, dedication, resilience, and passion in bringing this scheme to fruition.

List of Abbreviations

ACF	Active Curriculum Framework
AI	Artificial Intelligence
AIS	Association of Interdisciplinary Studies
AL&T	Anglia Learning & Teaching
ARU	Anglia Ruskin University
ASQC	Academic Standards and Quality Committee
AY	Academic Year
CATE	Collaborative Award for Teaching Excellence
CDI	Course Design Intensive
CIHE	Centre for Innovation in Higher Education
CoP	Community of Practice
CPD	Continuing Professional Development
DVC	Deputy Vice Chancellor
EfS	Education for Sustainability
EHRC	Equality and Human Rights Commission
ESD	Education for Sustainable Development
HE	Higher Education
HEA	Higher Education Academy
HECoS	Higher Education Classification of Subjects
HEI	Higher Education Institute
HESA	Higher Education Statistics Agency
IATL	Institute for Advanced Teaching and Learning
ILRM	Institutional Lead for Ruskin Modules
IMT	Interdisciplinary Metacognitive Thinking
JACS	Joint Academic Coding System
LMS	Learning Management System
LO	Learning Outcome
MDF	Module Definition Form
MS	Microsoft
OECD	Organisation for Economic Cooperation and Development
OfS	Office for Students

PAL	Peer-Assisted Learning
PBL	Project-Based Learning
PGCertHE	Postgraduate Certificate in Higher Education
PSRB	Professional, Statutory and Regulatory Bodies
REF	Research Excellence Framework
RES	Race Equality Strategy (Strategy for Advancing Race Equality at ARU)
RESA	Race Equality Student Advocates
RM	Ruskin Module
RML	Ruskin Module Leader
RMOS	Ruskin Module Open Studios
SALT	Student Associate Learning and Teaching
SDGs	Sustainable Development Goals
SU	Students' Union
TEF	Teaching Excellence Framework
TL	Transformative Learning
TP	Transformative Pedagogy
UK	United Kingdom
UKPSF	UK Professional Standards Framework
UKRI	UK Research and Innovation
UN	United Nations
UN DESA	United Nations Department of Economic and Social Affairs
UNESCO	United Nations Educational, Scientific and Cultural Organization
USA	United States of America
VLE	Virtual Learning Environment
WEF	World Economic Forum
WHO	World Health Organisation
ZPD	Zone of Proximal Development

Part I

Introduction and Context

Chapter 1

Introduction

*Simon Pratt-Adams, Mark Warnes, and
Elaine Brown*

Introduction and Context

This book is aimed at those involved in teaching or supporting learning in Higher Education (HE). It is also aimed at those who influence what goes on in HE, and we hope that the book will inspire and encourage awareness of the unique and distinctive qualities and importance of interdisciplinary breadth modules.

In this book, we describe Anglia Ruskin University's (ARU) Ruskin Modules (RMs), and how they rest on three pillars of interdisciplinarity, sustainability, and employability. We introduce the RM leaders, known as Trailblazers, and describe how through informal CPD support meetings, they spontaneously created a Community of Practice (Lave & Wenger, 1991). In addition, we explore the relevance of the United Nations Sustainability Development Goals (UN SDGs) (UN DESA, 2023), and wicked problems (Rittel & Webber, 1973) to RMs.

ARU provided students with the following definitions of the central topics:

Interdisciplinarity is integral to RMs – Ruskin modules combine your knowledge and skills with those from other courses that appear (at first) to be unrelated; discovering connections across different courses at ARU will better prepare you for a world of change, and at the same time create innovative, new solutions to complex challenges (ARU, 2021a).

Sustainability is integral to RMs – Business 'as usual' is destroying the planet. The way many countries consume the earth's natural resources is unsustainable. Inequality within many countries is growing. We need to think in new and creative ways to tackle these issues (ARU, 2021b).

Employability is integral to RMs – The nature of work and meaningful activity is changing. Critical thinking, creativity, problem-solving & flexibility are some of the skills we need to thrive. Ruskin modules are an opportunity to rehearse and amplify these skills (ARU, 2021c).

Wicked Problems – Ruskin modules bring together students from different courses to tackle 'wicked' challenges. With no single answer, wicked

DOI: 10.4324/9781003474593-2

challenges enable students to explore solutions outside their discipline and offer the opportunity to take different perspectives, develop innovative thinking, and creative problem-solving skills that the jobs of the future demand (ARU, 2021d).

Although these topics are common to all chapters (although some authors provide their own definitions), what separates them are the unique experiences of those members of staff (both academic and Professional Services) who took a leap of faith and embraced this bold, innovative initiative.

Interdisciplinary breadth modules have existed, in one form or another, for several years (French, 2015; Hennessy et al., 2010). Several Australian universities offer them (Krohn, 2016; Osborne & Dibben, 2017) and, recently, a smattering of UK universities have joined them (Power & Handley, 2019). However, the version developed and delivered at ARU is unique in many ways.

Introduced in the 2020/2021 academic year, RMs were compulsory for *all* Level 5 (second year) undergraduates (except when constrained by Professional, Statutory and Regulatory Body [PSRB] requirements). To overcome potential timetabling conflicts, all RMs were delivered online, simultaneously, on Wednesday mornings (although this proved challenging for students retaking modules during their third year).

Interdisciplinary Breadth Modules

It is essential to understand interdisciplinary breadth modules in the context of the current globalised landscape of HE. The global HE sector is evolving in this transformative and turbulent era (Garretson et al., 2021; Judijanto et al., 2024), and keeping pace with changing trends and advancements is necessary when redesigning curricula to ensure a clear focus. Interdisciplinarity has been interwoven into the strategic plans of some UK universities and the agendas of research councils and it is anticipated that this will grow (Evis, 2022). Focusing on successful curriculum innovation and designing, developing, and delivering interdisciplinary teaching and learning are necessary steps towards dynamic and strategic change (Blackmore & Kandiko, 2012; Turner et al., 2022). Central to this process are the people who desire change, their reasons for seeking it, and the leaders of such efforts (Thomas et al., 2021).

To ensure students receive the best possible education, HE providers need to explore the main drivers, barriers, and trends in HE interdisciplinary learning (Middleton et al., 2021; Turner et al., 2022). Several pedagogical approaches can be used for interdisciplinary learning, including project-based, problem-based, and team-based learning (Brassler & Dettmers, 2017; Telléus et al., 2023; Warr & West, 2020). However, successful and effective interdisciplinary learning requires a collaborative and supportive effort (Evis, 2022) from all stakeholders to challenge the status quo and provide transformative student learning experiences (Adagale, 2015; Brown et al., 2015; Turner et al., 2022).

Implementing interdisciplinary approaches can often be challenging due to their complex nature, which includes the lack of a coherent and standardised curriculum compared with a disciplinary-based curriculum. Additionally, assessing interdisciplinary learning outcomes (LOs) can be problematic due to the risk of disciplinary bias and dominance (Gantogtokh & Quinlan, 2017; Lyall et al., 2015; Turner et al., 2022). As interdisciplinary approaches draw upon multiple fields of study, 'the construction of appropriate bridges between the "great divide" [between individual disciplines]' (Shearer, 2007, p. 18) can be challenging to cover all the necessary aspects.

Notwithstanding these challenges, interdisciplinary learning has become an increasingly popular and evolving field in HE that requires careful planning, coordination, and evaluation (Shearer, 2007; Yang, 2009). For academic achievement and professional success, interdisciplinary learning involves integrating knowledge, skills, and perspectives from different fields of study to engage students in solving complex problems and developing innovative solutions. One way to address these challenges is to establish a university-wide interdisciplinary programme (Anakin et al., 2018; Brown & Acevedo, 2022) that integrates multiple fields of study to help students understand complex issues and develop assessment tools that assess interdisciplinary LOs.

Ruskin Modules

Students could choose from the 19 modules on offer, and some were more popular than others. Those students who, for whatever reason, did not choose a module were allocated to one.

1 AI and the Future: A threat to humanity?
2 To be or not be enterprising?
3 Is technology changing us?
4 Do we need humans as teachers?
5 How would you respond in a crisis situation?
6 Do I matter?
7 What's the real price tag on fashion?
8 What does social justice in the twenty-first century mean?
9 Does language affect the way I think?
10 Climate Justice and Social Inequality: Could you be an agent for change?
11 Can we design a better future?
12 How do you disagree with the majority view and still be respected?
13 Work: What is it good for?
14 Do numbers lie?
15 Who, me!!! Make a difference in my community?
16 Performing activism: How can we use our bodies for change?

17 Where do you belong in this city?
18 Why all the fuss over hair?
19 Digital accessibility: Why should it matter to you?

Posing the module titles as questions emphasised their exploratory nature and illustrated that RMs would not provide any simple answers. Instead, students would have to operate in interdisciplinary teams to forge a sustainable solution to a wicked problem that best met the interests of a range of stakeholders. Modules were designed to help students develop the skills demanded by industry, for a fast changing, uncertain future including critical thinking, teamworking skills, information literacy, digital literacy, communication skills, problem-solving and decision-making skills, and wide general knowledge, and thus enhance their employability in the Fourth Industrial Revolution (Coonan & Pratt-Adams, 2018; World Economic Forum (WEF), 2016, 2020).

This book is divided into two parts: *Part 1: Introduction and Context*, which includes this introductory chapter; and *Part II: Case Studies*, which contains reflections from 16 module tutors from the first iteration of the RM scheme. Each case study closes with a series of discussion points which we hope will encourage readers to take forward into their own practice.

Part I: Introduction and Context

In *Chapter 2: Disciplinarities*, Mark Warnes, Uwe Richter, and Elaine Brown explore a range of 'disciplinarities', including monodisciplinarity, crossdisciplinarity, multidisciplinarity, interdisciplinarity, and transdisciplinarity, and the model of interdisciplinarity which ARU adopted as one of the three pillars upon which RMs are based.

A central tenet of RMs is that they should, at least, attempt to be transformative. Students should be different somehow by the end of the module, no matter how small the change. It is for this reason that Elsa Lee, Simon Pratt-Adams, and Mark Warnes include *Chapter 3: Transformative Education*.

In *Chapter 4: Introduction to Ruskin Modules*, Elaine Brown, Institutional Lead for Ruskin Modules, describes the genesis of the RM scheme, through the design and building of a curriculum fit for the future, to implementation of RMs. A lengthy development period was necessary to ensure that all interested parties had the opportunity to provide their input, adjust and adapt internal policies and regulations, develop, and deliver CPD, create content, and finally roll out the modules. There was no pilot scheme: this was it!

Finally, in *Chapter 5: Creativity and Design for Innovative Interdisciplinary Education*, Beatriz Acevedo and Andrew Middleton describe the Ruskin Module Open Studios CPD workshops, in which activities were based on processes usually associated with the creative arts. Module leaders were encouraged to be innovative and imaginative and to explore new ways of teaching and learning that differed from a traditional lecture/seminar structure.

Part II: Case Studies

In *Chapter 6: To Team or Not to Team*, Uwe Richter discusses his module, *Where do you belong in this city?* Focused on ARU's two main campuses, Cambridge and Chelmsford, this module invited students to develop a sustainable, interdisciplinary solution to an urban planning wicked problem.

In *Chapter 7: A Ruskin Module from Idea to Implementation*, Isobel Gowers reflects on her journey to develop her RM, *Digital Accessibility: Why should it matter to you?* Isobel tackles the complex topic of digital accessibility and how we are all affected by this multifaceted issue.

In *Chapter 8: Blurred and En-Tangled Boundaries: A Case for Interdisciplinarity and Diversification*, Linda Brown views the subject of Hair through the lenses of equality, diversity, and inclusion and asks, *Why all the fuss over hair?*

In *Chapter 9: Undergraduate Learners as Emerging Agents of Sustainability and Environmental Justice*, the interdisciplinary team of Roxana Anghel and Victoria Tait discuss how they converted undergraduate learners into agents of change for climate and environmental justice via their RM, *Climate Justice and Social Inequality: Could you be an agent for change?*

In *Chapter 10: Ruskin Module and Community Organising*, Julia Carr and Jess Maddocks of Citizens UK (the only non-ARU contributor) discuss their transdisciplinary RM about community organising, including the involvement of US students.

Chapter 11: Developing Professional Learning through an Interdisciplinary Community of Practice contains John Parkin and Deborah Caws' history of the spontaneous creation of a Community of Practice (Lave & Wenger, 1991) centred around weekly RM support sessions.

In *Chapter 12: The Humanistic Temperament*, Michael Wilby offers a philosophical exploration of his RM, *AI and the Future*, and asks students to consider whether AI poses a threat to humanity.

In Chapter 13: Interdisciplinary Learning Design, the final case study, George Evangelinos and Neil Dixon incorporate contributions from their student Himara Govinnage to illustrate the methods they employed to embed interdisciplinarity into their RM, *Is Technology Changing Us?*

Conclusion

In the concluding chapter, we bring together key themes and issues discussed in previous chapters. We also offer some concluding remarks regarding the central concerns of the RM scheme. In this chapter, we consider both the opportunities and challenges that interdisciplinary breadth modules present and offer some reflections about the wider implications of pedagogic practices presented in the book.

We hope you enjoy reading this book and that you find inspiration from the case studies shared by the authors.

References

Adagale, A. S. (2015). Curriculum development in higher education. *International Journal of Applied Research, 1*(11), 602–605. Retrieved 5 July 2024, from https://www.allresearchjournal.com/archives/?year=2015&vol=1&issue=11&part=I&ArticleId=958

Anakin, M., Spronken-Smith, R., Healey, M., & Vajoczki, S. (2018). The contextual nature of university-wide curriculum change. *International Journal for Academic Development, 23*(3), 206–218. https://doi.org/10.1080/1360144x.2017.1385464

Anglia Ruskin University (ARU) (2021a). *Interdisciplinarity is integral to Ruskin modules.* Retrieved 5 July 2024, from https://canvas.anglia.ac.uk/courses/21834/pages/interdisciplinarity

Anglia Ruskin University (ARU) (2021b). *Sustainability is integral to Ruskin modules.* Retrieved 5 July 2024, from https://canvas.anglia.ac.uk/courses/21834/pages/sustainability

Anglia Ruskin University (ARU) (2021c). *Employability is integral to Ruskin modules.* Retrieved 5 July 2024, from https://canvas.anglia.ac.uk/courses/21834/pages/employability-and-entrepreneurship

Anglia Ruskin University (ARU) (2021d). *Wicked challenges.* Retrieved 5 July 2024, from https://aru.ac.uk/student-life/opportunities-at-aru/ruskin-modules

Blackmore, P., & Kandiko, C. (Eds.) (2012). *Strategic curriculum change in universities: Global trends.* Routledge.

Brassler, M., & Dettmers, J. (2017). How to enhance interdisciplinary competence – Interdisciplinary problem-based learning versus interdisciplinary project-based learning, *Interdisciplinary Journal of Problem-Based Learning, 11*(2). https://doi.org/10.7771/1541-5015.1686

Brown, E., & Acevedo, B. (2022). Interdisciplinary design for ambiguity: Work in a wicked world. In S. Norton, and A. Penaluna (Eds.), *3 Es for wicked problems: Employability, enterprise, and entrepreneurship: Solving wicked problems.* Advance HE (pp. 16–20). Retrieved 5 July 2024, from https://documents.advance-he.ac.uk/download/file/document/10288?_ga=2.224590746.1657932763.1713965132-1110606625.1713965132

Brown, M. K., Ralston, P. A., Baumgartner, K. B., & Schreck, M. A. (2015). Creating a supportive teaching culture in the research university context: Strategic partnering and interdisciplinary collaboration between a teaching center and academic units. *To Improve the Academy: A Journal of Academic Development, 34*(1–2), 234–269. https://doi.org/10.3998/tia.17063888.0034.102

Coonan, E., & Pratt-Adams, S. (2018). Building higher education fit for the future: How higher education institutions are responding to the Industrial Strategy. Advance HE/HEA. Retrieved 5 July 2024, from https://www.advance-he.ac.uk/sites/default/files/2019-05/Building-HE-Curricula-Fit-For-The-Future.pdf

Evis, L. H. (2022). A critical appraisal of interdisciplinary research and education in British Higher Education Institutions: A path forward? *Arts and Humanities in Higher Education, 21*(2), 119–138. https://doi.org/10.1177/14740222211026251

French, S. (2015). The benefits and challenges of modular higher education curricula. *Issues and ideas paper.* Melbourne Centre for the Study of Higher Education. Retrieved 5 July 2024, from https://melbourne-cshe.unimelb.edu.au/__data/assets/pdf_file/0006/2774391/Benefits_Challenges_Modular_Higher_Ed_Curricula_SFrench_v3-green-2.pdf

Gantogtokh, O., & Quinlan, K. M. (2017). Challenges of designing interdisciplinary postgraduate curricula: Case studies of interdisciplinary master's programmes at a research-intensive UK university. *Teaching in Higher Education, 22*(5), 569–586. https://doi.org/10.1080/13562517.2016.1273211

Garretson, C. J., McCormack, T. J., Waller, R. E., Lemoine, P. A., & Richardson, M. D. (2021). The impact of turbulence on global higher education during a pandemic. *International Journal of Innovative Research and Advanced Studies*, 8(1), 30–33. Retrieved 5 July 2024, from https://www.ijiras.com/2021/Vol_8-Issue_1/paper_7.pdf

Hennessy, E., Hernandez, R., Kieran, P., & MacLoughlin, H. (2010). Teaching and learning across disciplines: Student and staff experiences in a newly modularised system. *Teaching in Higher Education*, 15(6), 675–689. https://doi.org/10.1080/13562517.2010.507301

Judijanto, L., Triolita, N., Machfiroh, R., Yunanto, M. K., & Siminto, S. (2024). Navigating the landscape of higher education in the 21st century: Challenges, innovations, and future perspectives. *International Journal of Teaching and Learning*, 2(1), 297–312. Retrieved 5 July 2024, from https://injotel.org/index.php/12/article/download/66/94

Krohn, A. L. (2016). Breadth: The interdisciplinary experiment: An investigation of students' expectations of The University of Melbourne's breadth subjects and the 'Melbourne Model' [Master's degree thesis]. The University of Melbourne. Retrieved 5 July 2024, from https://minerva-access.unimelb.edu.au/bitstreams/68b14f57-0618-52f2-bd18-b822a53b826e/download

Lave, J., & Wenger, E. (1991). *Situated learning: Legitimate peripheral participation*. Cambridge University Press.

Lyall, C., Meagher, L., Bandola, J., & Kettle, A. (2015). *Interdisciplinary provision in higher education: Current and future challenges*. Advance HE. Retrieved 5 July 2024, from: https://www.advance-he.ac.uk/knowledge-hub/interdisciplinary-provision-higher-education-current-and-future-challenges

McCune, V., Tauritz, R., Boyd, S., Cross, A., Higgins, P., & Scoles, J. (2023). Teaching wicked problems in higher education: Ways of thinking and practising. *Teaching in Higher Education*, 28(7), 1518–1533. https://doi.org/10.1080/13562517.2021.1911986

Middleton, A., Pratt-Adams, S., & Priddle, J. (2021). Active, inclusive and immersive: Using course design intensives with course teams to rethink the curriculum across an institution. *Educational Developments*, 22(1), 9–13. Retrieved 5 July 2024, from https://www.seda.ac.uk/wp-content/uploads/2022/01/Ed-Devs-22.1.pdf

Osborne, J., & Dibben, M. (2017). 'Over the Edge of the Wild': Lessons of discovery through developing transdisciplinary (breadth) units in blended courses. *Journal of Open, Flexible and Distance Learning*, 21(1), 25–34. Retrieved 5 July 2024, from https://www.learntechlib.org/p/180234/

Power, E. J., & Handley, J. (2019). A best-practice model for integrating interdisciplinarity into the higher education student experience. *Studies in Higher Education*, 44(3), 554–570. https://doi.org/10.1080/03075079.2017.1389876

Rittel, H. W., & Webber, M. M. (1973). Dilemmas in a general theory of planning. *Policy Sciences*, 4(2), 155–169. https://doi.org/10.1007/BF01405730

Shearer, C. (2007). Implementing a new interdisciplinary module: The challenges and the benefits of working across disciplines. *Practice and Evidence of Scholarship of Teaching and Learning in Higher Education*, 2(1), 2–20. Retrieved 5 July 2024, from https://www.pestlhe.org/index.php/pestlhe/article/view/15/23

Telléus, P. K., Bertel, L. B., Velmurugan, G., & Kofoed, L. B. (2023). Problems, complexity and interdisciplinarity. In A. Kolmos and T. Ryberg (Eds.), *PBL in a digital age* (pp. 53–67). Aalborg Universitetsforlag. Retrieved 5 July 2024, from https://vbn.aau.dk/ws/portalfiles/portal/527963500/PBL_in_a_Digital_Age_ONLINE.pdf

Thomas, L., Pratt-Adams, S., & Warnes, M. (2021). An evaluation of the active curriculum framework, course design intensives, and the Ruskin modules (Internal Report). Anglia Ruskin University.

Turner, R., Cotton, D., Morrison, D., & Kneale, P. (2022). Embedding interdisciplinary learning into the first-year undergraduate curriculum: Drivers and barriers in a cross-institutional enhancement project. *Teaching in Higher Education, 29*(4), 1092–1108. https://doi.org/10.1080/13562517.2022.2056834

United Nations Department of Economic and Social Affairs (UN DESA) (2023). *Sustainable Development: The 17 Goals.* Retrieved 5 July 2024, from https://sdgs.un.org/goals

Warr, M., & West, R. E. (2020). Bridging academic disciplines with interdisciplinary project-based learning: Challenges and opportunities. *The Interdisciplinary Journal of Problem-Based Learning, 14*(1). https://doi.org/10.14434/ijpbl.v14i1.28590

World Economic Forum (WEF) (2016). *The future of jobs: Employment, skills and workforce strategy for the Fourth Industrial Revolution.* Retrieved 5 July 2024, from https://www3.weforum.org/docs/WEF_Future_of_Jobs.pdf

World Economic Forum (WEF) (2020). *The future of jobs report 2020.* Retrieved 5 July 2024, from https://www.weforum.org/reports/the-future-of-jobs-report-2020/in-full/infographics-e4e69e4de7

Yang, M. (2009). Making interdisciplinary subjects relevant to students: An interdisciplinary approach. *Teaching in Higher Education, 14*(6), 597–606. https://doi.org/10.1080/13562510903315019

Chapter 2

Disciplinarities

Mark Warnes, Uwe Richter, and Elaine Brown

Introduction

Ruskin Modules (RMs) stand on three pillars: sustainability, employability, and interdisciplinarity. Interdisciplinarity is one of a group of 'disciplinarities', each with often overlapping and conflicting definitions. Stock and Burton (2011, p. 1094), for example, criticise 'an unnecessarily varied nomenclature' noting how,

> under the umbrella of integrated research an inexhaustive list of terminologies is used to define the concept, including: collaborative, integral, integrated, complementary, combined, participatory, trans-epistemic, system-oriented, trans-professional, comprehensive, problem oriented, cross-boundary, holistic, multidisciplinary, crossdisciplinary, interdisciplinary, and transdisciplinary.

In a similar vein, Graff (2016, p. 775) highlights that 'Interdisciplinarity is among the most talked about but most misunderstood topics in education on all levels today' and that authors 'seldom … seek common terms; typically, they mean very different approaches when they refer to interdisciplinarity'. Additionally, interdisciplinarity is 'closely linked with the concept of "integrative" learning, a pedagogical approach whose focus is on helping students make sense of knowledge across curricula' (Ashby & Exter, 2019, p. 203).

In an academic context, discipline is one of many terms referring to a field or area of study, a branch of knowledge, or a subject, and these terms are frequently used interchangeably. In the UK, for example, the Higher Education Statistics Agency (HESA) (2024a, para. 1) notes that 'subjects are persistent areas or branches of knowledge or learning that are studied in higher education'. In essence, therefore, a discipline is a bounded academic field usually studied at a university, which, according to Tress et al. (2005, p. 484 [original emphasis]), '[a] *discipline* has its own coherent set of tools, methods, procedures, concepts and theories'.

DOI: 10.4324/9781003474593-3

In this chapter, we explore definitions of the four disciplinarities by Stock and Burton (2011) and conclude with the Anglia Ruskin University (ARU) description of interdisciplinarity for RMs.

Monodisciplinarity

Also known as 'unidisciplinarity' (Săvoiu et al., 2014, p. 711), monodisciplinarity, as the name suggests, refers to a single discipline, and, as Tress et al. (2005, p. 483 [original emphasis]) note, '*disciplinary* research [refers to] projects that take place within the boundaries of currently recognized academic disciplines, while fully appreciating the artificial nature of these bounds and the fact that they are dynamic'. Furthermore, monodisciplinary 'research activity is oriented towards one specific goal, looking for an answer to a specific question' (Tress et al., 2005, p. 483), and is the primary means by which the Higher Education (HE) sector is designated into discrete cognate areas.

However, the designation of individual subjects remains loosely defined. In the UK, HESA (2024a, para. 1) introduced a 'new subject coding system – the Higher Education Classification of Subjects (HECoS) … from 2019/20' which replaced the Joint Academic Coding System (JACS). While JACS listed 165 principal subjects contained within 19 subject areas (HESA, 2024b), the full HECoS subject list has 1,092 entries.

HE reward and recognition schemes such as the Research Excellence Framework (REF) and the Teaching Excellence Framework (TEF) primarily focus on single disciplines. The REF, for instance, assesses HEI research output across 34 monodisciplinary Units of Assessment (UK Research and Innovation (UKRI), 2023). Similarly, subject-level TEF assesses teaching excellence across 35 monodisciplinary units (Office for Students [OfS], 2024). However, Advance HE (2020, para. 1) recognises mixed-disciplinary endeavours through the Collaborative Award for Teaching Excellence (CATE), which

> recognises and rewards collaborative work that has had a demonstrable impact on teaching and learning. Introduced in 2016, the scheme highlights the key role of teamwork in higher education.

The UK HE sector focuses on monodisciplinary studies, and the plethora of subject-specific academic publications reflects this. Nevertheless, the bounded nature of monodisciplinarity has limited capacity to address certain issues, including 'wicked problems' (Rittel & Webber, 1973), which although technically unsolvable, definitely cannot be resolved from a monodisciplinary perspective and must be addressed using a range of disciplinary lenses.

Pluridisciplinarity

Ilter (2015) refers to 'monodisciplinary versus pluridisciplinary research', using the term pluridisciplinarity to refer collectively to cross-, trans-, multi, and interdisciplinarity. In an example of conflicting definitions, O'Rourke et al. (2016, p. 63) 'use "cross-disciplinary" as a cover term for both interdisciplinary and transdisciplinary activity'. Similarly, Evely et al. (2010, p. 442) note that

> A number of different terms can be used to indicate different degrees of integration of types of knowledge, disciplinary bases or stakeholder involvement. Within the academic literature, this knowledge integration is commonly referred to as multidisciplinary, interdisciplinary or transdisciplinary approaches. Cross-disciplinarity is used as an overarching term that encompasses these different forms.

Crossdisciplinarity

Ashby and Exter (2019, p. 203) note that 'the cross-disciplinary curriculum typically utilizes the borrowing of tools, ideas, or theories, mostly from neighboring fields, in order to explain specific phenomena'. Taking this further, Evely et al. (2010, p. 442) suggest that

> a crossdisciplinary research approach is likely to assist in understanding the complex dynamics of many key environmental problems in a socioecological context. Such research can: (1) provide new perspectives on complex, dynamic problems; (2) provide a more holistic view of a problem that is better suited to targeting the underlying drivers and processes…; (3) assist in the selection of more appropriate research methodologies; (4) provide greater flexibility in research approach and implementation; and (5) facilitate production of new information and insights that would not have been achieved by single disciplinary or epistemological perspectives alone.

Dellaportas et al. (2020, p. 2) note that the 'benefits of crossdisciplinary research come from being attentive to ideas and processes developed in diverse fields in an endeavour to find new meaning using fresh perspectives'.

Multidisciplinarity

Stock and Burton (2011, p. 1095) note that

> Multidisciplinarity is characterized within the literature as the least integrative form of integrated research – yet, equally, it is arguably the most attainable. Multidisciplinarity features several academic disciplines in a thematically based investigation with multiple goals … While researchers aim

to share knowledge and compare results from the studies there is no attempt to cross boundaries or generate new integrative knowledge. Each member is able to contribute a professional perspective on the issue. Thus the advantage of this approach is that, while the research approaches are disciplinary, the different perspectives on the issue can be gathered into one report for assessment.

Tress et al. (2005, p. 485 [original emphasis]):

suggest applying the term *multidisciplinarity* to research efforts of different academic disciplines that relate to a shared goal, but with multiple disciplinary objectives. Participants exchange knowledge, but they do not aim to cross subject boundaries in order to create new integrative knowledge and theory. The research process progresses as parallel disciplinary efforts without integration.

Ashby and Exter (2019, p. 203) define multidisciplinary teaching as 'integration of many disciplines, although theories and approaches introduced continue to be tied to specific disciplines', therefore emphasising the lack of synthesis across disciplines.

Interdisciplinarity

Tress et al. (2005, pp. 485–486) define interdisciplinarity 'as involving several unrelated academic disciplines in a way that forces them to cross subject boundaries. The concerned disciplines integrate disciplinary knowledge to create new knowledge and theory and achieve a common research goal'. Similarly, Stock and Burton (2011, p. 1096) describe how 'interdisciplinary studies focus on addressing specific "real world" system problems and, as a result, the research process forces participants (from a variety of unrelated disciplines) to cross boundaries to create new knowledge'.

In relation to integrated learning or programmes, Ashby and Exter (2019, p. 203) define interdisciplinarity as a 'subset of such integrative learning where the focus is on the synthesis of disciplines'. Therefore, central to interdisciplinarity is the production of new knowledge through the synthesis of several disparate disciplinary perspectives.

Transdisciplinarity

For Săvoiu et al. (2014, p. 713), transdisciplinarity

appears between disciplines (sciences), along them, and sometimes even over them, and is considered a superior final form of interdisciplinarity, which involves concepts, principles, language and finally even theory, in parallel with methods, methodology and models, which tend to become universal, dynamically generated by the action of the many levels of reality (systems theory, information theory, theory of scientific modelling, etc.).

Nevertheless, unlike other theorists, Săvoiu et al. (2014) do not refer to the inclusion of non-academic members. Tress et al. (2005, p. 487), for example, define transdisciplinary research 'as projects that involve academic researchers from different unrelated disciplines as well as non-academic participants, [including] the general public, to create new knowledge and theory and research a common' and note how 'Transdisciplinarity thus combines interdisciplinarity with a participatory approach' (Tress et al., 2005, p. 487).

Stock and Burton (2011, p. 1098) argue that 'transdisciplinarity is the highest form of integrated project, involving not only multiple disciplines, but also multiple non-academic participants … in a manner that combines interdisciplinarity with participatory approaches'. Similarly, Ashby and Exter (2019, p. 203) define transdisciplinarity as 'synthesis of disciplinary areas to the extent that knowledge may no longer be attributable to a specific field; it may also include active involvement and collaboration with community and other stakeholders to co-construct knowledge'.

Bernstein (2015, p. 1) explains how transdisciplinarity originated in the early 1970s, but was later 'characterized by its focus on "wicked problems" that need creative solutions, its reliance on stakeholder involvement, and engaged, socially responsible science'. Bernstein (2015, p. 13) also notes how transdisciplinarity

has grown into more than a critique of disciplinarity and has gained recognition as a mode of research applied to real world problems that need not only to be understood in new ways but also demand practical solutions.

Ndaguba and Ijeoma (2017, p. 11), for example, describe how, in South Africa, 'the transdisciplinarity approach is critical in offering broader universal vision from diverse disciplinary angles in order to arrive at a single conclusion … The need for transdisciplinarity in public policy and administration cannot be overlooked'.

Comparison of Disciplinarities

Lawrence (2010, p. 127) argues that

Multidisciplinarity, interdisciplinarity, and transdisciplinarity are complementary rather than being mutually exclusive. Both interdisciplinary and transdisciplinary research and practice require a common conceptual

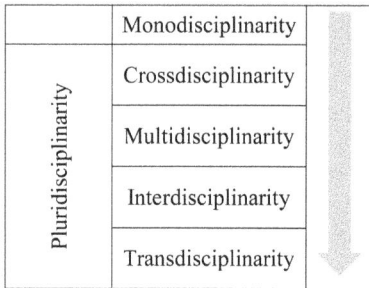

Figure 2.1 A hierarchy of disciplinarities

framework and analytical methods based on shared terminology, mental images, and common goals. Without specialised disciplinary studies, there would be no in-depth knowledge and data.

Stock and Burton (2011, p. 1095) point out that 'whereas with interdisciplinary and transdisciplinary studies researchers are able to resolve discrepancies and explore synergies through an iterative research process between participants, multidisciplinarity simply ensures that the required expert opinions on the issue are provided'.

A summary of the discussion concerning disciplinarities suggests the existence of a hierarchy (Figure 2.1).

Evolution of ARU's Interdisciplinary Ruskin Modules

As part of its *Corporate Strategy: Designing Our Future 2017–2026*, ARU (2017, p. 2) set out its vision to 'transform lives through innovative, inclusive and entrepreneurial education and research'. In their underpinning *Education, Research, & Innovation and Operating Strategies (2022–2027)*, ARU (2022, p. 8) reinforce this vision by 'engaging students in active, interdisciplinary curricula, tackling societal and environmental challenges with our local, regional and global communities … [and by] connecting staff and students in interdisciplinary knowledge exchange communities'. To realise these aims, ARU's (2018, p. 14) *Education Strategy 2018–2022* stipulates the following actions:

- Engage our students and employers in the co-design of courses that address environmental and societal challenges, and prepare our students for the world of work
- Develop our digital ecosystem to reshape the delivery and assessment of learning for greater personalisation

- Expand the interdisciplinary approach of our Ruskin modules and live briefs to wider audiences and deepen engagement with the UN Sustainable Development Goals (UN SDGs)
- Support our staff to effectively deliver active learning and engage with employers

RMs were conceptualised in the *Education Strategy 2018–2022* (ARU, 2018, p. 8):

> Our education provision will be shaped by our distinctive active learning approach, and the use of Ruskin modules to equip our students for the 21st century. Together they represent a radical restatement of the shape of a university education … We'll design Ruskin modules (breadth units) that creatively develop the capacity for critical reflection and reasoned argument, integrating the acquisition of graduate capitals with wider societal concerns and challenges, bringing together students from different disciplines around key challenges. Ruskin modules will form a core, credit-bearing part of the curriculum.

A briefing paper was submitted to ARU's Senate in November 2018, followed by discussions to draft the 'underlying principles and an accompanying operational framework for the introduction' of RMs, an institution-wide consultation, and the approval by ARU's Senate on 17 April 2019. In preparation for launching RMs, the ARU Education Committee defined them as inter- or transdisciplinary breadth modules to:

> broaden students' perspectives, developing their intellectual flexibility and creative capability to tackle complex problems and challenges in collaboration with others and effectively communicate in a way that is understandable to a wide audience. Thereby equipping them with key graduate level employability skills capitals and attributes (quoted in ARU, 2020).

Therefore, from their inception, ARU intended RMs (ARU, 2023a) to involve students from different disciplines in problem-solving activities, to develop novel solutions to significant social problems, either directly or indirectly related to sustainability. While interdisciplinarity and the UN SDGs are specified as part of RMs, they also strive to be co-designed with students, are delivered online to develop digital literacies in a digital learning environment, and subscribe to active, collaborative pedagogies. Therefore, RMs respond to the needs of a changing employment market and skills requirements (World Economic Forum, 2023) by supporting graduate and employability skills such as digital and information literacy, project and time management, inquiry-based learning, teamwork, and collaborative and communication skills.

The description of interdisciplinarity provided to students (ARU, 2021, para. 3) was that:

> Ruskin Modules combine your knowledge and skills with those from other courses that appear (at first) to be unrelated; discovering connections across different courses at ARU will better prepare you for a world of change, and at the same time create innovative, new solutions to complex challenges.

This description is informed by two definitions expressing interdisciplinarity in the RM scheme. According to Jacobs (1989, p. 8), an interdisciplinary curriculum 'consciously applies methodology and language from more than one discipline to a central theme, issue, problem, topic or experience'. Similarly, Klein and Newell (1997, pp. 393–394) define interdisciplinarity as

> a process of answering a question, solving a problem, or addressing a topic that is too broad or complex to be dealt with adequately by a single discipline or profession and draws on disciplinary perspectives and integrates their insights through construction of a more comprehensive perspective.

To help RM leaders understand the ARU description of interdisciplinarity, and to guide students in their studies, a common learning outcome was applied to all RMs: 'Critically reflect on the limitations of a single discipline to solve wider societal concerns by applying knowledge created through the discovery and exploitation of connections across disciplines' (Baxter & Brown, 2018, p. 4). While assessment of this learning outcome differs between modules, a common assessment rubric was introduced in 2022 to standardise the marking. The primary means of assessing students' understanding of interdisciplinarity was via written assignments such as reflective essays, reports, or portfolios.

The evaluation framework used in the evaluation of the first iteration of RMs (Thomas et al., 2021, p. 4) suggests:

> If Ruskin Modules are delivered to Level 5 students in the first trimester of 2021/22, and students attend the RMs, then students will have a positive learning experience, they will develop new knowledge and skills and they will have an opportunity to think differently about themselves and the world. If students benefit from RMs in these ways in the short-term, then in the medium-term they will be more effective learners, be more satisfied with their learning experience, have greater confidence in their personal and professional identities and future goals and they will embrace wider perspectives. In the longer-term students/graduates will be more employable, critical and flexible or open-minded.

The evaluation (Thomas et al., 2021) notes that although different models for breadth modules were identified in initial research (Norval et al., 2019, pp. 13–16), ARU introduced RMs as a compulsory module in all Level 5 undergraduate courses (except those with exemptions). While students can choose from over 20 RMs, they 'are deliberately situated outside the course, to offer students different disciplinary perspectives and experiences' (Thomas et al., 2021, p. 11).

Another reason for separating RMs from the core curricula, however, is that ARU does not offer elective modules in their courses. Therefore, embedding RMs as stand-alone interdisciplinary, yet compulsory, modules, in course curricula, was logistically the most sensible approach. Other UK universities, such as Leeds and Keele, which provide a greater choice of electives, offer 'study pathways' (i.e., a sequence of electives throughout a degree which forms a coherent pathway) or 'interdisciplinary clusters', such as Manchester's University College for Interdisciplinary Learning (Hallett, 2024). Lyall et al. (2015, x) described 'interdisciplinary electives' and 'core courses covering materials from different perspectives' and added 'research conducted for the initial stages of graduate school' as a further programme-level strategy. At ARU, the combination of Level 4 transition modules, Live Briefs at Levels 4 and 5 (ARU, 2023b), Level 5 breadth RMs (Level 5), and Level 6 major projects as depth modules was designed as a cluster constituting a coherent interdisciplinary and transdisciplinary learning narrative (Norval et al., 2019, p. 7).

Evaluation and Challenges

Thomas et al. (2021) found that as RMs are outside course curricula, their relevance and benefits need to be well communicated at all levels. Lyall et al. (2015, xi) recommend that 'the potential for interdisciplinary education to add value to an institution and its outputs should be articulated clearly: to staff but also to students, parents, employers, and other stakeholders'. While many RMs are co-taught by two tutors, only a few teams are interdisciplinary (Thomas et al., 2021).

RMs were designed for students to

- work collaboratively, respecting diversity, and being culturally sensitive
- critically reflect on the limitations of a single discipline to solve wider societal concerns
- create meaningful connections across disciplines, and apply new knowledge to key challenges
- participate as a responsible citizen in the life of local, national and global communities
- recognise, and critically reflect on issues of social responsibility, ethical conduct and sustainability
- encourage an appreciation of ambiguity (Norval et al., 2019, p. 5).

Ashby and Exter (2019, p. 204) define the benefits of interdisciplinary education as:

Provid[ing] students with knowledge and skills that allow them to look at the world through multiple lenses, synthesize disciplines to better understand the phenomena they explore, see the interdependencies among disciplines or individual topics, and understand larger systems in which individual disciplines exist.

Ashby and Exter (2019) further state that such environments develop students' critical thinking, problem-solving, creativity and innovation, collaboration, and communication skills. Lyall et al. (2015, v) identified similar demands of interdisciplinary education to develop 'future employees who have the skills to work in multi-professional teams and adopt holistic approaches to complex problems'. They found that interactive teaching methods were at the heart of interdisciplinary pedagogies summarised as 'project-based learning, case study methods, role-playing, simulations, virtual methods, peer-assessment and review, peer-assisted learning and small-group learning' (Lyall et al., 2015, x).

In their evaluation of how interdisciplinarity was embedded in RMs, Richter and Warnes (2024) arrived at similar results, however, with some tension between online, collaborative learning involving group- and teamwork, and students' (lack of) attendance and participation. Students appreciated authentic activities and assessments, but very few RMs were able to engage with outside stakeholders in real-life scenarios and wicked problems aiming at transdisciplinary learning.

The case study in Chapter 10 of this book, *Ruskin Module and Community Organising*, is an example of transdisciplinarity involving, as it does, both academic and non-academic players, supporting students to engage in community organising to address social problems at a local level. Richter and Warnes (2024) also found that assessed outcomes were frequently multidisciplinary rather than interdisciplinary as students often divided their team and group work along discipline lines but did not succeed in synthesising the different contributions to achieve an interdisciplinary outcome.

Conclusion

The introduction of interdisciplinary teaching and learning through RMs was unique for ARU, but also in the sector, as they sit outside the regular course curricula but are intended to be an integrated experience forming a cluster with modules within course curricula. This has involved a journey towards integration and embedding of interdisciplinarity within and across curricula as part of educational and institutional change.

Logistically, RMs are delivered online to enable students to attend from different geographically distributed campuses. However, online delivery brought challenges such as access, accessibility and digital poverty, digital literacy, social cohesion, and cooperation relating to online attendance and participation.

Future development of RMs involves further advances in evolving co-teaching in interdisciplinary teams recruited from across the institution providing a representative balance of disciplines and developing transdisciplinary approaches further by widening contributions from non-academic and external parties similar to the approach taken in Live Briefs.

The aim of the RMs is to help students develop a broader interdisciplinary skill set, preparing them to tackle complex situations and problems in their future careers. Our evaluations have shown encouraging results, identifying a range of skills that students were able to gain through the RMs and apply to their courses and lives.

References

Anglia Ruskin University (ARU) (2017). Designing our future 2017–2026. Our strategy. Anglia Ruskin University. Retrieved 5 July 2024, from https://www.aru.ac.uk/about-us/governance/strategy-and-leadership

Anglia Ruskin University (ARU) (2018). Education strategy 2018-2022. Anglia Ruskin University.

Anglia Ruskin University (ARU) (2020). The senate. Event report: Approval of Ruskin modules [Internal Report]. Anglia Ruskin University.

Anglia Ruskin University (ARU) (2022). *Underpinning strategies: Education, research & innovation, operating 2022-27*. Retrieved 5 July 2024, from https://www.aru.ac.uk/about-us/governance/strategy-and-leadership

Anglia Ruskin University (ARU) (2023a). Ruskin modules. Anglia Ruskin University. Retrieved 5 July 2024, from https://www.aru.ac.uk/anglia-learning-and-teaching/good-teaching-practice-and-innovation/ruskin-modules

Anglia Ruskin University (ARU) (2023b), *Innovative curriculum. Live Briefs*. Retrieved 5 July 2024, from https://www.aru.ac.uk/student-life/support-and-facilities/careers-and-employability/innovative-curriculum#live-briefs

Advance HE (2020). *Collaborative Award for Teaching Excellence*. Retrieved 5 July 2024, from https://www.advance-he.ac.uk/awards/teaching-excellence-awards/collaborative-award-for-teaching-excellence

Anglia Ruskin University (ARU) (2021). *Interdisciplinarity*. Retrieved 1 March 2022, from https://canvas.anglia.ac.uk/courses/21834/pages/interdisciplinarity

Ashby, I., & Exter, M. (2019). Designing for interdisciplinarity in higher education: Considerations for instructional designers. *TechTrends, 63*, 202–208. https://doi.org/10.1007/s11528-018-0352-z

Baxter, P., & Brown, E. (2018). *Education strategy: Ruskin modules*. Anglia Ruskin University.

Bernstein, J. H. (2015). Transdisciplinarity: A review of its origins, development, and current issues. *Journal of Research Practice, 11*(1), Article R1. Retrieved 5 July 2024, from https://academicworks.cuny.edu/cgi/viewcontent.cgi?article=1010&context=kb_pubs

Brown, E., & Acevedo, B. (2022). Interdisciplinary design for ambiguity: Work in a wicked world. In S. Norton and A. Penaluna (Eds.), *3 Es for wicked problems: Employability, Enterprise, and entrepreneurship: Solving wicked problems* (pp. 16–20). Retrieved 5 July 2024, from https://www.advance-he.ac.uk/knowledge-hub/3-es-wicked-problems-employability-enterprise-and-entrepreneurship-solving-wicked

Dellaportas, S., Xu, L., & Yang, Z. (2020). The level of cross-disciplinarity in cross-disciplinary accounting research: Analysis and suggestions for improvement. University of Nottingham Ningbo China. Retrieved 5 July 2024, from https://eprints.nottingham.ac.uk/64188/1/output%20%281%29.pdf

Evely, A. C., Fazey, I., Lambin, X., Lambert, E., Allen, S., & Pinard, M. (2010). Defining and evaluating the impact of crossdisciplinary conservation research. *Environmental Conservation, 37*(4), 442–450. https://doi.org/10.1017/S0376892910000792

Graff, H. J. (2016). The "problem" of interdisciplinarity in theory, practice, and history. *Social Science History, 40*(4), 775–803. https://doi.org/10.1017/ssh.2016.31

Hallett, R. (2024). Designing challenge-based interdisciplinary education: Curriculum structures & hybrid expertise. Paper presented at *Interdisciplinary Learning and Teaching Conference 2024*, University of Manchester (21 March). Retrieved 5 July 2024, from https://stories.manchester.ac.uk/interdisciplinaryconference/index.html

Higher Education Statistics Agency (HESA) (2024a). *The Higher Education Classification of Subjects (HECoS)*. Retrieved 5 July 2024, from https://www.hesa.ac.uk/support/documentation/hecos

Higher Education Statistics Agency (HESA) (2024b). *JACS 3.0: Principal subject codes*. Retrieved 5 July 2024, from https://www.hesa.ac.uk/support/documentation/jacs/jacs3-principal

Ilter, H. K. (2015). *Monodisciplinary vs Pluridisciplinary Research*. Retrieved 5 July 2024, from https://hkilter.com/index.php?title=Monodisciplinary_vs_Pluridisciplinary_Research

Jacobs, H. H. (1989). *Interdisciplinary curriculum: Design and implementation*. Association for Supervision and Curriculum Development. Retrieved 5 July 2024, from http://files.eric.ed.gov/fulltext/ED316506.pdf

Klein, J., & Newell, W. (1997). Advancing interdisciplinary studies. In J. Gaff, & J. Ratcliff (Eds.), *Handbook of the undergraduate curriculum: A comprehensive guide to the purposes, structures, practices, and change* (pp. 393–415). Jossey-Bass.

Lawrence, R. J. (2010). Deciphering interdisciplinary and transdisciplinary contributions. *Transdisciplinary Journal of Engineering & Science, 1*(1), 125–130. https://doi.org/10.22545/2010/0003

Lyall, C., Meagher, L., Bandola, J., & Kettle, A. (2015). *Interdisciplinary provision in higher education: Current and future challenges*. Advance HE. Retrieved 5 July 2024, from https://www.advance-he.ac.uk/knowledge-hub/interdisciplinary-provision-higher-education-current-and-future-challenges

Ndaguba, E. A., & Ijeoma, E. O. C. (2017). Exploring the epistemology of transdisciplinarity in public policy and administration in South Africa. *The Journal for Transdisciplinary Research in Southern Africa, 13*(1), a406. https://doi.org/10.4102/td.v13i1.406

Norval, A., Baxter, P., & Brown, E. (2019). SEN/19/06 – Education strategy: Introducing Ruskin modules [Internal report]. Anglia Ruskin University.

O'Rourke, M., Crowley, S., & Gonnerman, C. (2016). On the nature of cross-disciplinary integration: A philosophical framework. *Studies in History and Philosophy of Biological and Biomedical Sciences, 56*, 62–70. https://doi.org/10.1016/j.shpsc.2015.10.003

Office for Students (OfS) (2024). *Teaching Excellence and Student Outcomes Framework: Subject-level pilot guide*. Retrieved 5 July 2024, from https://www.officeforstudents.

org.uk/publications/teaching-excellence-and-student-outcomes-framework-subject-level-pilot-guide/

Rittel, H. W., & Webber, M. M. (1973). Dilemmas in a general theory of planning. *Policy Sciences*, *4*(2), 155–169. https://doi.org/10.1007/BF01405730

Richter, U., & Warnes, M. (2024). Embedding of interdisciplinarity into the curriculum through breadth modules: An evaluation of staff and student experiences. Paper presented at *Interdisciplinary Learning and Teaching Conference 2024*, University of Manchester (21 March). Retrieved 5 July 2024, from https://stories.manchester.ac.uk/interdisciplinaryconference/index.html

Săvoiu, G., Dinu, V., & Tachiciu, L. (2014). An inter-, trans-, cross- and multidisciplinary approach to higher education in the field of business studies. *The Amfiteatru Economic Journal*, *16*(37), 707–725. Retrieved 5 July 2024, from https://www.amfiteatrueconomic.ro/temp/Article_1307.pdf

Stock, P., & Burton, R. J. F. (2011). Defining terms for integrated (multi-inter-trans-disciplinary) sustainability research. *Sustainability*, *3*, 1090–1113. https://doi.org/10.3390/su3081090

Thomas, L., Pratt-Adams, S., & Warnes, M. (2021). An evaluation of the active curriculum framework, course design intensives, and the Ruskin modules: How well has the change process worked, what are the lessons for the future, and how can the impact be evaluated? [Internal Report]. Anglia Ruskin University.

Tress, B., Tress, G., & Fry, G. (2005). Clarifying integrative research concepts in landscape ecology. *Landscape Ecology*, *20*, 479–493. https://doi.org/10.1007/s10980-004-3290-4

UK Research and Innovation (UKRI) (2023). *REF2021: Units of Assessment*. Retrieved 5 July 2024, from https://archive.ref.ac.uk/panels/units-of-assessment/

World Economic Forum (WEF) (2023). *The Future of Jobs Report 2023*. World Economic Forum. Retrieved 5 July 2024, from https://www.weforum.org/publications/the-future-of-jobs-report-2023/

Chapter 3

Transformative Education

Elsa Lee, Simon Pratt-Adams, and Mark Warnes

Introduction and Context

The process of initiating a cross-institutional, interdisciplinary module as a mandatory element of the undergraduate degree programme at Anglia Ruskin University (ARU) has illuminated transforming and transformative aspects of the learning experience in contemporary Higher Education (HE).

In this chapter, we describe and explore these transformations and demonstrate how a commitment to interdisciplinarity can respond to them. We also use the notion of transformation as a form of theoretical analysis to draw together some of the outcomes from the different chapters in this book. We focus on:

1 The types of pedagogy employed at a time of uncertainty and change in wider society and the transformation in thinking among tutors who design and deliver interdisciplinary modules.
2 The transformation from disciplinary learning towards interdisciplinary learning within fluid organisational contexts and cultures and their impact on the management of knowledge flows and processes, the use of time, and physical and virtual space.
3 We conclude by critically considering the extent to which ongoing societal transformations are influencing universities as learning organisations.

As a widening participation university, a central aim of ARU's work is to provide students from backgrounds who do not traditionally attend HE an opportunity to improve their outcomes through learning. For example, ARU's (2017) corporate strategy, *Designing our Future 2017–2026* states, 'We're committed … to supporting access to university for students who may not have otherwise considered it or been able to afford it'. Similarly, the citation for ARU's 2023 Times Higher Education University of the Year award explains:

We're proud of all our staff and the transformational difference they're making to our students' lives. And we're equally proud of our students: what

DOI: 10.4324/9781003474593-4

they achieve when they're with us, and the positive change they bring to their world as graduates.

(ARU, 2023a)

ARU's mission is to serve its geographical region and transform lives through innovative, inclusive, and entrepreneurial education and research (ARU, 2023b). Inherent to this is a transformation relating to the journey of the student signing up for and completing the degree, as explicitly recognised in ARU's visions and values. The University's focus is on transforming the lives of the students who enter ARU's degree programmes. The Office for Students (OfS) recognised these values, and the transformative education offered, by presenting ARU with a Gold award in the Teaching Excellence Framework 2023 (OfS, 2024, p. 6). The TEF panel noted that

All students are required to take a Ruskin module (aligned to a UN [sustainable] development goal) alongside their main course of study. Internal survey data reported that 88 per cent of students valued this module. The panel considered this to be evidence of outstanding curriculum innovation.

In September 2021, ARU established a selection of interdisciplinary breadth modules which all second-year students take. In this chapter, we reflect on the ways in which the journey towards establishing this breadth curriculum has impacted the university. We briefly describe some of these impacts and focus on those with pedagogical significance.

Sustainability and Education for Sustainability

One feature at ARU which justifies the decision to consider transformation as a theoretical lens is its focus on sustainability and education for sustainability. Sustainability is one of ARU's areas for research and innovation (ARU, 2022), and also a central feature of Ruskin Modules (RMs), as illustrated by this statement on its website (ARU, 2023c, para 6):

Ruskin Modules are framed by the United Nations Sustainable Development Goals (SDGs), so you can gain the skills and knowledge required to respond to the world's most pressing challenges. ARU's commitment to sustainability means you'll acquire the skills and knowledge you need to make a difference.

The inclusion of sustainability as a central feature for RMs resulted in a Next Generation Learning and Skills prize at the 2023 Green Gown Awards (2024, para. 4). The judges welcomed the underlying objective to give all students more skills in how to apply climate change to their subject areas. There is a great range and number of modules, and codesign makes them relevant and useful and we like the compulsory and diversified nature that reaches a large number of students. The institutional-wide approach made this a winning application and highly transferable.

Sustainability and Education for Sustainability (EfS) are also key drivers of change in the HE sector nationally and internationally. For example, the *International Higher Education Declaration to Support the Implementation of the United Nations Sustainable Development Goals* (Big Tent Consortium, 2018) is a call to action to HEIs to commit to the UN SDGs and their focus on transformation for sustainability. Sustainability has always been centrally concerned with transformation (Sterling et al., 2018; United Nations, 2015). This point is particularly relevant in the case of EfS in HE and the influential work of Stephen Sterling. Sterling et al. (2018, p. 1) note, for example, that 'At heart, sustainability education seeks to nurture transformative learning (TL) experiences that can heal, empower, energise, and liberate potential for the common good'.

For Sterling (2004), transformative education changes a learner such that they become enabled to understand and respond to the risks of environmental and social degradation in its various forms. This is widely accepted within the sustainability and environmental education field (Wals & Corcoran, 2012). This has included the notion of critiquing discipline-bound knowledge and has led to a focus on the significance of trans- and interdisciplinary approaches (Lotz-Sisitka et al., 2015).

In the field of education more broadly, the idea of Transformative Learning (TL) has a long history. Jack Mezirow's work with adult learners in the US in the 1970s was seminal in developing an understanding of TL which involves a fundamental, multi-staged, change in identity, and what he refers to as meaning perspectives (Dirkx et al., 2006; Mezirow, 2003, 2018; Mezirow & Marsick, 1978). TL helps to reveal those implicit assumptions, and ideas assimilated through cultural and epistemological contexts, and deciding to change them. This has echoes of Freire's *conscientisation* (Freire, 1994; Sterling, 2011), hooks' *transgressive learning* (1994), and Biesta's *subjectification* (2011) in that TL involves breaking free from conditions imposed by context and gaining the ability to reshape and reform those contexts through political, cultural, and social engagement and influence. Typically, TL would apply to programmes with adults who return to university after a period of employment, to undertake a Master's Degree, for example, although it might also apply to younger groups of students. While a traditional notion of HE might not meet Mezirow and Marsick's (1978) criteria, widening participation institution populations include non-traditional student groups, including mature students, and students from under-represented backgrounds. First-in-family students are more likely to undergo a greater degree of social transformation than students from backgrounds with an expectation of university attendance straight after school. Therefore, TL theory may be more applicable in this context than in other HE settings, such as Russell Group universities.

Beyond transformation at the personal level, Sterling et al. (2018, p. 1) note that

> educational systems or institutions cannot adequately support such trans-formative education and transformative learning experiences unless they themselves have experienced or are experiencing sufficient transformative processes consistent with this ethos. While myriad "education for change" movements have long seen education as an agent or vehicle for personal and social change, the corollary – that educational thinking and policy must itself change sufficiently to allow it to fulfil this agency function – has received much less attention.

Sceptical of the degree to which education can actually lead to change, Sterling et al. (2018) point towards the success of educational endeavours under-pinned by transformations at institutional and macro-societal levels. Sterling (2004) also writes about the different ways in which HEIs can approach edu-cation in relation to sustainability and sets these out as four levels of response to the environmental challenge from HE (see Table 3.1).

Importantly, Sterling (2004) holds that the final level of response is only possible in the context of response-*ability*: when the socio-political and cul-tural conditions allow for it to happen because there has been a paradigmatic shift in the dominant economic paradigm. In his critique of Mezirow's trans-formative learning theory, Defoe (2000, p. 4) suggests that 'It may very well be that those who could benefit most from transformative learning are least likely to experience it'.

Table 3.1 Staged learning responses to the challenge of sustainability

	Type of response	Resultant change	Type of learning
1	No response	No change	Denial/ignorance (no learning)
2	Accommodation	Green gloss	Adaptive
3	Reformation	Serious reform	Critically reflective adaptation
4	Transformation	Whole system redesign	Transformative

Source: Sterling (2004, p. 7).

Ruskin Modules

In 2019, ARU initiated a wholescale curriculum change, implemented using a Course Design Intensive (CDI) approach (Benfield, 2008), which included the introduction of a 15-credit interdisciplinary breadth Ruskin Module at Level 5 (Second Year) (Middleton et al., 2021) by constructively aligning learning outcomes, assessment, and teaching and learning activities (Biggs, 1996).

Thomas et al. (2023) evaluated the first iteration of the RMs using a theory of change evaluation, which, along with the chapters in this book, informs our observations. We identify the following conceptions of transformation:

1 **Transforming student epistemologies** – Through exposure to theory and practices not addressed in discipline-specific degree pathways using an interdisciplinary focus (see Chapters 2 and 6).
2 **Transforming pedagogical approaches** – Critical pedagogy and pedagogic reimagining for educators to *unlearn* their approaches to teaching (see Chapters 5 and 8).
3 **Transforming organisational culture** – Realising the different ways in which administrative processes affect curriculum design leading to organisational change (see Chapters 5 and 8).
4 **Transforming student values** – Through, for example, participating in conversations about challenging topics including white privilege, gender norms, and animal rights, with students expressing views from a range of cultures and geopolitical backgrounds not normally encountered in discipline-specific pathways (see Chapter 6).
5 **Transforming thinking and values** – The impact of weekly RM leader meetings with academics from across the institution from different disciplines, and non-teaching staff, resulted in a RM Community of Practice (Fullan, 2016) (see Chapter 11).
6 **Digital transformation** – Digital transformation has been particularly important as ARU is based on multiple campuses, and RMs are delivered (almost) entirely online.
7 **Transforming social and environmental context** – The RM timeline cuts across the COVID-19 period, when students and staff were working exclusively from home, carrying out all teaching and learning activities online, during which questions of globalisation and sustainability became increasingly prevalent.

Transformative Pedagogy

Following the COVID-19 pandemic, institutions across the globe have embraced transformation (Marinoni et al., 2020). This change resulted in a significant shift in the structure of institutions as learning organisations, with a renewed focus on strategies promoting diversity, fostering inclusivity, and postcolonial and decolonising practices (Ngcamu & Mantzaris, 2023). By prioritising these values, institutions create a more equitable and inclusive learning environment that benefits everyone. Indeed, the transformation of learning requires whole institutions to operate with and engage with a different mindset than a business-as-usual approach (Fűzi et al., 2022; Sterling, 2011).

COVID-19 caused a notable disruption in the HE sector. This led to a challenge to the neoliberal models of HE that have existed since the late 1970s (Maisuria & Cole, 2017). These models are often characterised as more like businesses serving the private interest rather than the public and personal good (Galbraith, 1992; Lotz-Sisitka et al., 2015). The system has been deemed troubled, fragmented, underfunded, and incoherent (Hussey & Smith, 2010; Marginson, 2011; McMahon, 2009). As a result, alternative possibilities are emerging, such as the London Interdisciplinary School (2023), that are challenging the existing HE system. Furthermore, the post-COVID-19 'New Normal' (Corpuz, 2021) has also presented opportunities for alternatives and shifts in HE and the remaking of HE for the advancement of learning and knowledge. Hence, in their book, *The Good University*, Connell asks, 'Is it sensible to talk about "the university" – even in ruins – anymore?' (2019, p. 5).

These conditions necessitated reflection on the transforming aspects of the pedagogic experience, a pedagogy for uncertainty, ambiguity, and dynamism (Lotz-Sisitka et al., 2015), which suggests the HE context as being in a state of transformation. The world is no longer predictable and rational, but is now uncertain, relational, and complex (Gilbert & Pratt-Adams, 2022; Kromydas, 2017). Consequently, HE pedagogy is responding by changing its ways of working (Devecchi & Potter, 2020). By working together, learners and teachers can create a transforming pedagogic experience that prepares students to succeed in a rapidly changing world. The development of RMs during and after COVID-19 reflected the pace of educational transformation, in real-time, that RM module leaders were aware that as 'Trailblazers' they were 'breaking new ground'.

RMs are designed to promote collaboration among students from all disciplines across ARU, inspiring them to challenge their perceptions and appreciate diverse viewpoints. RMs are mandatory in the second year of all but a few undergraduate degrees (i.e., those with Professional, Statutory and Regulatory Body (PSRB) requirements are exempt) and provide a space for self-reflection, developing new skills, and enhancing existing ones. The challenges presented in RMs are 'wicked problems' (Lönngren & van Poeck, 2021; Norton & Penaluna, 2022; Rittel & Webber, 1973), which enhance student employability by fostering innovative thinking and creative problem-solving abilities (Coonan & Pratt-Adams, 2018; OECD, 2016). In addition, RMs help build students' confidence in questioning established ways of thinking, encouraging TL.

Thus, RMs embody a paradigm shift towards a Transformative Pedagogy (TP). TP, however, is not a one-off experience, but is ongoing with no determinable stopping point (Taimur & Onuki, 2022; Ukpokodu, 2009). TP is different from TL, which is about a personal change of identity and being-in-the-world (Heidegger, 1927). It is also different from Transformative Education, which is education leading to whole-scale system change. Thus, despite bearing many similar hallmarks, it differs from both as it focuses on the practice of pedagogy, and the ways in which pedagogy has a transforming effect (Freire, 1970).

TP is a complex process that involves various aspects. Transformation can affect learners, teachers, institutions, policies, and, ultimately, society at large (Fujino et al., 2018). A more holistic and engaged pedagogy may require the teacher and student to share their personal experiences, become empowered, and grow from the process (Palmer, 1998). In this context, a teacher facilitates a learning environment where students are encouraged to openly express their thoughts and ideas. Similarly, students are encouraged to take ownership of their learning by setting personal goals, reflecting on their progress, and seeking feedback from their peers (Doyle, 2023). An engaged and empowered pedagogy can have a far-reaching impact beyond the classroom as it contributes to developing a more inclusive and democratic society, where individuals are comfortable in expressing their thoughts and engaging in constructive dialogue. Therefore, it is important to invest in a pedagogy that fosters personal growth, critical thinking, and empathy.

A vital element of any breadth curriculum is a commitment to crossing disciplinary boundaries and embracing interdisciplinarity, something which is also critical to EfS-informed curricula (Lotz-Sisitka et al., 2015; Catallo et al., 2023). RM leaders adhere to this principle by designing their curricula in a way that brings together students and, in some instances, staff from various disciplines.

While each RM has a distinct focus, all modules share a common Learning Outcome (LO) 'to critically reflect on the limitations of a single discipline to solve wider societal concerns by applying knowledge created through the discovery and exploitation of connections across disciplines' (Baxter & Brown, 2018, p. 4). Assessment of this LO requires students to demonstrate their interdisciplinary ability to solve 'wicked problems' (Brown & Acevedo, 2022). Indeed, according to Freire (1998a), bringing knowledge and approaches from different disciplinary perspectives to tackle the problems involves teachers challenging rather than simply 'coddling' their students.

RM leaders design their curricula using a range of schools of thought. For instance, the RM, *What is the Meaning of Social Justice in the 21ˢᵗ Century*, includes theoretical input from, among others, sociology, education, psychology, philosophy, and politics. RM leaders need a high degree of interdisciplinary competence and breadth of knowledge, as well as a sense of humility in the knowledge that some of their students will have a fuller understanding of the range of tools from their own disciplinary perspectives.

The definition of organised knowledge is also changing, with a new focus on a global, digital impact and knowledge economy focused on outcomes, rather than being dependent on time and process set by HEIs (McGill, 2023). The conventional education model is no longer sufficient to cater to the ever-changing needs of the present. Traditionally passive students receive knowledge from the expert and controlling teacher (Freire, 1970), but this approach does not encourage creativity or transformation and creates a wall, with the teacher distanced from the students, merely 'play-act(ing) the teacher's part' (Palmer, 1998, p. 17). TP means moving away from the outdated 'sage on the stage' approach and embracing new ways of teaching that are relevant to the modern world (Pratt-Adams et al., 2020), where the capacities of both students and the lecturer, as active participants, collaborate in a learning relationship (Freire, 1970). Such a transformation requires challenging the restrictive structures themselves (such as discipline-specific teaching) to engage students in critical thinking, problem-solving, and reflective education, in dialogue with the teacher (Freire, 1970).

RMs are based on interdisciplinarity, via team and group work, and assignment setting with personally engaged foci, such as reflective writing. Such an approach has evolved into a TP, impacting values, epistemologies, and digital methods. However, the rapidly increasing digitalisation of pedagogy and the shift in thinking about its possibilities as an outcome of the COVID-19 lockdown conditions give a renewed impetus to new pedagogic strategies.

Pedagogic Practices

Grossberg (1994) developed three models of progressive pedagogic practices: (1) hierarchical, where the teacher assumes they know what the students need to learn; (2) dialogic, where the silenced are given a chance to speak for themselves; and (3) praxical pedagogy, which teaches people the skills to understand and intervene in their history. Grossberg (1994) based these models on assumptions about the social relations, positioning, and authority of teachers and students. Grossberg (1994, p. 18) also suggests a fourth model of pedagogy, which is a pedagogy of 'risk' and 'possibilities'. This model avoids traditional forms of intellectual authority and offers agency to students to help them communicate and understand their place in the world (Mostern, 1994). It also maintains the teacher's role as an expert producer of knowledge alongside the expertise of the students.

Progressive engaged pedagogic practices (hooks, 1994) require the educator to intervene democratically and establish a respectful relationship with the learner, including the social, cultural, and historical context that shapes their knowledge, and this takes effort that some teachers may be unwilling to expend. According to Freire (1970, p. 53), knowledge is not static but emerges through a constant process of invention and reinvention, which requires 'a restless, impatient, hopeful inquiry that human beings pursue in the world, with the world, and with each other'. If hooks' (1994) transgressive learning requires personal engagement by both teacher and learner, achieving such engagement in a virtual classroom can be challenging. Engaged pedagogy necessarily values student expression, but in the context of an online environment, where students might prefer to switch off their cameras and microphones, it is unclear whether this can be considered 'engaged learning'.

In a physical classroom setting, students are more likely to interact with their teacher. However, in a virtual space, students interact more with digital materials, which imbues them with a different and more influential role. The materials become the intermediary in the engagement between teacher and learner (Alenezi, 2020; Zhu et al., 2022).

Universities are dynamic educational environments where disciplines, practices, and issues are established, altered, challenged, and borders crossed. Those who work there may push boundaries of knowledge and may be viewed positively or negatively based on their positions and contributions (Giroux & McLaren, 1994). For example, digital technology has enhanced the opportunities for including overseas speakers during a lecture, or for teaching across geographically dispersed campuses. Thus digital technology has transformed ideas about borders and border crossing significantly (Giroux, 2005), and while some individuals may choose to remain within these boundaries, others, identified by Janmohamed (1994) as 'border intellectuals', may be inclined to challenge them.

Agency is also central to the transformational change of educational culture, influencing collaborative decision-making of the vision, policy, and practice through empowered and confident teachers, and students expressing agency and taking responsibility for decisions (Outram & Parkin, 2020). Agency also legitimates the right to practice pedagogy in a reimagined and different way. According to Jefferson and Anderson (2021, p. 47), 'Reimagined pedagogy allows educators and leaders to connect, combine and create learning with diverse pedagogical elements to generate a range of teaching approaches'.

Similarly, hooks' (1994) work on inclusion is important. In the context of the virtual world, teachers do what they can to ensure that their students feel, and are, fully included in the learning environment. In a traditional physical space, it is fairly straightforward for an informed and inclusive practitioner to judge whether their practice and the learning experience were connecting emotionally and intellectually with the learners. Given that virtual synchronous learning has become a norm, it is vital to ensure that every learner is given equal opportunities to participate and learn, particularly given the heightened significance of module materials and their design, as well as the constitution and management of online group workspaces, like breakout rooms, which are vital to the success of online collaboration and student engagement.

However, the act of teaching is not merely about sharing information, but as hooks (1994, p. 134) suggests, it is about partaking 'in the intellectual and spiritual growth of our students'. According to Palmer (1998), connection with themselves, their students, and their subject is an element of a good teacher, which comes not from their methods but their hearts, where intellect and emotion meet. In this way, a complete and deeper form of learning can take place when teachers create a climate of an open environment and are willing to transgress the boundaries of traditional 'banking' education and engage pedagogically with their students (Freire, 1970).

The relationship between educators and learners can be complex and at times difficult and requires a 'coherent' relationship between what teachers say and what they do. Teachers need to have the freedom to teach and be radical but also need to allow the freedom of learners to learn and to see that change is legitimate (Freire, 1998b). Freire (1998b, p. 56) emphasises the importance of a 'Commitment to justice, liberty, and individual rights, of our dedication to defend the weakest when they are being subjected to the exploitation of the strongest'.

Freire (1998b) talks about reconciling the teacher-student contradiction through, for example, critical hope, which involves sharing ideas between teachers and students in the learning-teaching relationship, discussing and planning for a better future depending on their particular contexts. However, taking an active and engaged pedagogical approach is more demanding on the teacher than conventional forms of pedagogy, and it can be a challenge to find time to build a learning community with large, online classes. Such a process requires a commitment to self-actualisation on the part of the teacher to empower the students and create a stimulating learning experience (hooks, 1994).

RM leaders have the opportunity for support from the course leader during debrief and decompression sessions that are given over to tutors to reflect on their teaching (see Chapter 11). This approach acknowledges the benefits for tutors to reflect on their own personal narratives they have shared during academic discussions. It also indicates how RMs that focus on complex and challenging social and environmental justice issues require a different approach to addressing them. Palmer (1998, p. 144) explains how,

> Involvement in a community of pedagogical discourse is more than a voluntary option for individuals who seek support and opportunities for growth. It is a professional obligation that educational institutions should expect of those who teach ... The growth of any craft depends on shared practice and honest dialogue among the people who do it.

hooks (1994, p. 204) argues that discussing and critically thinking about pedagogy is not considered 'the intellectual work that most folks think is hip or cool'. Nevertheless, educators who wish to improve their teaching practices and academic scholarship must communicate openly with colleagues who share the same goal (Palmer, 1998). By doing so, they can exchange ideas, identify common ground, and work together to create effective, engaging, and transformative pedagogical approaches.

Institutions can play a supportive role in enabling transformation and change and TP is central to that. Such an approach needs a clear, shared, and inclusive leadership approach (Outram & Parkin, 2020) to open up spaces and invite engagement with a group of early adopters, such as the RM 'Trailblazers'. Doing so allows for the development of deep (or more profound), mutually supported, connected, and authentic, active learning experiences (Palmer, 1998). And, as RMs have demonstrated, this type of learning should include interdisciplinary collaboration. Ultimately, this leads to a change in organisational culture; to hold a different set of values which are pivotal to the transformation process, as they can bring about and drive forward action to stimulate transformation and change development (Bishop et al., 2020). Thus, the values of the institution must reflect the integrity of the institution and enable the transformation to take place (Jefferson & Anderson, 2021).

Conclusion

HE is undergoing a significant transformation, resulting in the emergence of new forms of learning institutions. According to Sterling (2011), this shift in education might answer contemporary challenges by embracing change and laying the foundation for the future of education. Similarly, Lotz-Sisitka et al. (2015, p. 78) argue,

> There is need for more exploratory, transgressive forms of learning in our institutions. Ultimately these will require an integration of sustainability-oriented higher education teaching, research and community engagement processes into possibilities for learning that allows for the emergence of agency and lived experience in transformative praxis contexts.

RMs are a model for learning and teaching in relation to sustainability that fits comfortably on Sterling's (2004) third level of a reformatory response (EfS), which has had a range of transformational effects on students, tutors, and organisations. Hence, in widening participation institutions such as ARU, there is hope that HEIs can be, and in some cases are, learning institutions in line with Sterling's fourth level of a transformative response. Taken together, the changes that we have described might eventually lead to a societal systemic change that allows Freire's (1992) optimistic but cautious vision of a 'Pedagogy of Hope' to become reality.

Nevertheless, the contemporary approach of studying specific discipline-bound subjects in degree courses to qualify for a particular profession still has merit, as many professions would be impossible without specialist knowledge.

However, a breadth curriculum enhances degrees that train students in specific epistemological approaches. In viewing the knowledge they learn in their discipline through the lenses of other disciplines, students are likely to become more critically aware and, therefore, better informed about the essential knowledge and skills they will need to act effectively and equitably in their chosen field in the future. This critical capacity to identify and act on knowledge of systemic bias is key to creating a more equitable and just society, which is a central aim of RMs, and where much of the promise of a Transforming Pedagogy lies.

Recommendations

We recommend some guiding principles for a Transforming Pedagogy:

- The content taught and learned should be authentic, engaging, and stimulating.
- Adopt a realistic and unified approach, allowing all students in a given institution to participate from any location, making education a more fully inclusive experience.
- The content should be problem-focused, and assessed in such a way as to enable students to consider a range of solutions, informed by their own perspectives, to a problem.
- Tutors should have access to a wide range of pedagogic strategies, both formal and informal, to enable diverse, imaginative, and active teaching methods.
- The emphasis should be on creating a student-centred, lived, personal and relatable experience that fosters a sense of engagement, belonging, and personal growth.
- The curriculum should be inclusive, diverse, and socially balanced, with a compassionate approach.
- Include a commitment to Digital Literacy, Digital Technology, and Digital Capability to support the above principles.

References

Alenezi, A. (2020). The role of e-learning materials in enhancing teaching and learning behaviors. *International Journal of Information and Education Technology, 10*(1), 48–56. https://doi.org/10.18178/ijiet.2020.10.1.1338

Anglia Ruskin University (ARU) (2017). Designing our future 2017-2026: Our strategy. Anglia Ruskin University. Retrieved 5 July 2024, from https://www.aru.ac.uk/-/media/Files/about-us/governance/designing-our-future-2017-2026.pdf

Anglia Ruskin University (ARU) (2022). Designing our future: Underpinning strategies – Education, research & innovation and operating (2022-2027). Anglia Ruskin University. Retrieved 5 July 2024, from https://myaru.sharepoint.com/

sites/i-documentcentre/Corporate%20Documents/Forms/Default.aspx?id=
%2Fsites%2Fi%2Ddocumentcentre%2FCorporate%20Documents%2FARU%20
Underpinning%20Strategies%202022%2Epdf&parent=%2Fsites%2Fi%2Ddocument
centre%2FCorporate%20Documents&p=true&ga=1

Anglia Ruskin University (ARU) (2023a). University of the year 2023. Anglia
Ruskin University. Retrieved 5 July 2024, from https://london.aru.ac.uk/about-us/
why-aru-london/university-of-the-year-2023

Anglia Ruskin University (ARU) (2023b). Our vision and values. Anglia Ruskin
University. Retrieved 5 July 2024, from https://www.aru.ac.uk/about-us/our-
mission-and-values

Anglia Ruskin University (ARU) (2023c). Ruskin modules. Anglia Ruskin University.
Retrieved 5 July 2024, from https://www.aru.ac.uk/student-life/support-and-
facilities/careers-and-employability/innovative-curriculum/ruskin-modules

Baxter, P., & Brown, E. (2018). Education strategy: Ruskin modules. Anglia Ruskin
University.

Benfield, G. (2008). e-Learning course design intensives: Disrupting the norms of
curriculum design. *Educational Developments*, *9*(4), 20–22. Retrieved 5 July
2024, from https://www.seda.ac.uk/wp-content/uploads/2020/09/Educational-
Developments-9.4.pdf

Biesta, G. J. J. (2011). Theorising civic learning: Socialisation, subjectification and the
ignorant citizen. In G. J. J. Biesta (Ed.), *Learning democracy in school and society*.
Sense Publishers. https://doi.org/10.1007/978-94-6091-512-3_7

Big Tent Consortium, (2018). *International Higher Education Declaration to Support the Implementation of the United Nations Sustainability Goals*. Retrieved 5 July
2024, from https://unescochair-cbrsr.org/pdf/Big_Tent_Communique_English_
November_2018.pdf

Biggs, J. (1996). Enhancing teaching through constructive alignment. *Higher Education*, *32*, 347–364. https://doi.org/10.1007/BF00138871

Bishop, M., Gentle, P., & Parkin, D. (2020). Overcoming 'change without change':
Co-creation, creativity, and sustainable change. In J. Potter, & C. Devecchi (Eds.),
*Delivering educational change in higher education: A transformative approach for
leaders and practitioners* (pp. 32–43). Routledge.

Brown, E., & Acevedo, B. (2022). Interdisciplinary design for ambiguity: Work in a
wicked world. In S. Norton, & A. Penaluna (Eds.), *3 es for wicked problems: Employability, enterprise, and entrepreneurship: Solving wicked problems* (pp. 16–20). Advance HE.

Catallo, A., Lee, E., & Vare, P. (2022). *Curriculum for a changing climate: A track
changes review of the national curriculum for England* (Final report). Retrieved 5
July 2024, from https://cdn.prod.website-files.com/5f8805cef8a604de754618
bb/637d2a1bede15e6467a233dd_Curriculum%20for%20a%20Changing%20Cli-
mate_%20a%20track%20changes%20review%20of%20the%20national%20curricu-
lum%20for%20England.pdf

Connell, R. (2019). *The good university: What universities actually do and why it's time
for radical change*. Bloomsbury.

Coonan, E., & Pratt-Adams, S. (2018). *Building higher education fit for the future:
How higher education institutions are responding to the Industrial Strategy*. Advance
HE/HEA. Retrieved 5 July 2024, from https://www.advance-he.ac.uk/sites/
default/files/2019-05/Building-HE-Curricula-Fit-For-The-Future.pdf

Corpuz, J. C. G. (2021). Adapting to the culture of 'new normal': An emerging response to COVID-19. *Journal of Public Health*, *43*(2), e344–e345. https://doi.
org/10.1093/pubmed/fdab057

Defoe, T. (2000). *Perspectives on Mezirow's Transformative Learning Theory*. *Changing Minds*. Retrieved 5 July 2024, from https://www.academia.edu/attachments/
72763603/download_file?s=portfolio

Devecchi, C., & Potter, J. (2020). The reflective educational change leader: Conclud-ing remarks on a journey into delivering educational change. In J. Potter, & C. Devecchi (Eds.), *Delivering educational change in higher education: A transforma-tive approach for leaders and practitioners* (pp. 189–199). Routledge.

Dirkx, J. M., Mezirow, J., & Cranton, P. (2006). Musings and reflections on the mean-ing, context, and process of transformative learning: A dialogue between John M. Dirkx and Jack Mezirow. *Journal of Transformative Education, 4*(2), 123–139. https://doi.org/10.1177/1541344606287503

Doyle, T. (2023). *Helping students learn in a learner-centered environment: A guide to facilitating learning in higher education.* Routledge.

Freire, P. (1970). *Pedagogy of the oppressed.* Penguin.

Freire, P. (1992). *Pedagogy of hope: Reliving pedagogy of the oppressed.* Bloomsbury Publishing.

Freire, P. (1994). *Education for critical consciousness.* Continuum.

Freire, P. (1998a). *Pedagogy of freedom: Ethics, democracy and civic courage.* Rowman.

Freire, P. (1998b). *Teachers as cultural workers: Letters to those who dare teach.* Westview Press.

Fujino, D., Gomez, J., Lezra, E., Lipsitz, G., Mitchell, J., & Fonseca, J. (2018). A transformative pedagogy for a decolonial world. *Review of Education, Pedagogy, and Cultural Studies, 40*(2), 69–95. https://doi.org/10.1080/10714413.2018.1442080

Fullan, M. (2016). *"Enter change" the NEW meaning of educational change* (5th ed., pp. 107–120). Teachers College Press.

Fűzi, B., Géring, Z., & Szendrei-Pál, E. (2022). Changing expectations related to digitalisation and socialisation in higher education. Horizon scanning of pre- and post-COVID-19 discourses. *Educational Review, 74*(3), 484–516. https://doi.org/10.1080/00131911.2021.2023101

Galbraith, J. K. (1992). *The culture of contentment.* Sinclair-Stevenson Ltd.

Gilbert, J., & Pratt-Adams, S. (2022). *Soft systems methodology in education: Applying a critical realist approach to research on teacher education.* Springer.

Giroux, H. (2005). *Border crossings: Cultural workers and the politics of education.* Routledge.

Giroux, H., & McLaren, P. (Eds.) (1994). *Between borders: Pedagogy and the politics of cultural studies.* Routledge.

Green Gown Awards (2024). Anglia Ruskin University – Ruskin Modules: Collabo-ration for sustainable change. Green Gown Awards. Retrieved 5 July 2024, from https://www.greengownawards.org/anglia-ruskin-university1

Grossberg, L. (1994). Bringing it all back home: Pedagogy and cultural studies. In H. Giroux, & P. McLaren (Eds.), *Between borders: Pedagogy and the politics of cultural studies* (pp. 1–28). Routledge.

Heidegger, M. (1927 [1978]). *Being and time.* Wiley.

hooks, b. (1994). *Teaching to transgress.* Routledge. https://doi.org/10.4324/9780203700280

Hussey, T., & Smith, P. (2010). *The trouble with higher education: A critical examina-tion of our universities.* Routledge.

Janmohamed, A. (1994). Some implications of Paulo Freire's border pedagogy. In H. Giroux, & P. McLaren (Eds.), *Between borders: Pedagogy and the politics of cultural studies* (pp. 242–252). Routledge.

Jefferson, M., & Anderson, M. (2021). *Transforming education: Reimagining learning, pedagogy and curriculum.* Bloomsbury.

Kromydas, T. (2017). Rethinking higher education and its relationship with social inequalities: Past knowledge, present state and future potential. *Palgrave Communi-cations, 3*(1). https://doi.org/10.1057/s41599-017-0001-8

London Interdisciplinary School (2023). *The London Interdisciplinary School*. Retrieved 5 July 2024, from https://www.lis.ac.uk/

Lönngren, J., & van Poeck, K. (2021). Wicked problems: A mapping review of the literature. *International Journal of Sustainable Development & World Ecology, 28*(6), 481–502. https://doi.org/10.1080/13504509.2020.1859415

Lotz-Sisitka, H., Wals, A., Kronlid, D., & McGarry, D. (2015). Transformative, transgressive social learning: Rethinking higher education pedagogy in times of systemic global dysfunction, *Current Opinion in Environmental Sustainability, 16*, 73–80. https://doi.org/10.1016/j.cosust.2015.07.018

Maisuria, A., & Cole, M. (2017). The neoliberalization of higher education in England: An alternative is possible. *Policy Futures in Education, 15*(5), 602–619. https://doi.org/10.1177/1478210317719792

Marginson, S. (2011). Higher education and public good. *Higher Education Quarterly, 65*, pp. 411–433. https://doi.org/10.1111/j.1468-2273.2011.00496.x

Marinoni, G., van't Land, H., & Jensen, T. (2020). *The Impact of COVID-19 on Higher Education Around the World. IAU Global Survey Report.* Retrieved 5 July 2024, from https://www.iau-aiu.net/IMG/pdf/iau_covid19_and_he_survey_report_final_may_2020.pdf

McGill, L. (2023). *Digital Transformation in Higher Education.* Retrieved 5 July 2024, from https://www.jisc.ac.uk/guides/digital-transformation-in-higher-education

McMahon, W. (2009). *Higher learning, greater good: The private and social benefits of higher education.* Johns Hopkins University Press.

Mezirow, J. (2003). Transformative learning as discourse. *Journal of Transformative Education, 1*(1), 58–63. https://doi.org/10.1177/1541344603252172

Mezirow, J. (2018). Transformative learning theory. In K. Illeris (Ed.), *Contemporary theories of learning* (pp. 114–128). Routledge.

Mezirow, J., & Marsick, V. (1978). Education for perspective transformation: Women's re-entry programs in community colleges. Teacher's College, Columbia University.

Middleton, A., Pratt-Adams, S., & Priddle, J. (2021). Active, inclusive and immersive: Using course design intensives with course teams to rethink the curriculum across an institution. *SEDA Educational Developments, 21*(1), 9–13.

Mostern, K. (1994). Decolonization as learning: Practice and pedagogy in Frantz Fanon's revolutionary narrative. In H. Giroux, & P. McLaren (Eds.), *Between borders: Pedagogy and the politics of cultural studies* (pp. 253–271). Routledge.

Ngcamu, B. S., & Mantzaris, E. (2023). Challenges, recovery strategies and solutions to the COVID-19 pandemic in universities: An exploratory literature review. In P. Sultan (Ed.), *Innovation, leadership and governance in higher education* (pp. 61–82). Springer. https://doi.org/10.1007/978-981-19-7299-7_4

Norton, S., & Penaluna, A. (Eds.) (2022). *3 Es for wicked problems: Employability, Enterprise, and entrepreneurship: Solving wicked problems.* Advance HE.

Office for Students (OfS) (2024). *TEF 2023 Outcomes: Anglia Ruskin University.* Office for Students. Retrieved 5 July 2024, from https://tef2023.officeforstudents.org.uk/open-ancillary/?id=109b4e87-5189-ee11-be36-0022481b574a&finaloutcome=a85f867a-9d53-ee11-be6f-0022481b522f

Organisation for Economic Co-operation and Development (OECD) (2016). *Innovating education and educating for innovation: The power of digital technologies and skills.* OECD Publishing. https://doi.org/10.1787/9789264265097-en

Outram, S., & Parkin, D. (2020). A tailored undertaking: The challenge of context and culture for developing transformational leadership and change agency. In J. Potter, & C. Devecchi (Eds.), *Delivering educational change in higher education: A transformative approach for leaders and practitioners* (pp. 9–19). Routledge.

Palmer, P. J. (1998). *The courage to teach: Exploring the inner landscape of a teacher's life.* Jossey-Bass Inc.

Pratt-Adams, S., Richter, U., & Warnes, M. (Eds.) (2020). *Innovations in active learning in higher education*. University of Sussex/Fulcum. https://doi.org/10.20919/9781912319961

Rittel, H. W., & Webber, M. M. (1973). Dilemmas in a general theory of planning. *Policy Sciences, 4*(2), 155–169. https://doi.org/10.1007/BF01405730

Sterling, S. (2004). Higher education, sustainability, and the role of systemic learning. In P. B. Corcoran, & A. E. J. Wals (Eds.), *Higher education and the challenge of sustainability*. Springer. https://doi.org/10.1007/0-306-48515-X_5

Sterling, S. (2011). Transformative learning and sustainability: Sketching the conceptual ground. *Learning and Teaching in Higher Education, 5*, 17–33.

Sterling, S., Dawson, J., & Warwick, P. (2018). Transforming sustainability education at the creative edge of the mainstream: A case study of Schumacher College. *Journal of Transformative Education, 16*(4), 323–343. https://doi.org/10.1177/1541344618784375

Taimur, S., & Onuki, M. (2022). Design thinking as digital transformative pedagogy in higher sustainability education: Cases from Japan and Germany, *International Journal of Educational Research, 114*, 101994. https://doi.org/10.1016/j.ijer.2022.101994

Thomas, L., Warnes, W., & Pratt-Adams, S. (2023). Addressing the challenges of evaluating curriculum enhancement and learning development: An institutional case study using programme theory evaluation. *Innovations in Education and Teaching International*. https://doi.org/10.1080/14703297.2023.2293958

T-Learning (2024). *T-Learning*. Retrieved 5 July 2024, from https://transgressive learning.org

Ukpokodu, O. (2009). The practice of transformative pedagogy. *Journal on Excellence in College Teaching, 10*(2), 43–67.

United Nations (UN) (2015). *Transforming our world: The 2030 agenda for sustainable development*. UN General Assembly.

Wals, A. E. J., & Corcoran, P. B. (Eds.) (2012). *Learning for sustainability in times of accelerating change*. Brill. https://doi.org/10.3920/978-90-8686-757-8

Zhu, Y., Xu, Y., Wang, X., Yan, S., & Zhao, L. (2022). The selectivity and suitability of online learning resources as predictor of the effects of self-efficacy on teacher satisfaction during the COVID-19 lockdown. *Frontiers in Psychology, 13*, 765832. https://doi.org/10.3389/fpsyg.2022.765832

Chapter 4

Introduction to Ruskin Modules

Elaine Brown

Introduction

In September 2021, Anglia Ruskin University (ARU) introduced interdisciplinary breadth modules, 'Ruskin Modules', as a compulsory part of the undergraduate curriculum.

Ruskin Modules (RMs) were first proposed in ARU's (2018b) *Education Strategy 2018–2022*. The *Education Strategy* extended the commitment in ARU's Corporate Strategy (2017), *Designing our Future 2017–2026*, to transform lives through 'innovative, inclusive and entrepreneurial education and research' (ARU, 2017, p. 2).

The *Education Strategy* made explicit the vision of transformative education by 'being imaginative in the advancement of the knowledge and education of our students' (ARU, 2018b, p. 4). The development of RMs demonstrated this imagination, designed 'to equip students for the 21st century' by creatively developing 'students' capacity for critical reflection and reasoned argument, integrating the acquisition of graduate skills with wider societal concerns and challenges, bringing together students from different disciplines around key challenges' (ARU, 2018b, p. 8)

Research used to support the design and implementation of ARU's interdisciplinary curricula included consulting with colleagues across the higher education sector, along with two publications which were used as primary resources: Lyall et al.'s (2016) review of *Interdisciplinary Provision in Higher Education* and de Greef et al.'s (2017) practical handbook on *Designing Interdisciplinary Education*. Lyall et al. (2016) provide guiding principles and de Greef et al. (2017) provide a more discursive overview that was useful to develop continuing professional development (CPD) to support module developers.

The sequence of steps taken to implement RMs is described at institutional levels (i.e., regulatory, quality assurance processes) and educators (i.e., support for developing interdisciplinary modules). Interweaving the sequence of steps is a theme of assuring 'interdisciplinarity' in the modules, for educators and students.

DOI: 10.4324/9781003474593-5

The Journey

The need to respond to societal and environmental challenges and the skills and ways of thinking required to integrate different perspectives are arguments for implementing interdisciplinary curricula. These challenges cannot be addressed by a single discipline (Graybill et al., 2006; Repko et al., 2020). To address these challenges, interdisciplinary curricula encourage students to integrate different disciplinary perspectives by identifying and applying their own discipline in new ways, and by being exposed to other disciplinary perspectives. Understanding these different perspectives can be challenging (Repko et al., 2020), but an appreciation of this plurality can help develop an appreciation of diverse perspectives, critical thinking, and synthesis (de Greef et al., 2017; Howlett et al., 2016; Lyall et al., 2016). Exposure to different disciplinary perspectives can also enable students to reflect on the differences in their own perspectives and assumptions (Newell, 1992), which can foster personal growth and transformation (Ansari et al., 2023; Howlett et al., 2016).

Interdisciplinary learning offers unique opportunities to prepare 'students for a changing world' (Lyall et al., 2016, v) by bringing together and exposing students to different perspectives (Ansari et al., 2023). By offering interdisciplinary curricula as part of their courses, Higher Education institutions (HEIs) may better prepare students to respond to these challenges and encourage communication and collaboration, which in turn encourage critical, reflective thinking, and personal growth.

However, despite the need for 'new professionals' (de Greef et al., 2017, p. 10) and the perceived value of introducing interdisciplinary education (Lyall et al., 2016), the introduction of interdisciplinary curricula at HEIs is neither simple nor universally popular. Responding to these challenges requires a clear definition and conceptualisation of interdisciplinarity as well as institutional support for educators who develop the curricula.

HEIs are traditionally ordered by disciplinary approaches to learning and teaching which brings structural barriers (Noy et al., 2017) and potential cultural resistance (Howlett et al., 2016; Lyall et al., 2016; Turner et al., 2022). These existing systems and structures often prioritise resources for disciplinary endeavours making it difficult to challenge existing disciplinary narratives (Noy et al., 2017; Turner et al., 2022). The introduction of interdisciplinary curricula at an institution requires coordination and support as well as collaboration and learning between faculty and educators (Noy et al., 2017) and to achieve this the vision and rationale for interdisciplinary curricula within the institution needs to be articulated clearly (Lyall et al., 2016).

Pedagogic Rationale for Ruskin Modules

RMs were identified as part of an Active Curriculum Framework (ACF) within the *Education Strategy 2018–2022* (ARU, 2018b). The evidence base for the ACF described a student-centred approach to the curriculum 'designed to engage students as active participants in their own learning' (ARU, 2018b, p. 7). Active participation can involve discussion (Higher Education Academy (HEA), 2018), problem-based learning, and discovery (Hobbs & Brown, 2020).

Within the ACF, the pedagogic rationale for interdisciplinary breadth modules presented to ARU's (2018a, p. 14) Education Committee described that such curricula would,

> broaden students' perspectives, developing their intellectual flexibility and creative capability to tackle complex problems and challenges in collaboration with others and effectively communicate in a way that is understandable to a wide audience. Thereby equipping them with key graduate level employability skills capitals and attributes

with the aims of RMs described (ARU, 2018a, p. 8) as,

> creatively developing the capacity for critical reflection and reasoned argument, integrating the acquisition of graduate skills with wider societal concerns and challenges, bringing together students from different disciplines around key challenges.

The focus of RMs on societal concerns and challenges was important to the scheme. Basing the curricula on problems is an approach to designing interdisciplinary curricula and is a prerequisite for the necessary integration of insights that interdisciplinarity affords (Newell, 2002). Other approaches to interdisciplinarity such as cultural (Klein & Newell, 1997) or concept-based (de Greef et al., 2017) were not pursued as consistent, active, inclusive, and collaborative learning design would have been more challenging to assure.

Institutional Consultation

To create an initial proposal for the design of the scheme and the way in which RMs might be operationalised at ARU, the Institutional Lead for Ruskin Modules (ILRM) researched the literature and together with a researcher from ARU's Centre for Innovation in Higher Education (CIHE) identified institutions offering similar schemes of breadth modules. Key staff at these institutions were interviewed about their modules, asking about the perceived successes of such schemes and future developments.

Around 40 questions were asked about the rationale, aims of the scheme, how the modules were operationalised at those institutions, lessons learned, and any changes that were proposed. The ILRM and researcher collated and mapped answers to a core subset of 27 questions that acted as the basis for the proposed operational model for the RM scheme.

In their descriptions of institutional change, Klein and Newell (1997, p. 402) articulate the need to 'listen to the system' to surface motivations and concerns. Consequently, the proposal was presented to ARU's Academic Standards and Quality Committee (ASQC) in February 2019, and this proposal formed the basis of a formal consultation exercise on an institutional approach (Lyall et al., 2016) to interdisciplinary modules.

There was substantial engagement with the consultation exercise with 44 responses received including ten responses collated from organisational units such as faculties, Professional Services, and Trade Unions. Many respondents appreciated the notion of breadth modules evidenced by a belief in the breadth of an educational experience, and the opportunity to discuss the ways in which the educational provision could accommodate such an approach.

ARU's Education Committee considered the feedback from the consultation and addressed the points raised. The Students' Union was actively involved in thinking about RMs and suggested themes for modules they wanted to see in the institutional offer such as global health, laughter and happiness, and how to be an entrepreneur. More formally, in response to the proposal, feedback from students through focus groups organised and facilitated by the Students' Union was also considered.

As a direct result of the consultation exercise, several aspects of the original proposal were reconsidered; for example, the introduction of RMs in the first year of undergraduate study was dropped. The Senate approved the amended model in March 2019 which allowed time for the Academic Regulations to be revised and published in line with its annual cycle of circulation.

Establishing an Operational Model

ARU's curriculum structure is modular (ARU, 2022) with the credit of each module relative to the indicative hours of study. Module credit ranges from 15 credits through to 120-credit capstone projects. RMs were approved as 15-credit modules and a compulsory requirement of all undergraduate courses at Level 5. Space for RMs was created in the curriculum of all undergraduate courses as part of a systematic process of Course Design Intensives (CDIs) (Middleton et al., 2021) scheduled to support the adoption of the ACF. This active inclusive learning framework is a holistic course-level approach to curriculum design and delivery that articulates the educational dimensions and learning literacies that support students to learn and develop graduate capitals (ARU, 2021).

Further operational principles included that students would be presented with a variety of modules from which to choose, courses would offer an unrestricted range of RMs from which to choose, and students would, as far as practicable, be enrolled on their first choice of RM.

Exemptions from Ruskin Modules

The course (re)approval process was amended to provide an opportunity for individual courses to seek permission to implement an alternative model to the delivery of RMs approved by the Senate. Similarly, it was essential to not place at risk the continued accreditation of courses by Professional, Statutory and Regulatory Bodies (PSRB), which acknowledged the flexibility of some requirements and the highly prescriptive nature of others. Therefore, where Course Teams provided evidence 'that the continued accreditation of a course may be placed at risk by the inclusion of RMs, such a course will be required to follow an alternative format for satisfying the generic outcomes of Ruskin Modules' (ARU, 2019, p. 9), temporary exemption was approved for two years for course teams to discuss with PSRBs how to best integrate the outcomes of RMs into their course curricula.

Approving Curricula

Faculty-specific education committees normally approve new modules. RMs, however, are located outside the faculties, centrally within ARU's learning and teaching development unit, Anglia Learning & Teaching (AL&T). The Education Committee agreed to undertake separate approval events to consider RMs (ARU, 2021), and a new committee was later approved to oversee the development and quality assurance of RM curricula.

This committee consisted of two external panel members experienced with interdisciplinary curricula at their own institutions, the Academic Registrar, ILRM, faculty representatives, and a member of senior faculty management (Head of School) as the Chair. The Students' Union was invited to provide student representation for the approval panels.

The open, collegiate, and discursive nature of the panels meant that the design of curricula was not just approved but also improved. Two recommendations emerged from the approval event that were approved by both the ASQC and the Education Committee:

1 Titles of RMs should be framed as questions that provoke (curiosity).
2 RMs include a common learning outcome that makes explicit interdisciplinarity (ARU, 2020).

RM Titles as Questions

To entitle a RM as a statement of intent, for example, 'Introduction to design' implies that the outcomes of the module are predictable and known by the Module Leader (and not yet the student) and is the antithesis of the 'inherent ambiguity in addressing complex challenges' (ARU, 2020, p. 3) and the collaborative nature of the modules. Additionally, questions are more likely to engage students with the module. Questions relating to higher-cognitive levels (Bloom, 1956) are also more likely to engage students in higher-order thinking (Gall, 1970) and creative thinking (Antink-Meyer & Lederman, 2013).

Thus, each RM is titled as a question, rather than a statement, to provoke curiosity (LeBlanc et al., 2017) and make explicit that learning activities take an active, student-centred, problem-based approach to learning (Allen et al., 2011) rather than a didactic, educator-centred approach (Pratt-Adams et al., 2020).

Shared Learning Outcome

The aims of RMs were to bring students from different courses together to respond to contemporary challenges by integrating their perspectives. Exposing students to others with different personal and disciplinary perspectives provides the opportunities to develop mental flexibility while attempting to solve complex problems. By engaging with people and problems in this way, RMs are designed to better prepare students with skills for workplaces of the future.

A paper to ARU's (2020, p. 3) Education Committee stated that:

> a principle of Ruskin Modules is the ambiguity inherent in addressing complex challenges – to entitle a Ruskin Module as a statement of intent implies the broader outcomes of the module are known and predictable and is the antithesis of this philosophy. Questions are points of entry to the module that invite students to think of potential answers from their own point-of-view and are therefore accessible in a way that statements are arguably not accessible. Furthermore, a question that is framed to provoke makes Ruskin modules stand out from other modules; a module with this title that appears on a student's transcript may prompt an employer to ask about the module which in turn provides an opportunity for the student to articulate their engagement, skills, and experience gained.

A set of outcomes for the scheme, adapted from van der Waldt (2014), articulated in more detail the outcomes for students of the RMs:

- Work collaboratively, respecting diversity, and being culturally sensitive.
- Critically reflect on the limitations of a single discipline to solve wider societal concerns.
- Create meaningful connections across disciplines and apply new knowledge to key challenges.
- Participate as a responsible citizen in the life of local, national, and global communities.
- Recognise and critically reflect on issues of social responsibility, ethical conduct, and sustainability.
- Encourage an appreciation of ambiguity.

These six outcomes of the scheme were cross-checked with ARU's graduate capitals and condensed into a single learning outcome common to each RM (Baxter & Brown, 2018, p. 4):

Critically reflect on the limitations of a single discipline to solve wider societal concerns by applying knowledge created through the discovery and exploitation of connections across disciplines.

In this way, interdisciplinarity is addressed explicitly within each RM, and the distinctiveness of the scheme is underlined.

The first approval panel for RMs took place at the end of 2019 and resulted in the approval of the curricula of eight RMs. The panel requested that two proposals undergo further improvement and deferred the consideration of one module to the next meeting. Three subsequent approval panels from 2019 to 2021 approved further curricula.

Nineteen RMs were offered to students during the process of Module Planning in Spring 2021, and 2,022 students were enrolled at Teaching Week 1 in the 2021/22 Academic Year. The most popular RM, *AI and the Future: A Threat to Humanity?*, was chosen by 214 students, with enrolments on the seven most popular RMs exceeded 100; enrolments on the smallest RM numbered 46.

Timetabling Ruskin Modules

A working model for RMs assumed that 3,500 Level 5 students would be involved, and ARU estimated that 20–25 RMs would need to be implemented in the first year. Discussions about the logistics of RMs included the challenges of timetabling, the capacity of available rooms, and the practicalities of running the modules simultaneously at two campuses. Additionally, as RMs were open to all students whose courses were not temporarily exempt, a time slot was identified in the timetable and protected across the timetables of all courses. Wednesday mornings were chosen, as Wednesday afternoons were already protected for sporting activities and societies, and this provided conceptual consistency.

The COVID-19 pandemic from March 2020 meant that RMs were designed to be facilitated online rather than face-to-face. Not only was this necessary due to the pandemic but also pragmatically facilitating RMs online better enabled the timetabling of classes as sessions were not restricted by room capacity, nor did they have to be repeated, or delivered simultaneously at two geographically remote campuses.

Engaging Educators

Preliminary research (ARU, 2020) suggested that interdisciplinary, breadth modules facilitated by passionate educators are more successfully received by students. Models at other institutions included modules designed and run centrally or designed centrally and tutors sought by their expertise. Additionally, in their recommendations for institutional change, Klein and Newell (1997) describe identifying 'what motivations exist' (Klein & Newell, 1997, p. 402) within the institution rather than assuming what may work. The ILRM therefore opened a call for Expressions of Interest for staff members who were interested in developing a RM (ARU, 2020). Thus, a call for educators interested in developing interdisciplinary curricula was circulated to staff shortly after the approval of the operating model of RMs by the Senate, including an invitation to representatives from the Students' Union. Such was the level of interest that the venue for the workshop was twice relocated to accommodate additional attendees. These early enthusiasts were named 'Trailblazers' in recognition that they were breaking new ground.

The RM Trailblazer Day ran in June 2019, during which an external consultant facilitated a 'sandpit' together with the ILRM and Deputy Vice Chancellor (Education). Based on the sandpit model used by the Engineering and Physical Sciences Research Council (EPSRC) to generate research bids, the Trailblazer Day provided an opportunity for academic and Professional Services staff to come together in multidisciplinary groups to generate ideas. The outcomes of the Trailblazer Sandpit were to:

- Establish a community of pioneers to drive the development of RMs
- Foster the discussion and sharing of initial ideas
- Identify approximately 20 RMs with initial cross-disciplinary groups to take ideas forward.

Staff and students were grouped into 12 teams comprising people from multiple disciplines. The Trailblazer Day included a series of activities where staff and students were encouraged to think creatively and collaboratively, designing learning experiences rather than designing 'modules' based on implicit beliefs about curriculum design which may hinder innovation.

Teams considered the core themes of their proposed RM, suggesting both a title and learning outcomes; these proposals were presented to the whole group for feedback, and posters were hung on the walls for a 'gallery walk', where additional feedback could be added. Designs for 28 RMs sprung from the Trailblazer Day with proposals ranging from an exploration of the senses such as 'Hear and Taste' to 'Future Proofing' and 'Privilege'.

The Next Steps Workshops

Trailblazers from the day were invited back together in their teams to develop their proposals from posters to Module Definition Forms (MDFs) through two smaller Next Steps workshops facilitated by the ILRM and the Academic Registrar. These workshops asked educators to take 'the next steps' to reflect on their passions in HE, identify the desired outcomes for students, and question assumptions that might be held about the ways a module should run. The ILRM and Academic Registrar were keen that Trailblazers design their RMs to best fit their envisioned pedagogic design and were interested where the Academic Regulations might preclude this.

The design of only six proposals from the Trailblazer Day was developed further and taken to an approval event. The ideas for the other 14 RMs were created at the Next Steps workshops or independently of development workshops by educators.

The Trailblazer Day elicited 'buzz', fun, excitement, innovation, and design activity with more colleagues interested in designing interdisciplinary curricula than anticipated (Klein & Newell, 1997). Unfortunately, only a small proportion of these colleagues committed to the design and facilitation of a RM. Most of the educators who became Trailblazers contacted the ILRM independently of the Trailblazer Day.

Conceptualising Interdisciplinarity

Following the approval of the curricula as both appropriate and interdisciplinary, RMs needed to be 'fleshed out' with learning activities and assessments. It was not assumed that staff who were able to design and deliver the course-based disciplinary curriculum of familiar subjects could design and deliver an interdisciplinary curriculum where integration of disciplines was the focus (Lyall et al., 2016) and that these skills needed to be developed.

Trailblazers were also encouraged to explore their conceptualisations of interdisciplinarity (Klein & Newell, 1997), which may have been shaped by their disciplinary epistemologies and educational philosophies. Klein and Newell (1997) caution that as a complex concept 'interdisciplinarity will not be a matter of agreement, conceptually, practically, or politically' (Klein & Newell, 1997, p. 342) and this lack of shared understanding can stall implementation (Holley, 2009). Not only this, but ARU wanted to ensure that RMs were truly interdisciplinary rather than multidisciplinary or crossdisciplinary.

This exploration of interdisciplinarity was guided by a series of CPD workshops, discussions, and a conceptualisation of interdisciplinarity articulated for the RM scheme. This central conceptualisation (Brown, 2020) is important not only for a consistent basis from which the curricula develop but also for a consistent message articulated for students. This conceptualisation articulates the ways in which RMs are interdisciplinary and defines crossdisciplinarity and multidisciplinarity, which are commonly misconstrued as interdisciplinarity (Lyall et al., 2016; Spelt et al., 2009). Educators could then expand upon this conceptualisation and innovate their curriculum according to their philosophies and the context of the challenge to which their RM responds.

Two definitions of interdisciplinarity in curricula were used to support a consistent conceptualisation for RM Leaders. Jacobs (1989, p. 8) describes a 'curriculum approach that consciously applies methodology and language from more than one discipline to a central theme, issue, problem, topic of experience'. This first definition makes explicit the Module Leader's responsibility to facilitate the conscious and proactive (Klein, 2006; Spelt et al., 2009) integration of at least two disciplines (Blom et al., 2020; Stein, 2007) rather than leaving this activity to the student (Lyall et al., 2016) (or to chance).

The second definition from Klein and Newell (1997, p. 3) describes 'a process of answering a question, solving a problem, or addressing a topic that is too broad or complex to be dealt with adequately by a single discipline or profession' and 'draws on disciplinary perspectives and integrates their insights through construction of a more comprehensive perspective'. This makes it clear that our curriculum approach is centred on responding to the question that is the title of the RM and that the application of methodology or language is not just 'additive' but 'transformative' (Klein, 2006) and creates (Knight et al., 2013) a new perspective (Klein, 1990) which advances our current view (Repko, 2008; Spelt et al., 2009). This definition signalled the need for RMs to be problem-centred, and for Trailblazers to support the integration of, rather than solely the introduction of, different disciplinary perspectives.

Continuing Professional Development

A series of CPD workshops continued the theme of exploring the design and implementation of interdisciplinarity through three 'Bringing Interdisciplinarity to Life' sessions, which guided RM Leaders through theories of interdisciplinarity, integrative activities, and designing interdisciplinary assessment. Furthermore, a series of Ruskin Module Open Studios (see Chapter 5) offered Trailblazers (and students) regular time to explore and reflect on themes relating to interdisciplinarity, employability, and sustainability through facilitated art-based activities. In addition, three regular meetings with Trailblazers were introduced. 'T-time' (i.e., Trailblazer Time) ran weekly from May to December 2021. Initially, T-time provided an informal and agenda-less space for Trailblazers to ask questions and share anxieties. As teaching started, T-time became a space for Trailblazers to share what was working well in their RM and morphed into a space for 'just in time' CPD. 'Morning Espresso' was trialled to share information quickly with Trailblazers, and to answer any questions. However, discussion was frequently required and so the concept of Morning Espresso was abandoned. As RMs all ran on Wednesday mornings, 'Decompress and Debrief' was scheduled for Wednesday afternoons for Trailblazers to discuss how the morning's activities had gone and for the ILRM to address any challenges quickly. One of the remits of 'Decompress and Debrief' was to support Trailblazers' wellbeing. In addition, the ILRM added an end of Trimester 'Synchronisation Day' to align the marking of assessment to the Ruskin Module Learning Outcome, and a 'Blue Skies' workshop to reflect on what went well, and the further support required to inform new CPD.

Reception

RMs were not embraced by all stakeholders at ARU, but the development and maturation of interdisciplinary curricula can involve a considerable change in culture and take time (Lyall et al., 2016). This is still early in the implementation of interdisciplinary curricula and different views are to be expected 'in a healthily diverse higher education system' (Lyall et al., 2016, xi). Similarly, feedback from students is mixed with some students unable to see the benefits of skills development through to students experiencing profound personal transformation.

Conclusion

The introduction of RMs was a significant institutional initiative. Creating credit-bearing, interdisciplinary breadth modules, unrelated to any specific subject, was in itself a risky endeavour, but making them compulsory for a third of the student body (i.e., all Level 5 undergraduates, except those on PSRB-governed courses) was a considerable gamble. As this meant a change and a challenge to the accepted order of learning and teaching, it is hardly surprising that the reaction was divided. This abrupt and revolutionary change to established practice will take time to form part of the educational furniture at ARU. Only with hindsight will staff and students truly recognise the impact of RMs in producing graduates with an interdisciplinary perspective on complex global issues, particularly sustainability, and enhanced employability through the acquisition of those skills prized by employers.

Recommendations

- Involve students and colleagues across the institution in the introduction of interdisciplinary curricula and be clear and consistent about the outcomes of the curricula in all communications.
- Support students to tell stories of transformation that can be shared.
- Be prepared to support educators with interdisciplinary pedagogy, through institutional processes, and emotionally.

References

Allen, D. E., Donham, R. S., & Bernhardt, S. A. (2011). Problem-based learning. *New Directions for Teaching and Learning, 128*, 21–29. https://doi.org/10.1002/tl.465

Anglia Ruskin University (ARU). (2017). Designing our future 2017-2026: Our strategy. Anglia Ruskin University.

Anglia Ruskin University (ARU). (2018a). Active curriculum development update. Anglia Ruskin University.

Anglia Ruskin University (ARU). (2018b). Education strategy 2018-2022. Anglia Ruskin University.

Anglia Ruskin University (ARU). (2019). SEN/19/06 – Education strategy: Introducing Ruskin modules [Unpublished internal document]. Anglia Ruskin University.

Anglia Ruskin University (ARU). (2020). *Education strategy: Ruskin modules.* Cambridge, Chelmsford and Peterborough: Anglia Ruskin University.

Anglia Ruskin University (ARU). (2021). Briefing document for approval panel members: Ruskin modules approval phase 4 [Unpublished internal document]. Anglia Ruskin University.

Anglia Ruskin University (ARU). (2022). Academic regulations: Fifteenth edition. Anglia Ruskin University.

Ansari, H., Holland, M., Tozer, S., Vessey, T., & Brown, E. (2023). *Tales of transformation* [Paper presentation]. Interdisciplinary Learning and Teaching Conference: Interdisciplinary Experiences: Transforming Perspectives, Anglia Ruskin University, 20 April 2023.

Antink-Meyer, A., & Lederman, N. G. (2013). Inventing creativity: An exploration of the pedagogy of ingenuity in science classrooms. *School Science and Mathematics, 113*(8), 400–409. https://doi.org/10.1111/ssm.12039

Baxter, P., & Brown, E. (2018). Education strategy: Ruskin modules. Anglia Ruskin University.

Blom, M., Scager, K., & Wiegant, F. (2020). *Assessment of Interdisciplinary Competencies.* Retrieved 5 July 2024, from https://teaching-and-learning-collection.sites.uu.nl/wp-content/uploads/sites/982/2021/08/18122-B2_Rapport-Assessment-Interdisciplinary-Competencies-final.pdf

Bloom, B. S. (1956). *Taxonomy of educational objectives, handbook: The cognitive domain.* David McKay.

Brown, E. (2020). Ruskin modules summary [Unpublished internal document]. Anglia Ruskin University.

Gall, M. D. (1970). The use of questions in teaching, *Review of Educational Research, 40*(5). https://doi.org/10.3102/00346543040005707

Graybill, J., Dooling, S., Shadas, V., Withey, J., Greve, A., & Simon, G. (2006). A rough guide to interdisciplinarity: Graduate student perspectives. *Bioscience, 56*(9), 757–763. https://doi.org/10.1641/0006-3568(2006)56[757:ARGTIG]2.0.CO;2

de Greef, L., Post, G., Vink, C., & Wenting, L. (2017). *Designing interdisciplinary education: A practical handbook for university teachers.* Amsterdam University Press.

Higher Education Academy (HEA) (2018). *Active Learning.* Retrieved 5 July 2024, from https://www.heacademy.ac.uk/knowledge-hub/active-learning

Hobbs, M., & Brown, E. (2020). The 1-2-3 feedback cycle. In S. Pratt-Adams, U. Richter, & M. Warnes (Eds.), *Innovations in active learning in higher education.* University of Sussex. https://doi.org/10.20919/9781912319961

Holley, K. A. (2009). Understanding interdisciplinary challenges and opportunities in higher education. *ASHE Higher Education Report, 35*(2), 1–131. https://doi.org/10.1002/aehe.3502

Howlett, C., Ferreira, J.-A., & Blomfield, J. (2016). Teaching sustainable development in higher education: Building critical, reflective thinkers through an interdisciplinary approach. *International Journal of Sustainability in Higher Education, 17*(3), 305–321. https://doi.org/10.1108/IJSHE-07-2014-0102

Jacobs, H. H. (1989). *Interdisciplinary curriculum: Design and implementation.* Association for Supervision and Curriculum Development. Retrieved 5 July 2024, from https://files.eric.ed.gov/fulltext/ED316506.pdf

Klein, J. T. (1990). *Interdisciplinarity: History, theory, and practice.* Wayne State University Press.

Klein, J. T. (2006). A platform for a shared discourse of interdisciplinary education. *JSSE-Journal of Social Science Education.* Retrieved 5 July 2024, from http://digitalcommons.wayne.edu/englishfrp/3

Klein, J. T., & Newell, W. H. (1997). Advancing interdisciplinary studies. In J. G. Gaff, & J. L. Ratcliff (Eds.), *Handbook of the undergraduate curriculum: A comprehensive guide to the purposes, structures, practices, and change* (pp. 393–415). Jossey-Bass.

Knight, D. B., Lattuca, L., Kimball, E., & Reason, R. (2013). Understanding interdisciplinarity: Curricular and organizational features of undergraduate interdisciplinary programs. *Innovative Higher Education*, *38*(2), 143–158. https://doi.org/10.1007/s10755-012-9232-1

LeBlanc, H. J., Nepal, K., & Mowry, G. S. (2017). Stimulating curiosity and the ability to formulate technical questions in an electric circuits course using the question formulation technique (QFT), *IEEE Frontiers in Education Conference (FIE)*, pp. 1–6.

Lyall, C., Meagher, L., Bandola, G., & Kettle, A. (2016). *Interdisciplinary provision in higher education: Current and future challenges*. Retrieved 5 July 2024, from https://documents.advance-he.ac.uk/download/file/document/4604

Middleton, A., Pratt-Adams, S., & Priddle, J. (2021). Active, inclusive and immersive: Using course design intensives with course teams to rethink the curriculum across an institution. *SEDA Educational Developments*, *21*(1), 9–13.

Newell, W. H. (1992). Academic disciplines and undergraduate interdisciplinary education: Lessons from the School of Interdisciplinary Studies at Miami University, Ohio. *European Journal of Education*, *27*(3), 211–221. Retrieved 5 July 2024, from https://www.jstor.org/stable/pdf/1503450.pdf

Newell, W. H. (2002). Integrating the college curriculum. In J. Klein (Ed.), *Interdisciplinary education in K-12 and college* (pp. 119–138). The College Board.

Noy, S., Patrick, R., Capetola, T., & McBurnie, J. (2017). Inspiration from the classroom: A mixed methods case study of interdisciplinary sustainability learning in higher education. *Australian Journal of Environmental Education*, *33*(2), 97–118. Retrieved 5 July 2024, from https://www.jstor.org/stable/pdf/26422963.pdf

Pratt-Adams, S., Richter, U., & Warnes, M. (Eds.) (2020). *Innovations in active learning in higher education*. University of Sussex/Fulcum. https://doi.org/10.20919/9781912319961

Repko, A. F. (2008). Assessing interdisciplinary learning outcomes. *Academic Exchange Quarterly*, *12*, 171–178.

Repko, A. F., Szostak, R., & Phillips Buchberger, M. (2020). *Introduction to interdisciplinary studies* (3rd ed.). SAGE Publications.

Spelt, E. J. H., Biemans, H., Tobi, H., Luning, P., & Mulder, M. (2009). Teaching and learning in interdisciplinary higher education: A systematic review. *Educational Psychology Review*, *21*, 365–378. https://doi.org/10.1007/s10648-009-9113-z

Stein, Z. (2007). Modeling the demands of interdisciplinarity: Toward a framework for evaluating interdisciplinary endeavors. *Integral Review*, *4*(1), 91–107. Retrieved 5 July 2024, from https://www.integral-review.org/issues/issue_4_jun_2007_full_issue.pdf

Turner, R., Cotton, D., Eidse, N., Thompson-Fawcett, M., & Fitzsimons, S. (2022). Embedding interdisciplinary learning into the first-year undergraduate curriculum: Drivers and barriers in a cross-institutional enhancement project. *Teaching in Higher Education*. https://doi.org/10.1080/13562517.2022.2056834

Van der Waldt, G. (2014). Public administration and transdisciplinarity: A modalistic approach toward knowledge co-construction. *International Journal of Humanities and Social Science*, *4*(6), 120–134. Retrieved 5 July 2024, from https://www.ijhssnet.com/journals/Vol_4_No_6_April_2014/12.pdf

Yair, G. (2008). Can we administer the scholarship of teaching? Lessons from outstanding professors in higher education. *Higher Education*, *55*(4), 447–459. Retrieved 5 July 2024, from https://www.jstor.org/stable/29735195

Chapter 5

Creativity and Design for Innovative Interdisciplinary Education

The Case of the Ruskin Module Open Studios

Beatriz Acevedo and Andrew Middleton

Introduction

Ruskin Modules (RMs) are interdisciplinary breadth modules aimed at fostering creative and critical thinking while addressing complex social and environmental problems. They establish an opportunity for innovation in curriculum design by integrating elements of the United Nations Sustainable Development Goals (UN SDGs) (United Nations, 2015), addressing global citizenship, and responding to the challenges and opportunities presented by employability and entrepreneurship imperatives. RMs are compulsory modules for every Level 5 (Year 2) undergraduate student at Anglia Ruskin University (ARU), and one of their key characteristics is interdisciplinarity. The RM ethos supports ARU's commitment to an active curriculum (Pratt-Adams et al., 2020), including authentic learning and assessment, diversity and inclusivity, accessibility, sustainability, and employability (ARU, 2017, 2018a, 2018b, 2018c). Although there is a growing interest in developing such interdisciplinary education (Higher Education Academy (HEA), 2015), the RMs take this further by fostering cooperation, dialogue, and creativity in their design.

Responding to an open call, lecturers, and Professional Services colleagues, including ourselves, volunteered to become part of the experience. From the outset, ARU was determined that RM development would not follow a typical pattern. Consequently, the Institutional Lead for Ruskin Modules (ILRM) (see Chapter 4) and the Academic Developer (Acevedo) adopted a twofold approach: firstly, we designed a series of interdisciplinary workshops focused on 'Bringing Interdisciplinarity to Life', following a Continuing Professional Development (CPD) of sharing scholarship and good practice on interdisciplinarity while encouraging co-creation among passionate pioneer RM innovators, or 'Trailblazers'. The entire process of RM development was aimed at embodying the spirit of the Trailblazers, who are risk-takers with a passion for innovative educational experiences and an acceptance of uncertainty are both innovators and entrepreneurs (Hasanefendic et al., 2017). The innovative aspects of RMs are related to the processes which combine key ideas of

DOI: 10.4324/9781003474593-6

interdisciplinary education, sustainability, and employability. For example, we sought to collaborate as we developed our tools and materials for interdisciplinary learning activities and assessment.

Secondly, based on studio-based learning approaches, the ILRM and Academic Developer created the Open Studios as a space in which to apply this creative thinking to a wider realm of working with academics from different faculties and Professional Services, working towards the common purpose of developing the RMs. The idea was extended by the authors of this chapter, Acevedo and Middleton, using their dual identities as artists/educators and experience in using aesthetic and creative methodologies for management learning, education, and staff development (Acevedo et al., 2022; Middleton, 2021). Using the Open Studios, we aimed to foster creativity by encouraging module leaders to go beyond the constraints of traditional lectures and encouraging them to experiment and innovate in developing more active and immersive learning environments.

In this chapter, we discuss the development of the Open Studios model and situate this in the specialisms of studio-based learning design for non-studio-based disciplines in higher education. Our aim was to explore the idea of studio-based learning and its potential in higher education and curriculum design. In our approach, the studio is both a physical and a virtual space where participants can play, experiment, and question the module development process and learn from each other. As we were working with the RM Trailblazers, who already possessed what bell hooks (1994) calls a 'passion for education', we were able to be imaginative in creating conditions that would allow them to amplify their enthusiasm by devising a space for open conversations.

In addition, we describe the various aspects of designing interdisciplinary modules, integrating experimentation and playfulness as part of the process. We expand on some of the creative methods used for the development of the key aspects of the RMs.

In the following section, we present a critical assessment of Open Studios as a creative space, including their potential and challenges. We draw upon formal and informal group evaluations (i.e., 'reflective moments') and focus groups which examine the impact of Open Studios on RM development. Finally, we offer a critical summary of Open Studios while sharing some ideas for further application and development. In the spirit of Open Studios, this chapter emerges from our authentic voices, bringing out the playful and non-prescriptive aspects of the Open Studios experience.

Studio-Based Learning Fostering Innovation and Interdisciplinarity in Higher Education

Imagine stepping into a garden. A path crosses through a lawn bordered with plants. The air is fresh, and the sound of birds twittering is a welcome distraction to the oppressive squares confronting you in your Teams meetings. Then a door opens, and we enter the studio. Inside it is a bit messy, strips of paper, dots of paint, pencils, brushes, and scissors, are all scattered on a big table. The mess is somehow relaxing and inviting. There is no need for perfection or dexterity; on the contrary, the space signals that mistakes are encouraged. A small bell indicates the beginning of the session, followed by a very brief welcome and a breathing exercise.

We include our sensorial description to bring the virtual and physical sensuality of the Open Studios to life. Although the delivery of the workshops was virtual, our aim was to take people outside of their virtual offices into a space filled with birdsong and the visual stimulation of an actual messy studio, with its materials and tools. This setting is full of inviting affordances (Gibson, 1979); influences that solicit actions and which invite the participant to feel drawn to act in a certain way (Withagen et al., 2017). Here we refer to the studio as both a physical space and a virtual space as we explore the potential of studio-based learning in the context of academic development and curriculum design, although its meanings also have ontological, pedagogical, technological, epistemological, and cultural significance.

The word 'studio' is loaded with artistic connotations. The artist's studio or *atelier*, or the architect's studio, where tools, materials, and prompts have inviting affordances (e.g., visual material, models, groups of pencils, books, paper, cuttings) look like the 'magical objects of creative folks'. However, the word studio stems from the Latin *studium* referring to a specific space or room. As Grant (2021, p. 19) explains, the term *studium* refers to the origin of European universities:

> it derives from the idea of being incorporated or being part of a collective movement ... based on this story, the more accurate word to describe the university was actually 'studium' suggesting that we should be referring the Studium of Cambridge, Studium of Bologna, etc.

The evolution of universities replaced this notion of *studium*, implying the free exchange of ideas and experiences and cooperation among faculties and scholars, with a complex structure of power, hierarchies, and independent faculties (Rüegg, 2004). The studio became associated with creative disciplines and their ways of working and scholarship. Indeed, Long (2012) reminds us that arts and architecture schools have adopted the studio as a place to work on real-life problems and client briefings. However, Long (2012) argues that the studio is not only a physical place but also an epistemological space that fosters cooperation and learning among peers. The studio accommodates diverse ways of working including, for example, a series of structured conversations between instructor(s), students, and outside experts: those who may be invited in, for example, to provide context, set a brief, perform as an audience, or assess exhibited work. An individual's work is peer-assessed in a group 'crit', which provides a supportive system, creating a sense of community around critique, and contributing to the individual development of projects or artefacts. This emphasis on the cooperative nature of the studio recognises that the individuality of the endeavours is a key quality in studio-based learning and, in our case, studio-based educational design. Nevertheless, the individual endeavour is situated within a cooperative ethos of 'working alongside' (Harrop & Turpin, 2013).

In our view, the concept of 'studio' disrupts the dualistic conceptions of formal/informal, and physical/virtual learning space. Instead, we present a multifaceted and multi-layered site of doing, being, belonging, becoming, and connectivity as an alternative way to conceptualise the studio as a place of learning. Drawing upon Gibbs (2013), educational development in the context of the RMs fostered interdisciplinarity and creativity, sharing good practices and anxieties in bringing together such an innovative project. To nurture innovation and development in educational settings, it is useful to consider the notion of a 'hybrid learning studio' as 'a site of unbounded and liminal experience in which a learner's agency is situated in a socially networked and cooperative paradigm' (Middleton, 2021, p. 4). This concept can be applied to non-artistic disciplines in several ways:

- a functional setting for enacting learning, having tools, affordances, and practices
- a networked assemblage and ecology of practices
- a place of professional and disciplinary practice and shared identity
- a social space for collaboration, cooperation, and affinity

(Middleton, 2021, pp. 43–44)

We illustrate the multifaceted potential of Open Studios in Figure 5.1.

Following the distinctive nature of the RMs, the purpose of using the studio for educational development was not collaboration but cooperation. Collaboration normally involves a group of people working together towards an aim or project, while cooperation recognises the individual integrity of each of the participants and their own aims (Kolgar, 2010). The differences between collaboration and cooperation are location-based: a typical CPD session, for example, has clearly defined learning outcomes, limited time assigned to each aspect of the programme, a focus on developing, and, in many cases, working on, a joint project, while in the art studio, each person is working on their own painting or project yet supported by others. The studio, although having learning aims, has a looser structure, allowing time to follow a path when the dynamic requires it. The Open Studios, in this case, recognised that although each Trailblazer focused on their own distinctive module, they learnt from each other and felt supported by the community through the design process and shared values.

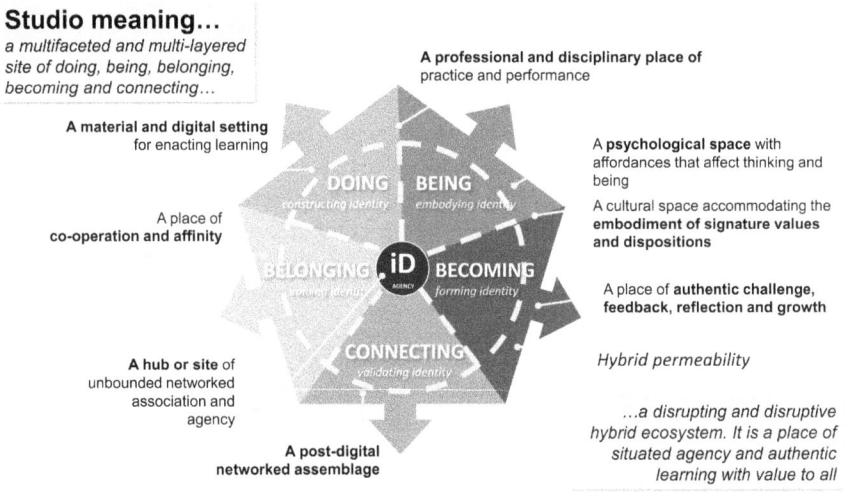

Figure 5.1 The Hybrid Learning Studio model: a place of doing, being, belonging, becoming, and connecting (Middleton, 2021, p. 7)

Fostering Innovation through RMs

From the outset, ARU considered RMs to be innovative, involving the expansion of boundaries in the design, delivery, and assessment of the experience (ARU, 2022). Yet innovation is one of those terms whose ubiquity and overuse can lead to a multitude of meanings. In the context of neophilia, innovation is the ultimate ambition, the 'shiny label' for every project, but educational innovation is challenging to prove. According to the Organisation for Economic Cooperation and Development (OECD) (2016, pp. 13–15), educational innovation can,

> i) improve learning outcomes and the quality of education, ii) contribute to the enhancement of equity and equality, iii) have positive effects of efficiency, and iv) update the educational system to keep track and not loose [sic] pace compared to societal and economic changes that are occurring simultaneously.

For others, the importance of innovation links to what Etzkowitz and Leydesdorff (1995) called the Triple Helix: a model used to understand the dynamic interactions between three key innovation actors (university, industry, and government) which support entrepreneurship, innovation, and economic growth. Cai (2015) adds institutional change and institutional capacity building to this model. Furthermore, innovation needs to be situated in a specific context and policy framework (Jacobs, 2000) and needs to be understood in terms of products and processes.

In the RM context, the notion of interdisciplinary education responds to the economic, environmental, and social complexities of the twenty-first century. Hawkey et al. (2019), for example, noted that contemporary problems are too multifaceted for a single perspective to address. In this regard, interdisciplinarity in education concerns a process of answering a question, solving a problem, or addressing a topic that is too broad or complex for a single discipline (Newell, 1990). Conklin (2006) describes such a challenge as a 'Wicked Problem' which, while being cumbersome and unwieldy, is disingenuous to ignore. Kolko (2012, para. 1 [original emphasis]), for example, defines a wicked problem as,

> a social or cultural problem that is difficult or impossible to solve for as many as four reasons: incomplete or contradictory knowledge, the number of people and opinions involved, the large economic burden, and the interconnected nature of these problems with other problems.

Our approach to interdisciplinarity involved an active learning approach, which embraced the difficulties involved in interdisciplinary education. As de Greef et al. (2017, p. 18) reminds us,

> Being involved in interdisciplinary education means that we ourselves must adhere to what we ask of our students: to be open-minded, to have intellectual courage and empathy, to create a safe environment for discussion, to be reflective on our own role, to develop shared understanding and to resolve differences.

Our challenge in the Open Studios was to encourage innovative approaches to RM design while guaranteeing interdisciplinarity. We sought to generate a creative ecosystem to nurture creative approaches and encourage innovation and experimentation, within existing boundaries of academic quality, project management, and academic regulations.

A further task was to maintain a pragmatic balance between specified systemic constraints (e.g., a specific learning outcome bounded by a curriculum deadline) with the need for academic autonomy and freedom. Thus, the problem we faced was how to create space within a structure, which Limpanowicz and McCandless (2014, p. 2) define as a 'liberating structure', which is the methods, places, and approaches aimed at 'transforming how people interact and work together to achieve much better results than what is possible with presentations, reports, and other conventional methods'. Consequently, the Open Studios model is located between the formal aspects of workshops and the less structured dynamics of creative endeavours.

Limpanowicz and McCandless (2014) explain how small structural changes can afford big differences, for example, the way in which questions are asked (e.g., appreciative interviews), or by promoting communication in teams through 'conversation cafés' or 'drawing sessions'. Their experience stems from the corporate world which readily adopts many of these creative methods and design thinking ideas (Taylor & Ladkin, 2009). These methods are not new but framing them as liberating structures creates a platform for exploring breaking barriers, overcoming fears, and offering possibilities to participants (i.e., students, educators, managers, decision-makers) to escape the trappings of conventional learning and development spaces.

Inspired by hooks (1994), the Open Studios channelled the RM's spirit of passion and transgression by questioning the 'banking' language of curriculum design and academic development (Freire, 1970). We interrogated many of the current ideas in curriculum design such as what inclusivity means for the student, the concept of education for sustainability, and developing active learning. The Open Studios became a space for questioning and creativity, and its aims were to:

1 embed interdisciplinarity values and practices in the development of the RMs,
2 offer creative-based methodologies for the participants to apply in the development of their RMs and to enhance their own professional practice,
3 nurture a sense of innovative community, based on cooperation and sharing the emotional and practical weight of this experience, complementing the ethos of the development of the project, and
4 provide a 'liberating structure' for the expansion of ideas, experimentation, and free discussion of alternatives in the design of the RMs.

How Open Studios Cooperate

The 14 two-hour Open Studios sessions supported the design of the RMs by following ideas drawn from Design Thinking (Razzouk & Shute, 2012) such as empathy, problem definition, shared understanding of interdisciplinarity, student-centred design, sustainability, and storytelling.

The liberating structure of the Open Studios addressed issues and/or questions of RM design using creative-based methods tailored through a divergent/convergent approach. According to Reddy et al. (2016, p. 191),

convergent thinking competencies are providing a single solution for a given problem by following conventional problem-solving procedures and judging decisions. Divergent thinking abilities are providing multiple solutions for a given problem by thinking outside of the box and refining the process.

The divergent aspect of the Open Studios introduced creative exercises and an expansion of ideas. For example, in the first hour of the Open Studios sessions, the divergent aspect started by inviting participants to adopt the studio mindset by metaphorically walking from the garden to the studio, followed by a wellbeing exercise to get 'in the zone'. This ritual complemented a managerial approach to the development of the RMs, and it symbolically and epistemologically marked an entering of a creative space (Han, 2019).

After this gentle beginning, we shared the purpose of the Open Studios and used creative methods to promote an opening up through divergent thinking about the theme of each session. We presented a pedagogical foundation and scholarship for every creative exercise, sharing the research behind the exercises, including, for example, using art-based methods for leadership development (Taylor & Ladkin, 2009), and creativity in higher education (Stone & Ashton, 2018), among others.

For the exercises in the Open Studios, we scaffolded different creative tasks, such as introducing drawing with simple sketches and later adding complexity. As, in our experience, people tend to be cautious when working with creative-based methods, we created a set of stepping stones to support Trailblazers to gradually take them towards a safe space in which to realise their creative skills, while avoiding the trap of perfection (Lamott, 1980). Following the creative exercises, participants shared their digital artefacts or images through the Teams Chat channel or on the online *Padlet* (a virtual 'corkboard') which we used to prompt a rich discussion about the creatively expressed ideas. This activity drew upon the spirit of the 'studio crit-group' of the art world in which participants receive feedback from peers. In our case, the benefit of this discussion was to feed-forward the participants' own thinking process. One of the few ground rules in the Open Studios is that peer comments in crits should focus on the implications for the module design and not on the technical quality of the creative output. By being a catalyst for sparking discussions based on participants' representation of problems, the Open Studios also helped participants to articulate a shared conceptualisation of emerging issues.

This dialogical space led to the convergence stage of the Open Studios, in which participants together applied their different ideas to the process of module design. Each Open Studios session finished with a 'gratitude and breathing' exercise, as a ritual closure of the space.

Examples from the Open Studios

Table 5.1 lists the 14 Open Studios sessions: Column 1 contains the session titles; Column 2 contains the purpose of the session; and Column 3 contains the creative tools used for each of them, along with suggested additional resources.

The Open Studios session *What do we mean by interdisciplinarity?* was challenging as a common misconception about interdisciplinarity is that it is simply about working together (HEA, 2015). We asked participants to use drawing, Lego, or domestic objects to visually represent what they understood by 'multi-disciplinarity', 'interdisciplinarity', and 'transdisciplinary'. In

Table 5.1 Open Studios for RM development

Session title	Purpose	Creative tools
1. What and why are we doing these RMs?	Empathy and purpose	Hand-drawn map of expectations: participants draw a map or write down their expectations about RMs (Kantrowitz, 2022)
2. What do we mean by interdisciplinarity?	Co-created meaning	3D and visual representations using Lego or domestic objects (James, 2013)
3. What is the change we want in the students?	Student-centred design	Participants create a paper puppet and give it life while reflecting on who exactly they are designing for/with (Gayá Wicks & Rippin, 2010)
4. Can I tell you a story?	The purpose of our RM	Participants shared a favourite story. Key elements of the story are identified and used to tell the story of their RM: Context, (S)Hero, Challenge, Magic Powers, Difficulties, and Resolution (Booker, 2006; Murdock, 2020)
5. How are we now?	Reflective Learning	Using meditative drawing to reflect on how the process of developing the RMs
6. Why the students should take this module?	Storytelling	Visually representing the purpose of the RM using the elements of storytelling to prepare a 1-minute video for students (Lupton, 2017)
7. What is your wicked problem?	Visual Thinking	Using visual thinking tools, participants bring different approaches to their questions or wicked problems (Conklin, 2006). Using visual metaphors, participants refine what it is what they are working on
8. Reflective Learning	Reflective practice	Diverse ways to capture progress through tools from autoethnography (Haynes, 2018), drawings, and 'jelly baby trees'
9. How can we make the UN SDGs real?	Education for sustainability	Participants go outside and focus on an element they find in the landscape and identify links and interdependences with its surroundings (Fretwell & Greig, 2019)

(Continued)

Table 5.1 (Continued)

Session title	Purpose	Creative tools
10. How games can help RMs education?	Playful learning	Participants are introduced to computer games to represent complex situations
11. How to activate the Graduate Capitals in the RM?	Employability	Using Angela Brew's (2020) *Tree Meds*, participants are encouraged to imagine their own development adopting the tree life: from seed to branches, flowers, and fruits. This is a performative exercise focused on identity and the development of skills (Tomlinson, 2017)
12. How can I trust you?	Teamwork and interdisciplinarity	Using some of the *36 Questions to Fall in Love* (Aron et al., 1997), participants establish a closer relationship and work around trust issues. The exercise is complemented with letter writing
13. How to use e-portfolios for reflective learning?	Using different online platforms	Examples of participants in the use of e-portfolios like MyShowcase, and how to make the best of Canvas (ARU VLE) (Attia, 2010)
14. What works for us?	Evaluation, feedback, and next steps	Participants return to the visual maps of expectations and are encouraged to identify what has changed, how we have changed, and what comes next in RM design?

this divergent phase of the Open Studios, we approached the topic of interdisciplinarity using lateral thinking to activate cognitive and emotional responses to develop our shared understanding. Consequently, participants developed imaginative visual representations of this complex topic (see Figure 5.2).

The convergent phase of the Open Studios brought together various aspects of the representations to explore how students understood and interpreted interdisciplinarity. In this phase, we used their visual representations (photographs and drawings) to elicit a rich conversation among participants (Vince & Warren, 2012). By focusing on the visual representations, we were able to relate our own perceptions about the differences between the three terms and their relation to interdisciplinarity to something concrete. We encouraged participants to consider how different disciplines would respond to the

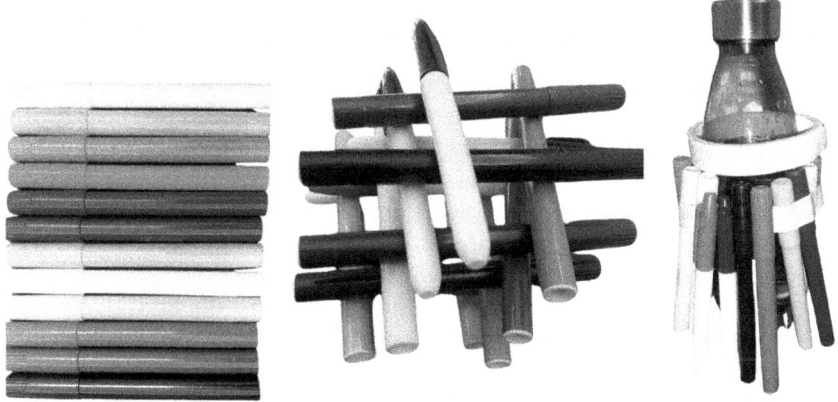

Figure 5.2 3D representations of multidisciplinarity, interdisciplinarity, and trans-disciplinarity (Lakhani, 2021)

same question and to create a reading list on interdisciplinarity to investigate how the same topic can be seen from different perspectives. Most importantly, however, the aim was to weave together those different approaches and the methods used to tackle them.

This shared understanding was later reinforced through additional Continual Professional Development workshops called *Bring Interdisciplinarity to Life*. We used the visual representation exercise in the development workshops and colleagues later reported on adapting it for their own RM sessions. The possibility of using the creative tools at home was also a key purpose of the Open Studios: granting permission and freedom to be creative through easy to apply tools in different settings.

The Open Studios were influenced by three major threads:

1   Drawing upon hooks' (1994) ideas of passionate engagement with education, we spent considerable time talking to Trailblazers to elicit their desire and passion in the development of their RMs. We followed hooks' (1994) advice to go beyond 'banking' ways of teaching (Freire, 1970), those practices focused on content delivery and outcomes, for example, to encourage transgressive teaching: teaching that stimulates questions, imagination, and creativity
2   Applying ideas of active learning and studio-based learning to the design of the modules and opening a safe space for the participants to rekindle their own creative talents, being inclusive of diverse ways of expression, from drawing to calligraphy, storytelling, performance, collage, or 3D
3   Underlying the whole approach were ideas adapted from Design Thinking

Methodology and Findings

Due to the experimental nature of the Open Studios, we factored in two 'reflective moments' during the implementation period (i.e., the half-way and final sessions) and another six months after the first iteration of the RMs had been delivered. In these reflective moments, participants shared how we were advancing as a group and the usefulness of the Open Studios, as part of the wider strategy of RM development. The first two reflective moments helped to adjust the approach and were anecdotical and conversational. For the impact evaluation six months later, we implemented a more formal evaluation method, including the consideration of ethical issues. We also included a semi-structured focus group in which we invited participants 'to evaluate your experience of the RM Open Studios, in the development of the RMs and the impact in your personal and professional life'.

A significant challenge faced by RM leaders was the limited time available to attend the Open Studios sessions. Over time, participation diminished as the Trailblazers needed to attend to competing external deadlines, and the number of participants varied between a maximum of 30 participants (especially at the beginning) to a minimum of five. Nevertheless, this is common to any CPD programme, although to the detriment of potential innovation and restricts the necessary time to expand and innovate (Blass & Hayward, 2014).

One of the most common threads in the conversations with participants was their encounter with creative methods:

> I felt it was pushing outside our comfort zone and doing the Open Studios again … just some of the creative things we did, was pushing me outside my normal … But equally, it's about being creative with everyday things and being inspired. So, either, you know, getting an idea or and having inspiration.

Another important aspect of the Open Studios was active learning with participants having space to develop their creative agency so they could use the resulting tools in their teaching and learning practice. For example, participants reported that they asked their students to represent interdisciplinarity with objects as we did in the workshops.

The Open Studios model as experienced in the design of the RMs reveals the possibilities of integrating creativity within time frameworks and project management boundaries. This is important in the development of innovative (and transformative and transgressive) pedagogical projects. Both rationales, innovation and delivery, can co-exist, and playfulness within structured spaces such as the Open Studios presents alternatives to the traditional CPDs and workshops.

Conclusion and Further Development

In this chapter, we considered studio-based learning and ways in which it can be adapted for academic development (that of the curriculum and its designer) through the experience of the Open Studios. Our intention has been to establish a viable balance between the structural drivers that support curriculum design and the emancipatory opportunity of designing new curricula. We have been intent on fostering innovation, building creative skills, and opening a space for dialogue, playfulness, and experimentation. The 14 Open Studios sessions and the evaluations show the opportunities and challenges of bringing creativity into a curriculum design project, and the need for creativity in academic development (Waddington, 2016).

We have previously delivered design thinking workshops and creative toolkits in other contexts, but the potency of the Open Studios model relies on the continuity of creating habits (Cameron & Bryan, 1992) and the adaption of creative habitual practices to different contexts of action (Dalton, 2004). Nevertheless, it is unclear whether Open Studios could work as free-standing workshops on creativity.

In conclusion, we reiterate that the development of innovative projects such as RMs requires openness and flexibility in the provision of support. The Open Studios process offered both divergent and convergent aspects that allowed time for imagination and focus on module development and deadlines. Essentially, we designed Open Studios to stimulate disruption, transgression, and imagination, all of which are crucial elements of innovation in higher education.

Points to Consider

Readers of this chapter may wish to consider the following:

- Considering how the physical spaces you use for teaching can be arranged to engender creative exchanges.
- Engaging participants who have not previously experienced the uncertainties that come with ideation and decision-making in their learning.
- Collaborating with friends and/or colleagues to generate arguments for adopting design thinking.

References

Acevedo, B., Malevicius, R., Fadli, H., & Lamberti, C. (2022). Aesthetics and education for sustainability. *Culture and Organization*, 28(3–4), 263–278. https://doi.org/10.1080/14759551.2022.2028147

Anglia Ruskin University (ARU) (2017). Designing our future 2017-2026. Anglia Ruskin University. Retrieved 5 July 2024, from https://aru.ac.uk/anglia-learning-and-teaching/about-us/our-strategy

Anglia Ruskin University (ARU) (2018a). Education strategy 2018-2022. Anglia Ruskin University. Retrieved 5 July 2024, from https://aru.ac.uk/anglia-learning-and-teaching/about-us/our-strategy

Anglia Ruskin University (ARU) (2018b). Active curriculum framework. Anglia Ruskin University. Retrieved 5 July 2024, from https://aru.ac.uk/anglia-learning-and-teaching/about-us/our-strategy

Anglia Ruskin University (ARU) (2018c). Employability strategy 2018-2023. Anglia Ruskin University. Retrieved 5 July 2024, from https://aru.ac.uk/anglia-learning-and-teaching/about-us/our-strategy

Anglia Ruskin University (ARU) (2022). Student life. Ruskin modules. Anglia Ruskin University. Retrieved 5 July 2024, from https://aru.ac.uk/student-life/support-and-facilities/careers-and-employability/ruskin-modules

Aron, A., Melinat, E., Aron, E. N., Vallone, R. D., & Bator, R. J. (1997). The experimental generation of interpersonal closeness: A procedure and some preliminary findings. *Personality and Social Psychology Bulletin, 23*(4), 363–377. https://doi.org/10.1177/0146167297234003

Ashton, S., & Stone, R. (2018). *An a-z of creative teaching in higher education.* Sage Publishing.

Attia, M. A. (2010). Student Teachers' Perceptions about the E-Portfolio as a Performance Assessment Tool. *Proceedings of the European Conference on Information Management and Evaluation*, pp. 6–14.

Blass, E., & Hayward, P. (2014). Innovation in higher education; will there be a role for 'the academe/university' in 2025? *European Journal of Futures Research, 2*, Article 41. https://doi.org/10.1007/s40309-014-0041-x

Booker, C. (2006). *The seven basic plots: Why we tell stories.* Bloomsbury.

Brew, A. (2020). *Tree Meds.* Retrieved 5 July 2024, from https://www.brewdraw.com/tree-meds

Cai, Y. (2015). What contextual factors shape 'innovation in innovation'? Integration of insights of the Triple Helix and the institutional logics perspective. *Social Science Information, 54*(3), 299–326. https://doi.org/10.1177/0539018415583527

Cameron, J., & Bryan, M. A. (1992). *The artist's way: A spiritual path to higher creativity.* G.P. Putnam's Sons.

Conklin, J. (2006). Wicked problems and social complexity. In J. Conklin (Ed.), *Dialogue mapping: Building shared understanding of wicked problems.* Wiley.

Dalton, B. (2004). Creativity, habit, and the social products of creative action: Revising Joas, incorporating Bourdieu. *Sociological Theory, 22*, 603–622. Retrieved 5 July 2024, from https://www.jstor.org/stable/3648935

de Greef, L., Post, G., Vink, C., & Wenting, C. (2017). *Designing interdisciplinary education: A practical handbook for university teachers.* Amsterdam University Press.

Etzkowitz, H., & Leydesdorff, L. (1995). The Triple Helix: University-industry-government relations: A laboratory for knowledge based economic development. *EASST Review, 14*(1), 14–19. Retrieved 5 July 2024, from https://papers.ssrn.com/sol3/Delivery.cfm/SSRN_ID2480085_code819652.pdf?abstractid=2480085&mirid=1

Freire, P. (1970). *Pedagogy of the oppressed.* Penguin.

Fretwell, K., & Greig, A. (2019). Towards a better understanding of the relationship between individual's self-reported connection to nature, personal well-being and environmental awareness. *Sustainability, 11*(5), 1386–1407. https://doi.org/10.3390/su11051386

Gayá Wicks, P., & Rippin, A. (2010). Art as experience: An inquiry into art and leadership using dolls and doll-making. *Leadership, 6*(3), 259–278. https://doi.org/10.1177/1742715010368767

Gibbs, G. (2013). Reflections on the changing nature of educational development. *International Journal for Academic Development, 18*(1), 4–14. https://doi.org/10.1080/1360144X.2013.751691

Gibson, J. J. (1979). *The ecological approach to visual perception.* Houghton Mifflin.

Grant, J. (2021). *The New Power University: The social purpose of higher education in the 21ˢᵗ century.* Pearson.

Han, B.-C. (2019). *The disappearance of rituals.* Polity.

Harrop, D., & Turpin, B. (2013). A study exploring learners' informal learning space behaviours, attitudes, and preferences. *New Review of Academic Librarianship, 19*(1), 58–77. https://doi.org/10.1080/13614533.2013.740961

Hasanefendic, S., Birkholz, J. M., Horta, H., & van der Sijde, P. (2017). Individuals in action: Bringing about innovation in higher education. *European Journal of Higher Education, 7*(2), 101–119. https://doi.org/10.1080/21568235.2017.1296367

Hawkey, K., James, J., & Tidmarsh, C. (2019). Using Wicked problems to foster interdisciplinary practice among UK trainee teachers. *Journal of Education for Teaching, 45*(4), 446–460. https://doi.org/10.1080/02607476.2019.1639263

Haynes, K. (2018). Autoethnography. In C. Cassell, A.L. Cunliffe, & G. Grandy (Eds.), *The sage handbook of qualitative business and management research methods.* SAGE Publications Ltd. https://doi.org/10.4135/9781526430236

Higher Education Academy (HEA) (2015). *Interdisciplinary provision in higher education: Current and Future challenges.* Retrieved 5 July 2024, from https://www.advance-he.ac.uk/knowledge-hub/interdisciplinary-provision-higher-education-current-and-future-challenges

hooks, b (1994). *Teaching to transgress.* Routledge.

Jacobs, C. (2000). The evaluation of educational innovation. *Evaluation, 6*(3), 261–280. https://doi.org/10.1177/13563890022209280

James, A. R. (2013). Lego serious play: A three-dimensional approach to learning development. *Journal of Learning Development in Higher Education, 6*, Article 6. https://doi.org/10.47408/jldhe.v0i6.208

Kantrowitz, A. (2022). *Drawing thought: How drawing help us observe, discover and invent.* MIT University Press.

Kolgar, O. (2010). Towards better group work: Seeing the difference between cooperation and collaboration. *English Teaching Forum, 2,* 16–23. Retrieved 5 July 2024, from https://files.eric.ed.gov/fulltext/EJ914888.pdf

Kolko, J. (2012). *Wicked problems: Problems worth solving.* Austin Centre for Design. Retrieved 5 July 2024, from: https://ssir.org/books/excerpts/entry/wicked_problems_problems_worth_solving

Lakhani, F. (2021). *3D representations of multidisciplinarity, interdisciplinarity, and transdisciplinarity* [Photo].

Lamott, A. (1980). *Bird by Bird. Some instructions on writing and life.* Bantam Double Day Dell Publishing.

Limpanowicz, H., & McCandless, K. (2014). *The surprising power of liberating structures: Simple rules to unleash a culture of innovation.* Liberating Structures Press.

Long, J. G. (2012). State of the studio: Revisiting the potential of studio pedagogy in US-based planning programs. *Journal of Planning Education and Research, 32*(4), 431–448. https://doi.org/10.1177/0739456X12457685

Lupton, E. (2017). *Design is storytelling.* Cooper-Hewitt Museum.

Middleton, A. (2021). *The situated agency of studio learning and its value for non-studio disciplines.* Doctoral Thesis. Sheffield: Sheffield Hallam University.

Murdock, M. (2020). *The Heroine's journey: Woman's quest for wholeness.* Shambhala Publications.

Newell, W. H. (1990). Interdisciplinary curriculum development. *Issues in Integrative Studies, 8*, 69–86. Retrieved 5 July 2024, from https://interdisciplinarystudies.org/wp-content/issues/vol8_1990/05_Vol_8_pp_69_86_Newell.pdf

Organisation for Economic Co-operation and Development (OECD). (2016). *Innovating education and educating for innovation: The power of digital technologies and skills.* OECD Publishing.

Pratt-Adams, S., Richter, U., & Warnes, M. (Eds.) (2020). *Innovations in active learning in higher education.* University of Sussex/Fulcrum. https://doi.org/10.20919/9781912319961

Razzouk, R., & Shute, V. (2012). What is design thinking and why is it important? *Review of Educational Research, 82*(3), 330–348. Retrieved 5 July 2024, from https://www.jstor.org/stable/23260048

Reddy, D., Iyer, S., & Sasikumar, M. (2016). Teaching and Learning of Divergent and Convergent Thinking through Open-Problem Solving in a Data Structures Course. *2016 International Conference on Learning and Teaching in Computing and Engineering (LaTICE)*, pp. 178–185. https://doi.org/10.14738/aivp.92.9974

Rüegg, W. (Ed.). (2004). *A history of the university in Europe: Volume III: Universities in the nineteenth and early twentieth centuries (1800-1945).* Cambridge University Press.

Taylor, S. S., & Ladkin, D. (2009). Understanding arts-based methods in managerial development. *Academy of Management Learning & Education, 8*(1), 55–69. Retrieved 5 July 2024, from https://www.jstor.org/stable/40214571

Tomlinson, M. B. (2017). Forms of graduate capital and their relationship to graduate employability. *Education + Training, 59*(4), 338–352. https://doi.org/10.1108/ET-05-2016-0090

United Nations (2015). *The 17 Goals.* Retrieved 5 July 2024, from https://sdgs.un.org/goals

Vince, R., & Warren, S. (2012). Participatory visual methods. *Qualitative organizational research: Core methods and current challenges* (pp. 275–295). SAGE Publications, Inc. https://doi.org/10.4135/9781526435620

Waddington, K. (2016). The compassion gap in UK universities. *International Practice Development Journal, 6*(1), article 10. https://doi.org/10.19043/ipdj.61.010

Withagen, R., Araujo, D., & de Poel, H. J. (2017). Inviting affordances and agency. *New Ideas in Psychology, 45*, pp. 11–18. https://doi.org/10.1016/j.newideapsych.2016.12.002

Part II

Case Studies

Chapter 6

To Team or Not to Team

Embedding Interdisciplinarity into the Curriculum

Uwe Matthias Richter

Introduction

In this chapter, I investigate how interdisciplinarity was embedded into the curriculum of my Ruskin Module (RM), *Where do you belong in this city?* I designed the module to introduce interdisciplinarity conceptionally through activities to frame the subsequent teamwork and reflection. The teams of students from different disciplines were set up and supported to work on a wicked problem as a project and produce an assessed digital artefact as a project outcome. Finally, students were asked to reflect on their interdisciplinary team and project work in an assessed reflective essay.

I consider the motivation and background to designing and delivering this module and then describe the module in more detail including the activities and literature informing the module. I conclude the chapter with research into students' reflections on interdisciplinarity and teamwork, and recommendations.

Background

The idea for proposing the interdisciplinary breadth module, *Where do you belong in this city?*, goes back to my experience as a student of Geography and German Studies at a German university. As part of urban geography, we explored my medieval university and hometown. City development, past and present, gave me a greater insight into my hometown and my identity within it. Studying German language and literature provided me with the opportunity to explore my town's linguistic landscape represented in the continuum between dialect, colloquial and standard German, professional and vocational variations as well as German spoken by immigrants.

However, my first experience goes back to a class I took at a high school in San Francisco in the 1970s which combined different subjects to look at contemporary issues through different lenses. We explored topics such as the preservation of the Redwood National Park in northern California versus the commercial interests of logging companies and the concerns of residents. Besides the desk research, we went on a field trip to the Park and talked to the

DOI: 10.4324/9781003474593-8

logging company, Sierra Club (a US environmental organisation), and residents, which gave us a close insight into the complexity of the issue.

These unique experiences motivated me to provide such an opportunity to students at Anglia Ruskin University (ARU) in the form of a RM. I decided to design a RM which provides students with a deep insight into an aspect of their university city (i.e., Cambridge or Chelmsford) as part of a team project. Team formation was based on themes chosen by students. Students could choose from four themes:

- The city and green spaces
- City development through the ages
- Communities, identity, and space
- Sensing the city (music, art, media scene)

I then allocated students from different disciplines to teams of five to seven. The teams were asked to define and refine their inquiry within the chosen theme and develop an assessed digital artefact (first assignment) to present the outcomes of their research. Teams had a choice of media to present their project to provide opportunities for students to express themselves in different ways and to use their skills in media and art.

The process was structured using a waterfall project management approach (McCormick, 2012; Petersen et al., 2009) with peer and tutor feedback at each development stage (i.e., proposal, blueprint, storyboarding, presentation). The waterfall approach broke down the project into sequential steps and thus scaffolded the learning process. Theoretical background information on teamwork, city development, space and place, sustainability, and interdisciplinarity was delivered alongside the project lifecycle and informed the project throughout its stages.

The first iteration of the module ran over 12 weeks (September to December 2021) as three-hour, timetabled, online, synchronous workshops, with an introduction to the topic, teamwork, and the project at the module beginning (Weeks 1 and 2), followed by the theoretical topics alongside time for teams to work on their project (see Figure 6.1).

The module used the virtual learning environment, Canvas, for content and asynchronous activities (e.g., preparation for synchronous sessions) and MS Class Teams as a synchronous collaborative platform. Each team had a private channel in Class Teams in which they could communicate using text chat, meet using Teams Meetings, and collaborate on documents. The open General channel was used for the timetabled synchronous sessions and to share documents and resources across teams.

The module concluded with the presentation of, and peer feedback on, the team artefacts in Week 11 using a virtual gallery in *Spatial* (Spatial, 2022) (see Figure 6.2) and an online writing workshop to scaffold the reflective essay (second assignment) in the final week.

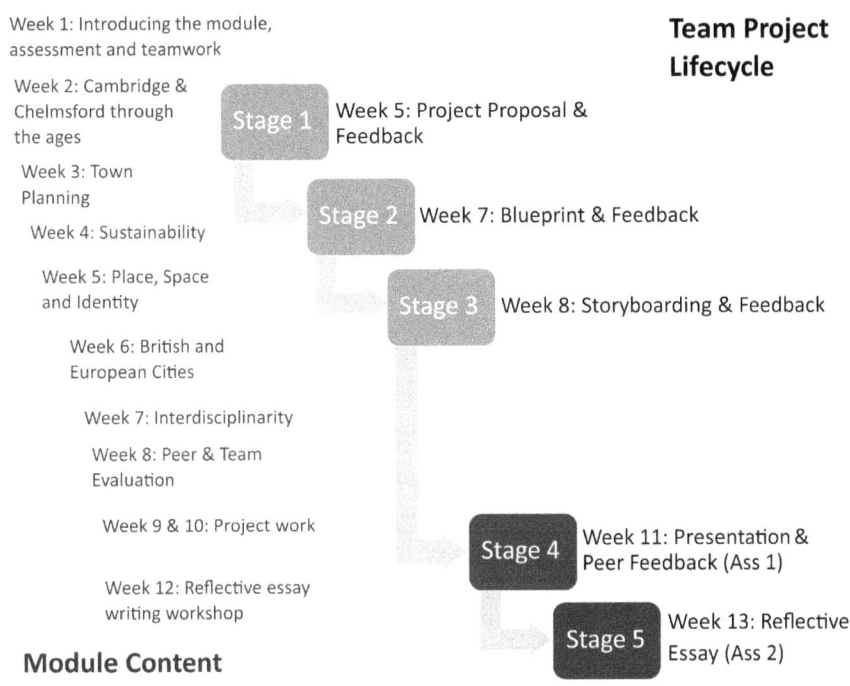

Week 1: Introducing the module, assessment and teamwork

Week 2: Cambridge & Chelmsford through the ages

Week 3: Town Planning

Week 4: Sustainability

Week 5: Place, Space and Identity

Week 6: British and European Cities

Week 7: Interdisciplinarity

Week 8: Peer & Team Evaluation

Week 9 & 10: Project work

Week 12: Reflective essay writing workshop

Module Content

Team Project Lifecycle

Stage 1 Week 5: Project Proposal & Feedback

Stage 2 Week 7: Blueprint & Feedback

Stage 3 Week 8: Storyboarding & Feedback

Stage 4 Week 11: Presentation & Peer Feedback (Ass 1)

Stage 5 Week 13: Reflective Essay (Ass 2)

Figure 6.1 Outline of module content and project lifecycle

The second assessment was linked to the first and I asked students to reflect on their teamwork, development of the artefact, and interdisciplinarity and sustainability as reflected in their teamwork and artefact.

I was the module designer and tutor in the first delivery of this module which resulted in a high workload. While I had a background in urban

Figure 6.2 Exhibition of artefacts in the virtual gallery (Spatial, 2022)

geography from my previous studies, and teamwork as a team-based learning facilitator, interdisciplinarity and sustainability had to be developed as topics to relate to the module and the assessments. However, input from different disciplines to support the four themes with resources, tasks, and support would have been advantageous. In subsequent deliveries, it proved beneficial to share delivery with another tutor to distribute the workload, but also provide more opportunities for interdisciplinary collaboration within the tutor team.

Literature Review

As Lyall et al. (2015, v) put it,

> The term 'interdisciplinarity' is often contested and it may seem that there are as many definitions of its nature and purpose as there are commentators. In particular, the phrase 'integrative learning' is often used as an umbrella term for activities that bridge, for example, experiences inside and outside the classroom, theory and practice, and disciplines and fields while interdisciplinary studies is a subset of integrative learning.

According to Appleby and Weller (2021), interdisciplinarity allows the student to learn by making connections between ideas and concepts across different disciplines [and] '[s]tudents learning in this way are able to apply the knowledge gained in one discipline to another different discipline as a way to deepen the learning experience' (2021, para. 12). Ivanitskaya et al. (2002, p. 135), note that,

> Multidisciplinary learning "refers to the involvement of several different professional areas, though not necessarily in an integrated manner" (Shafritz et al., 1988). By contrast, Rowntree (1982) defines the interdisciplinary approach as "one in which two or more disciplines are brought together, preferably in such a way that the disciplines interact with one another and have some effect on one another's perspectives".

For Jones (2009, p. 76), interdisciplinarity involves

> "inquiries which critically draw upon two or more disciplines, and which lead to an integration of disciplinary insights" (Haynes, 2002: 17) … The interdisciplinary approach is uniquely different from a multidisciplinary approach, which is the teaching of topics from more than one discipline in parallel to the other, nor is it a crossdisciplinary approach, where one discipline is crossed with the subject matter of another.

Chausson and Cole (2021, paras. 9–11) also offer definitions:

1 Multidisciplinarity: different disciplines work in parallel, with little or no integration of ideas, methods, or outputs
2 Interdisciplinarity: crossing disciplinary boundaries to create new knowledge, theory, or methodologies
3 Transdisciplinarity: integrating different knowledge systems (the interwoven coloured strings), or ways of knowing, beyond academia, such as practitioner knowledge, or local and Indigenous knowledge

According to Chettiparamb (2007), interdisciplinary teaching can be differentiated by the teaching approach (e.g., team teaching with teachers from different disciplines), interaction between different disciplines (e.g., service teaching, generic competencies, skills, and research, cross-disciplinary studies, bringing in different disciplinary perspectives and approaches into a disciplinary context), and the foci or objectives (e.g., to address a specific educational or societal need or requirement such as employability and sustainability).

The US-based Association of Interdisciplinary Studies (AIS) defines the purpose of interdisciplinarity as 'integrating the insights of knowledge domains to produce a more comprehensive understanding of complex problems, issues, or questions' (AIS, 2022, para. 1). In addition, Repko (2007, p. 131) proposed four elements for an interdisciplinary curriculum:

(1) addressing a complex problem or focus question that cannot be resolved by using a single disciplinary approach, (2) drawing on insights generated by disciplines, interdisciplines, or schools of thought, including non-disciplinary knowledge formations, (3) integrating insights, and (4) producing an interdisciplinary understanding of the problem or question.

Chettiparamb (2007, p. 33) comments that,

most instructional approaches associated with interdisciplinarity are based on active learning strategies and promote higher-order critical-thinking skills. These are analysis, synthesis, application and evaluation, and they include methods such as "collaborative/cooperative learning, discovery and problem-based learning, writing and math across the curriculum, and methods of assessment that are multi-dimensional, including qualitative and quantitative measures, normed measures, and self-assessments" (De Zure, 1999).

Table 6.1 Synthesis of interdisciplinary teaching strategies and pedagogical techniques

Strategy	Pedagogic techniques
Co-teaching	• Advanced planning and negotiation with co-teacher • Co-advising with industry representatives • Taking turns in teaching • Creating learning community • Co-creation of syllabus and case studies
Interactive methods	• Project-based learning (PBL) • Case study methods • Role-playing • Simulations • Virtual methods • Peer-assessment and review • Peer-assisted learning (PAL) • Small-group teaching
Programme-level strategies	• Interdisciplinary electives • Core courses covering material from different perspectives • Research conducted for the initial stages of graduate school

Source: Lyall et al. (2015, p. 23).

Based on their literature review, Lyall et al. (2015) identified three interdisciplinary teaching strategies: co-teaching, interactive methods, and programme-level strategies. These are summarised in Table 6.1.

The approaches I took for my RM were the use of interactive methods, including project-based learning in interdisciplinary teams based on authentic problems, virtual co-creation, and collaboration to produce a digital artefact, small-group teaching, and peer-assisted learning, evaluation, and review. While co-teaching was sought in the form of input of resources and expertise from subject experts, this was only achievable in subsequent iterations.

Embedding Interdisciplinarity into the Curriculum

The module introduced interdisciplinarity with the poem, *The blind men and the elephant: A Hindoo Fable*, by John Godfrey Saxe (1872), which was read out alongside a cartoon depiction of the poem by G. Renee Guzlas (Daigneault, 2013). Students were asked to define 'What the poem says about discipline-based versus interdisciplinary learning'. Students were then asked in groups to define the differences between multi-, trans/cross-, and interdisciplinarity by illustrating these concepts and sharing their illustrations with the plenary. Next, students were provided with definitions from the literature to compare including interdisciplinarity 'involving two or more academic, scientific, or artistic disciplines' (Merriam Webster dictionary), and 'when we consider interdisciplinary learning (and teaching), we are working across boundaries of knowledge and creating new knowledge from various sources' (Appleby & Weller, 2021, para. 3). Finally, students were asked to define the advantages and disadvantages of working in an interdisciplinary team as group work using a *Padlet* (Padlet, 2022).

These activities introduced interdisciplinarity conceptually by contrasting them against multi-, cross- and transdisciplinarity and provided students with initial insights into the benefits and challenges of working in interdisciplinary teams expressed in module learning outcomes.

Evaluation

My evaluation of the embedding of interdisciplinarity into RMS focused on two research questions:

1 How did students experience and reflect on interdisciplinarity?
2 How did teamwork and the project contribute to interdisciplinary learning?

For the second, individual, assessment element, students were invited to reflect on their team and project work, the development of the artefact, and how these reflected interdisciplinarity, specifically:

1 How the team decided on the project topic and what interested and motivated them in their topic.
2 How their team worked together and what they would do differently next time.
3 How they worked across disciplines in their team and what the benefits and challenges were over working in a single discipline team.
4 What they learned about sustainability relating to their topic.
5 What they enjoyed about the module and what they would do differently.

Fifty-three student reflective essays were thematically analysed (Braun & Clarke, 2006) using NVivo 12 (QSR International, 2022) to identify students' understanding of, and insight into, interdisciplinarity as part of the project and teamwork, and how that was expressed both in the team artefact and the individual reflection.

Analysis and Findings

Interdisciplinarity

About half of the students defined interdisciplinarity in line with the module understanding. Yet students defined interdisciplinarity in different ways. Most students defined interdisciplinarity in the context of working in a team with members from different disciplines. Student 48 (S48), for example, said:

> An interdisciplinary team is defined as being made up of at least two disciplines, with all members engaging in teamwork, sharing leadership, and dependent on one another to achieve team goals (Temkin-Greener et al., 2004). Interdisciplinary teams are encouraged to make and implement decisions, giving them the ability to affect change.

A different view is that interdisciplinarity may involve looking at an issue from different perspectives or with different mindsets.

> With everyone having a varied mindset, it is vital to be able to work alongside others and get a wider insight into the different knowledge and experiences that other people possess. This is embedded in interdisciplinary group work (S12).

An interesting comment from S17 concerned interdisciplinarity affording higher levels of inclusivity and intersectionality:

> The Interdisciplinary approach to solving wider societal issues is better as it is an approach that allows and aims for inclusivity for all when discussing different societal concerns. It gives room for intersectionality which in turn allows us to all live together harmoniously. Whereas single discipline limits itself as it only focuses on one ideal, for instance, they are different ways people can be marginalised such as gender, race, class, and sexual orientation.

Therefore, students strongly associated interdisciplinarity in the RM with teamwork with members from different disciplines, which was how the module and assessments were designed. However, interdisciplinarity was also defined as looking at an issue from different perspectives, with different views or mindsets, which could be within or across a discipline.

Process

Students described how they experienced learning in an interdisciplinary way through teamwork, different disciplines coming together, and skills and competencies involving diverse personalities and mindsets.

There were examples of how students brought in their different disciplines' knowledge and expertise to work together on the team project.

> We used [Student A]'s photographic skills to collect the photos for the presentation, as he has a degree in photography. [Student B] is studying psychology with a degree in criminology and has worked on the legal

side of sustainability. [Student C] is studying biomedical sciences and has worked on the bacteria that were found in the river. [Student D] is studying international trade and has researched the history of the river over the centuries. [Student E] is studying computer science and has been working on the social part of the project. Finally, I am taking a business and management course and have applied what I have learned to the economics of sustainability (S19).

The business students identified economic views, while the student who is studying graphic design enlightened the team on new creative software, to try and gain skills … The students who were involved with animal behaviour and conservation gave the team a broad view on the nature element of the reserve; they identified the animals and habitats which are important in their field of expertise (S51).

Other students explained how they were able to make connections between knowledge domains and bring them together as solutions.

The most valuable of these being the ability to look at facets of the work from other people's perspectives. I would look at a topic from my own viewpoint and consider how I would resolve it. On the other hand, another team member may have a different idea; I would then listen to their opinion and interpretation and take it into account (S25).

This often involved dividing up tasks by team members' strengths and skills and then bringing the different sections together at the end.

Within our team, one member was looking at sustainability as it correlated with their degree module, another having knowledge of web design set out to design a website. My discipline lends itself more to research, therefore I looked into the chosen places, and another peer's discipline provided insight into writing styles and presentation skills, so they offered to construct the information gathered (S9).

We solved societal issues by each member looking at an independent topic and then coming together as a team to present that issue and listen to what others had found. We would then discuss the matter and come to a conclusion on methods as to how we could resolve it (S25).

Other students described the social and personal learning aspects involved in interdisciplinarity:

We further managed our interdisciplinarity well, using internal disagreements to our advantage through their application to real-world solutions and ensuring that the value of each discipline was recognised, a significant learning curve for our team (S14).

> I found working within an interdisciplinary team interesting. None of us knew each other or what we were researching, which could have caused a barrier, but we broke through this barrier by learning about each other's differences before we started the process of the digital artefact. Once we got to know each other, we were able to combine our strengths, creating a variety of skills which could be used to understand what aspect of the project each person should research, as well as this we could understand what each person should organise, for example, who should take the role of leadership and so on. Splitting the work gave us more time to research the social artefact in depth (S23).

The process of experiencing interdisciplinarity for students in this module therefore centred on working on a project in teams which had students from different disciplines. As teams often divided project tasks by members' strengths and expertise, some teams may have been more multidisciplinary unless there were phases in the teamwork where team members exchanged notes, discussed across disciplines, and came to consensual decisions or compromises. There is evidence that these interdisciplinary processes took place in some teams but not in all. There were also references to potential personal and social benefits achieved through interdisciplinary learning such as leadership, inclusivity, and intersectionality.

Benefits

The benefits are closely linked to interdisciplinary teamwork and the process of engaging with each other to develop a solution to a problem or task. In this iteration of the module, student teams could choose their own topics within a theme but needed to develop a sustainable solution or approach to their topic. Based on their choice of theme, students were assigned to teams with members from different disciplines.

The main benefit students identified was to be able to look at a topic or problem from different perspectives provided by the discipline of the team members but also their diverse backgrounds and personalities. S24, for example, noted that,

> A huge advantage of interdisciplinary teamwork is that people within the team provide diverse perspectives and increase the chances of creative ideas, by providing the team with their own opinion on a problem and they then come to a decision based on all opinions and points gathered from the existing discussions they have had.

Some students also indicated that the experience they gained from interdisciplinary teamwork was beneficial for other modules and future employment:

We benefited greatly from this kind of instruction as interdisciplinarity requires making links between diverse concepts. It is because of this that the information is typically based on real-world experiences, giving it a real-world context and providing a genuine purpose for the learning (S20).

I had to work with students from different disciplines and different countries. As the students are from different subjects, I had to work with different mindsets and different thought processes. This made me understand how to work with different people which will be beneficial for my future professional life (S21).

A positive outcome and benefit from working as a team instead of singly was that we had different approaches to solv[ing] society issues, and this helped me gain skills in how I look at future problems like these (S34).

Many students mentioned the range of transferable skills and competencies they gained from working on a wicked problem across disciplines in a team, some relating to project work, others to teamwork, or a combination of both:

The skills I have gained from working in an interdisciplinary team include the ability to communicate with people from different disciplines, to understand and value different perspectives, and to find common ground. These skills are essential in solving societal issues, as they allow for a more holistic and inclusive approach … We employed and built critical thinking abilities as we learned to compare and contrast topics from other subject areas and go beyond the bounds of their own discipline. We begin to synthesize concepts from a variety of viewpoints and examine an alternative method of learning (S20).

The biggest advantage of interdisciplinary working is the promotion of critical thinking amongst participants, a skill that helps promote higher level questioning and learning (S50).

A few students commented on the supportive nature of teamwork which helped them succeed:

Working in a team allowed me to ask my teammates and they helped me understand that we had to create … if I was working alone, I would have found this very difficult (S23).

The one thing I enjoyed about this module was working with different people in a subject that we are all unfamiliar with and being able to work together to support each other through this (S31).

Several students commented on the personal experience, growth, and enrichment the team and project work gave them:

Working with people of different ages, social backgrounds, and academic disciplines has helped broaden my horizon (S7).

As students and, let's say, humans, we have also learned from each other, listening to all the ideas and thoughts that crossed our minds and working on every aspect of them (S8).

When it came to presenting ideas, everyone had their own ideas in mind on how they wanted things to be done which helped create great discussion and helped me learn how to be considerate of the way other people think and how they may not understand everything the way I may have looked at it at first, which has helped me to become more tolerant when working with other people from different backgrounds or academic studies (S33).

Students mentioned many benefits including the interdisciplinary approach to solving problems as part of teamwork, the engagement with students from different disciplines, and their personal and professional growth in skills, competencies, and experiences which are transferable beyond the module, thus developing their employability.

Challenges

While students found many benefits in working on a project in interdisciplinary teams, there were also challenges. The main challenges were around getting team members to meet, and fully engage and participate. This was also observed in the low attendance in the synchronously taught sessions of this module. Students also said that discussions and finding consensus were more time-consuming because they involved more disciplines, opinions, and perspectives which needed to be negotiated to come to an agreed position:

One potential drawback of our interdisciplinarity was clashes of interests in assessing developments, a real-world consideration (S14).

The problem with having a mixture of disciplines is disagreement ... We had different points of view, and this could cause the team to look at the project in different ways, and we had trouble coming to a collective agreement on how to tackle a problem (S16).

Sometimes it did not always make it easy to help motivate everyone in the same way as it felt the level of effort some individual people were putting into the project/team discussions was lacking at times which definitely held back the project as a whole, whereas if it had been just a disciplinary approach, you would have everyone in the same headspace from the beginning which means you all have similar mindsets on how you want the project to work which can help have the team move in one direction (S33).

Participation and cooperation are some of the key aspects to work on an interdisciplinary project and those are some of the factors the team was missing since the start … However, in interdisciplinary research, there is a high risk of unreliable partners. It does regularly happen that partners who try to figure out the same goals do not work in the same way we do. It often happens that in a team with multilingual communication when their mother language is not English [, it] sometimes confuses things (S49).

Students also observed that working in interdisciplinary teams meant taking longer to agree positions, communicate, and arrange meetings.

Another challenge of working in an interdisciplinary team was organising meetings and communication. Being an interdisciplinary team means more time is needed, throughout the process, to clarify what each team member needs to do and how it fits into the goal of the artefact. This was particularly tricky as we all had different work and study commitments so [it] was hard to organise meetings where everyone could join (S10).

While the benefits far outweigh the challenges, the challenges students raised can seriously constrain the effectiveness of interdisciplinary team and project work. Consistent and equal participation and contribution of team members to the successful outcome of their teamwork, arranging meetings, and clear communication were mentioned which were exasperated by students from different disciplines, languages, and cultural backgrounds. Similarly, coming to agreements and consensus in discussions was more difficult and often took more time. These challenges need to be considered when designing interdisciplinary teamwork and projects to provide adequate support and scaffolding.

Conclusion

The analysis of student reflections provided a good insight into the effectiveness, challenges, and processes of using teamwork and projects to embed interdisciplinarity into the curriculum.

Interdisciplinarity was mainly facilitated through teams with a mix of students from different disciplines who were asked to work together on a project of their choice within defined themes. The project was scaffolded in different stages which enabled working within a team and across teams through peer review activities. Therefore, students were encouraged and enabled to look at their chosen topic through their discipline lenses, share their perspectives, and find compromises and synergies where there were differences in perspectives. The reflections on the processes both in teamwork and interdisciplinary engagement showed, however, that teams would divide up projects by tasks usually along team members' strengths and discipline, which could result in a multidisciplinary rather than an interdisciplinary approach.

For the following delivery of this module in Trimester 1 of the 2022–2023 academic year, activities were developed to strengthen the interdisciplinary exchange within teams, especially at the beginning of the project where teams had to agree on how they wanted to work together (i.e., a team agreement), a plan and decision-making (i.e., project plan and risk assessment), and how they divided the work (i.e., task and role distribution as part of the project plan). At the end of the projects, team members were asked to work across the team to develop a coherent digital artefact.

A further approach to embedding interdisciplinary in the second iteration of the module was to ask students to choose from a range of well-articulated wicked problems (Coyne, 2005; Lönngren & van Poeck, 2021; Termeer et al., 2019) which focused the project work from the outset. Teams were formed based on students' choices of these wicked problems. The wicked problems were designed to require students to look at a specific issue through different lenses and pitch their sustainable solutions to different stakeholders. Therefore, interdisciplinarity was embedded by how a team approached a wicked problem and presented solutions.

Team and project work was introduced and supported in a scaffolded way which helped students to engage in team and project work through stages including:

- getting to know each other (sharing pen portrait),
- agreeing on how to work together (team agreement),
- agreeing on roles, project leadership, project plan, and risk assessment,
- working through the project in stages with (peer and tutor) feedback on each stage,
- peer and team evaluation (survey),
- guidance on media approaches for digital artefacts,
- peer feedback on digital artefacts arranged as a virtual exhibition,
- continuous reflection on teamwork, the project, and digital artefact feeding into the final reflective essay.

While student feedback clearly showed the effectiveness of teamwork for embedding interdisciplinarity into the curriculum, team and project work relies on students attending, participating, and engaging regularly. Students not attending, attending irregularly, and/or joining late are disruptive to teamwork. Low participation and poor contributions to teamwork can cause tensions within teams and are notorious problems for teamwork.

Measures taken to address such attendance and participation challenges included:

- setting out attendance expectations at the beginning of the module referencing ARU's Student Charter (ARU Students' Union, 2022), and timetabling synchronous online taught sessions,
- forming teams later in the module when student numbers were stable,
- signposting and scaffolding project stages and communicating these with teams,
- encouraging teams to engage all their members through a team agreement,
- requesting teams to create a credit section in their team artefact identifying team members' contributions. Non-contributing team members would fail this assessment,
- openness to alternative assessments as part of students' reasonable adjustments to be inclusive for those who cannot work in teams.

These measures were applied in the second delivery of this module. The more focused approach to wicked problems has led to better team artefacts reflecting deeper interdisciplinary engagement and providing sustainable interdisciplinary solutions. Failure and poor performance due to non or poor engagement were also considerably reduced. Ultimately, what students put into their teamwork defines the depth of learning they achieve.

Points to Consider

Readers of this chapter may wish to consider:

- Using an active collaborative learning approach such as team-based learning
- Embedding interdisciplinarity in their teaching
- Using project-based learning to develop employability skills

References

Appleby, M., & Weller, M. (2021). What are the benefits of interdisciplinary study? *OpenLearn*. The Open University. Retrieved 5 July 2024, from https://www.open.edu/openlearn/education/what-are-the-benefits-interdisciplinary-study

ARU Students' Union (2022). *Student charter*. Retrieved 5 July 2024, from https://www.aru.ac.uk/-/media/Files/about-us/governance/student-charter.pdf

Association of Interdisciplinary Studies (AIS) (2022). *Mission, vision & core values*. Association for Interdisciplinary Studies. Retrieved 5 July 2024, from https://interdisciplinarystudies.org/mission-vision-core-values/

Braun, V., & Clarke, V. (2006). Using thematic analysis in psychology. *Qualitative Research in Psychology*, *3*(2), 77–101. https://doi.org/10.1191/1478088706qp063oa

Chausson, A., & Cole, L. (2021). Talking transdisciplinarity. *International Institute for Environment and Development* (Blog post), 16 April. Retrieved 5 July 2024, from https://www.iied.org/talking-transdisciplinarity

Chettiparamb, A. (2007) *Interdisciplinarity: A literature review*. The Interdisciplinary Teaching and Learning Group, Subject Centre for Languages, Linguistics and Area Studies, School of Humanities, University of Southampton, SO17 1BJ. Retrieved 5 July 2024, from https://oakland.edu/Assets/upload/docs/AIS/interdisciplinarity_literature_review.pdf

Coyne, R. (2005). Wicked problems revisited. *Design Studies*, 26, 5–17. https://doi.org/10.1016/j.destud.2004.06.005

Daigneault, P. (2013). The blind men and the elephant: A metaphor to illuminate the role of researchers and reviewers in social science. *Methodological Innovations*, 8(2), 82–89. https://doi.org/10.4256/mio.2013.015

Ivanitskaya, L., Clark, D., Montgomery, G., & Primeau, R. (2002). Interdisciplinary learning: Process and outcomes. *Innovative Higher Education*, 27(2), 95–111. https://doi.org/10.1023/A:1021105309984

Jones, C. (2009). interdisciplinary approach: Advantages, disadvantages, and the future benefits of interdisciplinary studies. *ESSAI*, 7(1), Article 26. Retrieved 5 July 2024, from https://dc.cod.edu/essai/vol7/iss1/26

Lönngren, J., & van Poeck, K. (2021). Wicked problems: A mapping review of the literature. *International Journal of Sustainable Development & World Ecology*, 28(6), 481–502. https://doi.org/10.1080/13504509.2020.1859415

Lyall, C., Meagher, L., Bandola, J., & Kettle, A. (2015). *Interdisciplinary provision in higher education: Current and future challenges*. Advance HE. Retrieved 5 July 2024, from https://www.advance-he.ac.uk/knowledge-hub/interdisciplinary-provision-higher-education-current-and-future-challenges

McCormick, M. (2012). *Waterfall vs. agile methodology*. MPCS. Retrieved 5 July 2024, from http://www.mccormickpcs.com/images/Waterfall_vs_Agile_Methodology.pdf

Padlet (2022). *Padlet*. Retrieved 19 March 2024, from https://en-gb.padlet.com/

Petersen, K., Wohlin, C., & Baca, D. (2009). The Waterfall Model in Large-Scale Development. In F. Bomarius, M. Oivo, P. Jaring, & P. Abrahamsson (Eds.), *Product-Focused Software Process Improvement, 10th International Conference, PROFES 2009, Oulu, Finland, June 15–17, 2009, Proceedings*. Springer Nature. https://doi.org/10.1007/978-3-642-02152-7_29

QSR International (2022). *NVivo*. Retrieved 5 July 2024, from https://www.qsrinternational.com/nvivo-qualitative-data-analysis-software/

Repko, A. F. (2007). Interdisciplinary curriculum design. *Academic Exchange Quarterly*, 11(1), 130–137.

Rowntree, D. (1982). *A dictionary of education*. Barnes & Noble Books.

Saxe, J. G. (1872). The Blind Men and the Elephant. *All About Philosophy*. Retrieved 5 July 2024, from https://www.allaboutphilosophy.org/blind-men-and-the-elephant.htm

Spatial (2022). *Spatial Systems*. Retrieved 5 July 2024, from https://spatial.io/

Temkin-Greener, H., Gross, D., Kunitz, S. J., & Mukamel, D. (2004). Measuring interdisciplinary team performance in a long-term care setting. *Medical Care*, 42(5), 472–481. Retrieved 5 July 2024, from https://www.jstor.org/stable/4640776

Termeer, C. J., Dewulf, A., & Biesbroek, R. (2019). A critical assessment of the wicked problem concept: Relevance and usefulness for policy science and practice. *Policy and Society*, 38(2), 167–179. https://doi.org/10.1080/14494035.2019.1617971

A Ruskin Module from Idea to Implementation

Isobel Gowers

Background and Context

Digital accessibility is often associated with disability and will impact all of us at some point during our lifetimes. We might have a permanent disability, for example, or a temporary disability, such as a broken arm, a situational disability (i.e., trying to listen in a noisy environment), and many of us will end up with age-related sight and hearing loss. Globally, approximately one billion people are living with a disability, which equates to 12.5% of the population (World Health Organisation (WHO), 2021), meaning that everyone is likely to work with someone or have a customer/client with a disability.

Kulkarni (2019, p. 91), for example, states that:

> Accessibility refers to the extent to which a product, device, service, or environment is available and navigable for persons with disabilities, or for persons with other special needs or functional limitations. Digital accessibility … centres on access to technology products, resources and services across hardware and software.

This definition suggests that digital accessibility is solely related to people with acknowledged disabilities. The AbilityNet approach that 'web accessibility is about universality and making something that can be used by as many people as possible' (2023, para. 3) is much more inclusive and could be considered a better structure for digital accessibility.

Digital accessibility can be aligned with some of the UN's Sustainable Development Goals (SDGs) (UN, 2023). For example, *SDG 4: Quality Education* states, 'Ensure inclusive and equitable education'; *SDG 8: Decent Work and Economic Growth*, 'Promote sustained, inclusive and sustainable economic growth, full and productive employment and decent work for all'; and the most obvious, *SDG 10: Reduced Inequalities*, which has specific targets including 10.2: 'empower and promote the social, economic and political inclusion of all, irrespective of age, sex, disability, race, ethnicity, origin, religion or economic or other status' (The Global Goals, 2023, para. 3), and

DOI: 10.4324/9781003474593-9

10.3: 'Ensure equal opportunity and reduce inequalities of outcome, including by eliminating discriminatory laws, policies and practices and promoting appropriate legislation, policies and action in this regard' (The Global Goals, 2023, para. 4).

The importance of digital inclusion to the SDGs is highlighted in the report of the UN Secretary-General's High-Level Panel on Digital Cooperation (UN, 2019). Microsoft also demonstrated interest in the SDGs in their report, *Microsoft and the United Nations Sustainable Development Goals* (Art & Emejulu, 2020), supporting the link between digital accessibility and SDGs.

Digital accessibility can be considered a wicked problem (Rittel & Webber, 1973). Although improving digital accessibility seems a straightforward idea, there are many barriers that cause it to be a wicked problem. Firstly, the cost associated with improving accessibility which requires expertise or investment in specialist help to make digital materials accessible. Secondly, the need to raise awareness and help people realise that accessibility is an issue that we all can do something about. Coupled with these points is education, and the need to teach people how to make their digital assets more accessible.

One complex issue involves balancing the needs of people with different impairments, as improving accessibility in one instance might decrease it for others. For example, high contrast between text and background colours helps individuals with vision impairments to read digital material but can make it harder for people with dyslexia (Rello & Baeza-Yates, 2012). In addition, it is important to balance accessibility, usability, and aesthetics. A website, for example, needs to be attractive to encourage people to engage with it, yet it needs to be usable by all users, whatever their abilities or disabilities. Thus, digital accessibility is not as straightforward as it initially seems.

As university graduates will become the employers and entrepreneurs of the future, it is important to find ways to increase students' awareness of digital accessibility. Previously, I had promoted accessibility for staff, but I was interested to discover how many graduates with disabilities struggled once they reached the workplace. Often this is due to employers not providing the reasonable adjustments staff need, despite legislation (i.e., the Equality Act 2010), which requires employers to take action to remove barriers caused by disability. Examples of reasonable adjustments include, but are not limited to, the provision of materials in alternative formats including braille, the provision of hearing loops or British sign language interpreters, or ensuring buildings are accessible for people with mobility issues (see Equality and Human Rights Commission, 2019).

This lack of accessibility provision was brought home to me during a CPD session at the University of Essex which focused on the differences in inclusive practice between students' experience in HEIs and graduates' experiences in employment. The difference in approach to inclusive accessibility between the university and the workplace inspired me to make students aware of accessibility so they can shape workplace attitudes in the future.

With hindsight, I could have designed a module about widespread accessibility, but at the time I was working on a project ensuring the University was meeting the requirements of the *Public Sector Bodies (Websites and Mobile Applications) Accessibility Regulations 2018*, and my focus was digital accessibility. This was the catalyst for my interest in enhancing students' awareness of accessibility.

Ruskin Modules: The Spark of an Idea

Upon learning of the interdisciplinary Ruskin Modules (RMs), I immediately thought of them as a perfect vehicle for improving students' understanding of digital accessibility. I focused on how accessibility applies to all disciplines rather than how each discipline contributes to an understanding of accessibility.

The introduction of the RMs was a new initiative for ARU and was directed by the *Education Strategy 2018–2022* (ARU, 2018). Yet this can be problematic because, as Macdonald (2013, p. 11) points out, significant educational change happens because people think it is for their own, the students', and the institution's good. In technology terms, there needed to be enough 'early adopters' who were excited about interdisciplinary education, and the transformation it could make to create a sense of excitement about this new university wide initiative.

The next stage was to prepare the RM proposal form, which contained the details needed for the Module Definition Form. One of the challenges I faced was that the form did not include space for accompanying detail, so I felt a little constrained, as I wanted to put more information on the form than was requested. I felt like it needed a narrative to contextualise what would happen in the module. During the initial RMs, we had engaged in activities and developed a sense of excitement about how our RMs would work, but the form only collects information to populate the student information system, and it is difficult to capture innovation and the excitement on the form.

As the topic of digital accessibility is relevant to multiple disciplines, it was suitable for a breadth module. Consequently, during the planning stages, I worked with colleagues from different schools: two from the Business School and one from the Cambridge School of Art. We discussed ideas using Jacobs (1989) as a framework around students developing their own brand, whether as an individual or an entrepreneur, and the benefits of having an awareness of digital accessibility. We discussed issues such as typography and the tension between choosing font types for accessibility versus brand awareness. As my background is in science and education, working with academics in the arts and business schools helped broaden my perspectives. Having these discussions was important to further clarify my ideas as each disciplinary perspective brought something unique to the discussion and allowed creation of further ideas, such as a 'personal brand', that I had not thought of before. I had considered the effect of an inaccessible website excluding potential customers, but it was only by talking to someone specialising in marketing that I was able to think 'outside the box' and see the added value of integrating knowledge from different disciplines.

Once the proposal was completed, I submitted the module for validation, which gave me the opportunity to provide the information excluded from the form. Overall, the feedback was positive, but as the panel wanted the name of the module changed to something more stimulating, I changed it from *Why does digital accessibility matter?* to *Digital Accessibility: Why should it matter to you?*

The panel also wanted interdisciplinarity to be more explicit in the module paperwork. This is when I started to realise that, although the topic of digital accessibility was relevant to all disciplines, I had not explored the idea of interdisciplinarity itself in enough detail. Interdisciplinary thinking goes beyond a topic being important to any given discipline. Boix Mansilla et al. (2000, p. 219) defined interdisciplinarity as:

> the capacity to integrate knowledge and modes of thinking in two or more disciplines or established areas of expertise to produce a cognitive advancement – such as explaining a phenomenon, solving a problem, or creating a product – in ways that would have been impossible or unlikely through single disciplinary means.

Subsequently I explored how I could integrate information from different disciplines to solve the wicked problem of digital accessibility. I used Jacobs' (1989, p. 52) Interdisciplinary Concept Model, which is described as 'A step-by-step approach for developing integrated units of study'. The model consists of an Organising Centre surrounded by six radiating disciplinary spokes. My Organising Centre was digital accessibility but from the conversations I had prior to creating, and feedback after sharing, the model, my wheel had more than six spokes. For accessibility reasons, I changed the diagram to plain text for the Module Definition Form (see Table 7.1).

Both the name change and the additional consideration of how interdisciplinarity would be included in the module satisfied the validation panel and the module was validated.

Delivering the Module

It had always been my intention to deliver this Digital Accessibility RM online; therefore, I was already prepared when ARU decided that all RMs would be delivered remotely. The benefit of delivering these modules online was that students were from both Chelmsford and Cambridge. Delivering online did present some challenges, however. The students were all from different faculties and courses, so they did not know one another, and as very few students chose to turn their cameras on, it was difficult for

Table 7.1 Themes from the Interdisciplinary Concept Model

Discipline	Perspectives
Science	Engineering IT accessible solutions Neuroscience of accessibility Making complex scientific notation accessible
Philosophy	Personal ethics and morals compared to society's ethics and morals
Law	Legal requirements for digital accessibility
Maths	The challenges of making numbers accessible
Health and Medicine	Digital accessibility and public sector bodies, understanding the implications of different disabilities
Social studies	Inclusion, social justice, equality vs. equity, social model of disability, transient and situational disability
Linguistics	Simplifying language to make it accessible
The Arts	Aesthetics, designing accessible fonts, making art, media, and games accessible
Business	The effect of inaccessible content on customers, lost customers because content is not accessible

students to develop any sort of relationship with their peers. This was also challenging for me. A few students would turn on their cameras and microphones and offer contributions but by far the highest engagement was through the chat.

The module was developed around an active learning philosophy. This meant minimal delivery via lectures, and students would have more control over what they were learning. The first half of each weekly session was a facilitated discussion, and I used the second half for students to work on their group assessment tasks. I used a Team-Based Learning approach and provided students with weekly pre-session activities and post-session reflections. Students could use the latter to help with the reflective essay which was part of their assessment. The pre-session activity was often a video with questions to think about that would then be discussed in class.

From the outset, it was obvious that the students were not completing the pre- and post-session tasks. Students who did engage in the pre-session activity were able to contribute to the class discussion in greater depth. I realised that some students saw this as an additional module unrelated to their degree and therefore that it was less important. It was difficult to ascertain if students would have engaged better if this was face-to-face, or whether they were struggling with active learning as it was something new to them, or finally if they just were not interested in the subject matter of the module.

Only 19 of the 57 students who were initially enrolled on this module had selected this module. The remaining 38 students had been automatically enrolled as they had not made module selections for their optional modules including the RM. This may also have contributed to their lack of engagement.

Interdisciplinarity

Klaassen (2018) describes present-day education as bounded by discipline whereas Spelt et al. (2009) consider that interdisciplinary learning develops boundary crossing skills. Thus, part of the focus of this module was to encourage students to think outside of the boundaries of their current discipline. However, when the students and I started to discuss the ideas around disciplinary and interdisciplinary thinking, it was clear that many students did not yet identify as belonging to a discipline. They saw themselves as students of science or programming, for instance, but not as scientists or programmers. One of the few students who identified as belonging to a discipline was an illustrator, which I found surprising as Tomlinson and Jackson (2021) have shown that students from science subjects, rather than the arts and humanities, are more likely to have started to develop a professional identity rather than seeing themselves as novice students. Tomlinson and Jackson (2021) also found professional identity developed further as students moved up through the levels of study. This might be partly because student identity develops from participating in disciplinary research and scholarly activities (Davis & Wagner, 2019), and perhaps students lacked this experience at the beginning of their second year.

I divided the students into multidisciplinary teams which included students from at least three different faculties and not just discipline areas. This design, where students were put into teams rather than self-selecting, weakened the development of cohesive groups. The students felt very much this was something they had no control over, and in future I plan to give the students greater autonomy in choosing their multidisciplinary teams.

On reflection I do not think it was necessary that every member of the group came from a different discipline and that having 'course buddies' might give students more confidence to get involved. As team members develop trust over time, I wanted the group work to run the entire length of the module, as this would give them the time to develop and coalesce as a team that hopefully trusted each other. I wanted to maximise the development of social skills needed to form an effective team which Mendo-Lázaro et al. (2018) found worked better when cooperative teamwork is used over a longer period.

With hindsight I needed to include more activities to develop the team and to help them work together. Both collective energy and enthusiasm (Müceldili & Erdil, 2016 and an individual's tendency to cooperate (Bravo et al., 2019) are positively associated with team cohesiveness. I had hoped my own enthusiasm and passion for the topic of digital accessibility would carry the students along into cohesive teams, but I am not sure it was enough. Interestingly, Bravo et al. (2019) also concluded that task factors, such as workload and complexity, had a negative effect on team cohesion. On reflection, I wonder whether students perceived the task as overly complex and requiring substantial effort. Integrating different discipline perspectives is difficult, and students are unlikely to be used to working in this way. I think students being worried about what they needed to do had a negative effect on team unity.

I found that students relied more on sharing their own experiences than their discipline expertise. This made me question whether I had scaffolded the sessions appropriately and whether the students had acquired sufficient discipline knowledge at this stage of their course to enable them to draw upon this for problem solving. Creating multidisciplinary teams should have resulted in students contributing disciplinary expertise to integrate into problem solving, yet it is still unclear whether students noticed when the module content related directly to their discipline.

I had thought it was valuable to let the students work in multidisciplinary groups and had assumed that they would be able to. This lack of experience in integrating disciplinary perspectives meant it was then difficult for students to gain insight into the benefits of interdisciplinary problem solving. This lack of insight in turn meant that higher marks were more difficult to attain for the RM common learning outcome.

Although I had expected students to learn through what I designed to be an authentic and immersive experience of interdisciplinary working, I found this was not the case. In future I will consider providing the initial exploration of what different disciplines can contribute to the issue and how these different contributions can be integrated, encouraging co-creation with the students, rather than expecting the students to bring the necessary discipline expertise to their learning.

Active Learning

Active learning is not new or unique to RMs, and in the late 20th and early 21st centuries, there has been a growing interest in the field. Bonwell and Eison (1991) conclude that learners might have to problem solve but also engage in higher-order thinking, such as analysis, synthesis, and evaluation. Brame (2016, p. 1 [original emphasis]) notes that,

> active learning is commonly defined as **activities that students do to construct knowledge and understanding**. The activities vary but require students to do **higher order thinking**. Although not always explicitly noted, **metacognition** – students' thinking about their own learning – is an important element, providing the **link between activity and learning**.

For me, active learning has meant that students create their own learning. This might be when lecturers encourage students to think within a lecture, for example, or ask them to do or create something that facilitates learning of the subject matter. Students should have some control over their learning and are often required to engage in reflection to put their learning into context.

I delivered this RM using a holistic active learning approach. By this I mean that active learning was embedded in the learning outcomes, the assessment strategy, and the delivery of the content. The learning outcomes of the module were:

1 Critically reflect on the limitations of a single discipline to solve wider societal concerns by applying knowledge created through the discovery and exploitation of connections across disciplines (Baxter & Brown, 2018, p. 4)
2 Evaluate the role of digital accessibility in reducing inequality both nationally and internationally
3 Determine mechanisms for maximising digital accessibility for all whilst recognising the different needs of individuals means there is no perfect solution
4 Develop skills in producing a range of accessible digital content

The first of these learning outcomes is common to all RMs and not only focuses on the interdisciplinary nature but also requires students to reflect on how they have worked together and integrated knowledge from different disciplines, which is often a key component of active learning. I designed Learning Outcomes 2 and 3 to encourage students to explore the issues around digital accessibility and start to develop solutions to improve accessibility, recognising that there is no one quick fix to solve the problem. Finally, Learning Outcome 4 encouraged students to 'learn by doing' (Dewey, 1916; Freire, 1970) and apply the knowledge they had gained to developing accessible resources.

To facilitate the achievement of these learning outcomes and to enable this holistic approach, the assessment was integrated with the delivery. The second hour of each session (approximately half the contact time) was scenario-focused learning, where students came together as an interdisciplinary group working to produce digital resources to improve digital accessibility, which they later submitted as part of the assessment. This enabled students to work together to produce the resources, getting feedback from their peers and the tutor as they developed their digital assets. The students could choose what they created, giving them agency within the assessment.

I modelled the scenario on ARU's interdisciplinary accessibility working group, which was created to meet the requirements of the Public Sector Bodies Accessibility Regulations (2018). This working group was set up in March 2020 to ensure ARU complied with the new regulations by the September 2020 deadline and had members from Corporate Marketing, Anglia Learning & Teaching (ARU's learning and teaching development unit), Student and Library Services, Distance Learning, IT Services, and the Disability and Dyslexia team, who had to integrate disciplinary knowledge to ensure that the institution's digital assets were accessible. As scenarios can often feel contrived, I wanted to use a scenario that had application to real employment-related situations, and this scenario offered a level of authenticity.

Working in a group or team to create knowledge without it being driven by myself as a teacher again aligns with active learning. Pratt-Adams et al. (2020) highlight the fact that active learning is rooted in constructivist and social constructivist learning theories and the move towards more student-centred teaching approaches, and this is what I was trying to encapsulate. However, it did make me question at times whether students wanted a more student-centred approach to their teaching.

I was surprised how challenging students found this method of delivery. I gave them some direction about their meetings, having a chair and a scribe, but they found managing these meetings difficult and clearly needed more support for this than I had anticipated. I drew the idea of students recording meeting minutes and actions from my experience as an external examiner at another institution where students used the minutes as a record of their contributions to the group work, but also to gain skills in managing and minuting meetings that might be useful in their future careers. One of the issues I had faced was that, as this was the first time the module had run, I did not have exemplars of previous students' work to show to these students. I provided copies of some of the university working group minutes and a standard template, but few students chose to use these.

The second element of the assessment that students found difficult was having a choice. The students wanted to know what they should produce, while I wanted them to decide what digital assets to create. I gave them several examples of resources designed to improve accessibility, and while some students used these as a starter for producing their own resources, others were more creative. Two factors contributed to why students found this assignment challenging. Firstly, in line with the principle of least effort (Zhu et al., 2017; Zipf, 1949), students have learnt to be strategic in their studies and view assessments as a means to achieve a mark, and not as part of their learning. Consequently, students want a prescriptive assignment brief that tells them how to achieve a good mark. Secondly, students needed more scaffolding and checkpoints to help them navigate the process.

I really wanted to reward originality, creative thinking, and those students who had demonstrated learning through the process of the assignment rather than just trying to create an artefact to get them the mark they wanted. However, in another manifestation of the principle of least effort (Zipf, 1949), students sometimes only seem interested in the bare minimum needed to pass the assessment rather than what they need to learn from a module. Some students, for example, attended group meetings to be recorded as having attended, but then only made minimal contributions to the discussions. It is probably not possible to change this strategic approach (Jungert & Rosander, 2009) in one module alone. However, I tried to mitigate the culture of strategic study by designing the assessment to be as engaging as possible with students getting more out of it by putting more into it, both in construction of the assessment and through the assessment criteria. With hindsight engaging students who had not elected to take this module was likely to be a challenge.

In the first few weeks of the trimester, I went into each team meeting at least once per session to check that the students were on topic and engaged and to find out if they had any questions. Initially, students asked a lot of questions; however, many of these focused on what happens if a member of the team did not contribute fully to the work and whether they would get the same marks as those who had. There were also some groups that wanted more explanation of the task. For me, it appeared that students wanted reassurance about the task and elements that they felt they could control. I would have preferred them to delve deeper into integrating knowledge from different disciplines, but that was more of an unknown for the students. Nevertheless, although this might have worried students more, they were less willing to ask for help.

After the first six weeks, I told groups to call me into their meetings if they wanted feedback on the assets they were producing as part of the assessment but requests for feedback were few, with only two of the six active groups requesting formative feedback. It was frustrating that the students did not ask for more feedback, but it occurred to me that this might be because they were unfamiliar with a culture where they receive useful formative feedback and feedforward. In addition, I thought this was because they were worried about not having completed the task correctly. When students get feedback in real-time, they might find it more intimidating and might prefer getting written feedback where they do not feel the focus of attention. Thirdly, the students may have chosen not to ask for feedback as they did not want the additional work involved in responding to it. The lack of requests for feedback did make me reflect that I probably needed to add more formal formative feedback points in the assignment briefing. This creates an expectation of students that work will be submitted for feedback as part of the assessment process.

Conclusion

Delivering the RM on Digital Accessibility has been an invaluable learning experience for me. Digital accessibility remains an important topic for students to learn about and undoubtedly it is a wicked problem that benefits from an interdisciplinary approach. However, having taught this module, I think the students struggled to engage with unfamiliar content, delivery, and assessment style, and together this meant that all but the most interested students struggled to engage with both the content and the assessment.

The module has given me the opportunity to reflect on active learning in practice and some of the challenges faced by staff who embrace a holistic approach to active learning. This will not only help me support students that I teach going forward but also support other staff as I help them to utilise active learning pedagogies. One of the biggest takeaways I have from this module is ensuring that active learning, particularly assessment, is scaffolded. This is especially important when students are new to these techniques.

Points to Consider

Readers of this chapter may wish to consider:

- Providing students with a detailed introduction to active learning
- Co-creating content with students to reinforce their disciplinary identities
- Including formal formative feedback points

References

AbilityNet (2023). *What is Digital Accessibility?* Retrieved 05-07-24, from https://abilitynet.org.uk/accessibility-services/what-is-digital-accessibility

Anglia Ruskin University (ARU). (2018). Education strategy 2018-2022. Anglia Ruskin University.

Art, J.-Y., & Emejulu, D. A. (2020). *Microsoft and the United Nations Sustainable Development Goals.* Retrieved 5 July 2024, from https://query.prod.cms.rt.microsoft.com/cms/api/am/binary/RE4GSkV

Baxter, P., & Brown, E. (2018). Education strategy: Ruskin modules. Anglia Ruskin University.

Boix Mansilla, V., Miller, W. C., & Gardner, H. (2000). On disciplinary lenses and interdisciplinary work. In S. Wineburg, & P. Grossman (Eds.), *Interdisciplinary curriculum: Challenges of implementation.* Teachers College Press.

Bonwell, C., & Eison, J. (1991). Active learning: Creating excitement in the classroom. AEHE-ERIC Higher Education Report No. 1. Jossey-Bass.

Brame, C. (2016). *Active learning.* Vanderbilt University Center for Teaching. Retrieved 5 July 2024, from https://cft.vanderbilt.edu/active-learning/

Bravo, R., Catalán, S., & Pina, J. M. (2019). Analysing teamwork in higher education: An empirical study on the antecedents and consequences of team cohesiveness. *Studies in Higher Education, 44*(7), 1153–1165. https://doi.org/10.1080/03075079.2017.1420049

Davis, S. N., & Wagner, S. E. (2019). Research motivations and undergraduate researchers' disciplinary identity. *SAGE Open.* https://doi.org/10.1177/2158244019861501

Dewey, J. (1916). *Democracy and education: An introduction to the philosophy of education.* Macmillan Publishing.

Equality and Human Rights Commission (EHRC) (2019). Examples of Reasonable Adjustments in Practice. Retrieved 5 July 2024, from https://www.equalityhumanrights.com/en/multipage-guide/reasonable-adjustments-practice

Freire, P. (1970). *Pedagogy of the oppressed.* Penguin.

Jacobs, H. H. (1989). The interdisciplinary model: A step by step approach for developing integrated units of study. In H. H. Jacobs (Ed.), *Interdisciplinary curriculum: Design and implementation* (pp. 53–66). Association for Supervision and Curriculum Development.

Jungert, T., & Rosander, M. (2009). Relationships between students' strategies for influencing their study environment and their strategic approach to studying. *Studies in Higher Education, 34*(2), 139–152. https://doi.org/10.1080/03075070802596970

Klaassen, R. G. (2018). Interdisciplinary education: A case study. *European Journal of Engineering Education, 43*(6), 842–859. https://doi.org/10.1080/03043797.2018.1442417

Kulkarni, M. (2019). Digital accessibility: Challenges and opportunities. *IIMB Management Review, 31*(1), 91–98. https://doi.org/10.1016/j.iimb.2018.05.009

Macdonald, R. (2013). The nature of educational change. In R. Macdonald (Ed.), *Supporting educational change*. SEDA Special 33, p. 11.

Mendo-Lázaro, S., León-del-Barco, B., Felipe-Castaño, E., Polo-del-Río, M.-I., & Iglesias-Gallego, D. (2018). Cooperative team learning and the development of social skills in higher education: The variables involved. *Frontiers in Psychology, 9*, article 1536. https://doi.org/10.3389/fpsyg.2018.01536

Müceldili, B., & Erdil, O. (2016). Cultivating group cohesiveness: The role of collective energy. *Procedia—Social and Behavioral Sciences, 207*, 512–518. https://doi.org/10.1016/j.sbspro.2015.10.121

Pratt-Adams, S., Richter, U., & Warnes, M. (Eds.) (2020). *Innovations in active learning in higher education*. University of Sussex/Fulcrum. https://doi.org/10.20919/97819123

Rello, L., & Baeza-Yates, R. (2012). Optimal colors to improve readability for people with dyslexia. Retrieved 5 July 2024, from https://www.w3.org/WAI/RD/2012/text-customization/r11

Rittel, H. W., & Webber, M. M. (1973). Dilemmas in a general theory of planning. *Policy Sciences, 4*(2), 155–169. https://doi.org/10.1007/BF01405730

Spelt, E. J. H., Biemans, H. J. A., Tobi, H., Luning, A., & Mulder, M. (2009). Teaching and learning in interdisciplinary higher education: A systematic review. *Educational Psychology Review, 21*, 365–378. https://doi.org/10.1007/s10648-009-9113-z

The Global Goals (2023). *10: Reduced Inequalities*. Retrieved 5 July 2024, from https://www.globalgoals.org/goals/10-reduced-inequalities/

Tomlinson, M., & Jackson, D. (2021). Professional identity formation in contemporary higher education students. *Studies in Higher Education, 46*(4), 885–900. https://doi.org/10.1080/03075079.2019.1659763

UK Government (2010). Equality Act 2010. *The National Archives*. Retrieved 5 July 2024, from https://www.legislation.gov.uk/ukpga/2010/15/contents

UK Government (2018). The Public Sector Bodies (Websites and Mobile Applications) Accessibility Regulations 2018. *The National Archives*. Retrieved 5 July 2024, from https://www.legislation.gov.uk/uksi/2018/852/contents/made

United Nations (UN) (2019). *The Age of Digital Interdependence: Report of the UN Secretary-General's High-level Panel on Digital Cooperation*. Retrieved 5 July 2024, from https://digitallibrary.un.org/record/3865925?ln=en

United Nations (UN) (2023). *The 17 Goals*. Retrieved 5 July 2024, from https://sdgs.un.org/goals

World Health Organisation (WHO) (2021). *Disability and Health*. Retrieved 5 July 2024, from https://www.who.int/en/news-room/fact-sheets/detail/disability-and-health

Zhu, Y., Zhang, B., Wang, Q. A., Li, W., & Cai, X. (2017). The principle of least effort and Zipf distribution. *Journal of Physics: Conference Series, Volume 1113, 5th International Workshop on Statistical Physics and Mathematics for Complex Systems (SPMCS2017) 12–15 October 2017, Wuhan, China*. https://doi.org/10.1088/1742-6596/1113/1/012007

Zipf, G. K. (1949). *Human behavior and the principle of least effort: An introduction to human eoclogy*. Addison-Wesley Press.

Chapter 8

Blurred and En-Tangled Boundaries

A Case for Interdisciplinarity and Diversification

Linda Brown

Introduction

Other chapters in this book include Anglia Ruskin University's (ARU) thinking behind the development of Ruskin Modules (RM), but it is worth repeating the ambitious rationale behind these breadth modules:

> We'll design Ruskin modules (breadth units) that creatively develop the capacity for critical reflection and reasoned argument, integrating the acquisition of graduate capitals with wider societal concerns and challenges, bringing together students from different disciplines around key challenges. Ruskin modules will form a core, credit-bearing part of the curriculum. (ARU, 2019, p. 8)

This outreach aimed to connect local and global understanding, challenges, and priorities. The inclusion of graduate capitals within this statement incorporates ARU's framework to encourage the development of knowledge, skills, and attributes 'required to achieve successful outcomes and lifelong learning' (ARU, 2018a, p. 11). The six capitals aim to develop Knowledge, Identity Capital, Cultural Capital, Social Capital, and the Whole Person. In essence, our community had the opportunity to engage in learning and teaching which would create new communities of learners who could bring their lived experiences, subject knowledge, and passions into a shared space to shine the light on local and global matters by harnessing the potential of interdisciplinarity.

Strategic Encouragement

In addition to the call for RMs emerging from ARU's (2018b) *Education Strategy 2018–2022*, another institutional strategy plays an equally significant leading role in the background of this chapter: the ARU's (2021a) Strategy for Advancing Race Equality at ARU (known as the Race Equality Strategy (RES)), which was launched in November 2021. My role in its development

DOI: 10.4324/9781003474593-10

influenced me and provided me with an early appreciation of its role regarding RM design, themes, and assessment practice.

Years of work directed at promoting inclusion, probing awarding gaps, and recognising disparate and often negative experiences for students and staff inspired the RES. An institutional approach was essential if it were to have any chance of success and lasting impact. Linked to an extensive action plan, the RES sets out an ambitious programme aimed at all parts of the institution.

The RES rests upon the three interlinked foundations of Leadership and Strategy, Diagnosis and Data, and Communication. Contained within these foundations are five workstreams, two of which apply directly to learning, teaching, assessing, and development: Curriculum Change, and CPD/ Unlearning and Conversations (see Figure 8.1). While at the strategy's core, the aim of 'Race equality achieved through cultural change' (ARU, 2021a, p. 3) chimes well with the global and ambitious vision of RMs. Although the Curriculum Change workstream provided space for developing a RM, it is the CPD workstream which delineates their clearest role: 'Develop further "unlearning" opportunities for students including workshops, Ruskin modules, Advocate- and Students' Union (SU)-led events and activities which explore whiteness, privilege, structural racism, microaggressions, allyship, etc.' (ARU, 2021b, p. 7).

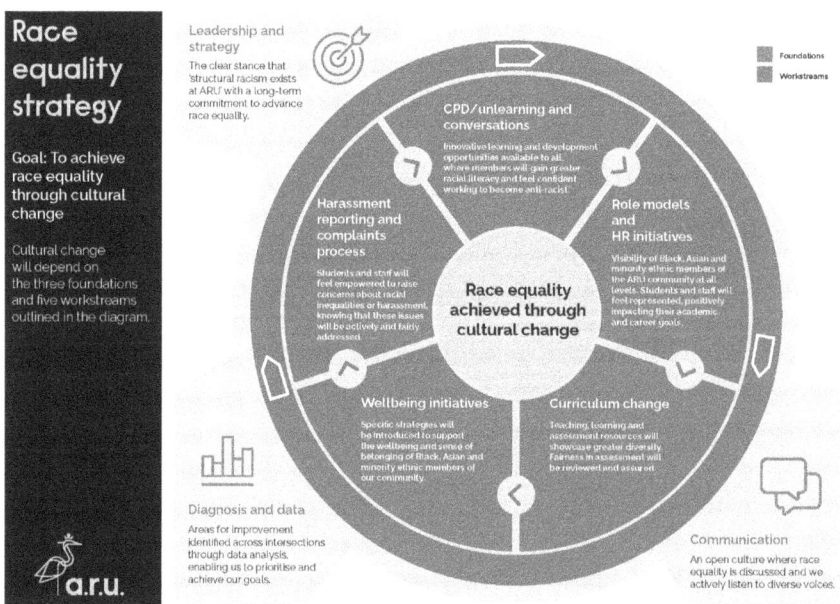

Figure 8.1 Race Equality Strategy diagram (ARU, 2021b)

Multiple Voices and Visions

Collaborations and Co-designing

In this chapter, I use my experiences of co-designing an interdisciplinary RM that relied upon and showcased diversification. The strength of student partnerships and collaborations has been highlighted and demonstrated in a number of contexts and institutions. Not without detractors, the potential of such collaborations has nevertheless influenced a range of planning conversations and initiatives in higher education. Understanding these collaborations from a wider perspective has led to a self-perpetuating system of potential benefits. Gannon-Leary et al. (2011, p. 108) observe how 'Involving students more closely in educational decision-making and listening seriously to their stories of experiences as learners are essential first steps which, in turn, will reinforce students' commitment and academic progress'. In other words, student involvement can lead to greater student success.

Pressure from sources peripheral to teaching in higher education has made explicit demands for universities to work more closely with their students as partners. For example, the Office for Students (OfS) (2022, p. 200) has included student partnerships in its regulatory framework:

> Seeking to engage students as partners is an important part of the academic governance and management of academic standards and quality, as is effective oversight of the information which the organisation produces about its provision for all its stakeholders, especially prospective, current, and completed students.

ARU has recognised the contributions made by students in a range of roles and conversations, including a long-term partnership with our Race Equality Student Advocates (RESAs). ARU formally launched this programme during the 2017–2018 academic year. Currently representing all four faculties and different levels of study, our RESAs play a positive, proactive role in promoting diversification, a sense of belonging, and racial literacy. In 2021, ARU Vice Chancellor, Professor Roderick Watkins (2021, para. 11), recognised their work:

> Our Student Advocates continue to play a major role in our work on race equality. This year they have been raising awareness of anti-racism, whiteness, privilege, and related themes, and developing tools for the university to diversify curricula.

Although my role is formally defined as staff-facing, I have increasingly sought out and developed opportunities to work closely with a range of students, but none more closely than with our RESAs. As a member of ARU's learning and teaching unit, Anglia Learning & Teaching (AL&T), I have worked across a vast spectrum of areas and initiatives, but the core of my role has been our institutional commitment to inclusion. This momentum has led me to a clear focus on race equality, and it has been this focus which has enabled rich and meaningful partnerships with students.

A major part of this collaboration has involved diversification and decolonisation efforts to embed the principles from the RES as well as the principles and recommendations of ARU's *Inclusive Curriculum Framework* (Brown et al., 2018). These curriculum efforts encompass broader goals such as closing awarding gaps, fostering an open, welcoming learning environment, and scrutinising ourselves regarding bias, stereotypes, and Euro-centric assumptions. As such my day-to-day work involves conversations with colleagues and students to listen and learn. The result has been engagement with honest, often painful, lived experiences alongside ambitious, practical, and hopeful ideas.

First Steps to Fusion

In leading on inclusive learning communities and partnerships, I seek connections that can advance more than one aim. Such an approach led to conversations with two RESAs with whom I collaborated in ancillary work alongside the larger diversification and decolonisation project. We established a splinter group as we undertook a project to research, probe, and engage with the intersection of interdisciplinarity and diversification. In the end, we took our aims a step further and, after determining that nothing of this sort already existed, decided to create a guidance tool which supported this intersection.

One of the RESAs had taken part in the RM CPD sessions and therefore understood the structure, rationale, and aims of RMs. The other RESA had not attended the sessions but possessed a strong understanding of interdisciplinarity which had emerged from secondary education in an international school. Their experiences brought a rich set of social, academic, and racial literacies and capital to the project. Our ongoing projects as team members in the RE work enabled expansive and productive conversations as we kept the relationship between diversification and interdisciplinarity foremost in our minds.

We regularly consulted a basic diversification and decolonisation tool that the RESAs had previously co-created. This template for staff and students was not subject-specific and therefore malleable in its generic guidance. Thus, against the backdrop of the RM priorities, and with reference to the generic diversification tool, the shape and format of a guide, designed for those at ARU involved in developing RMs, *Fusion: the interplay between interdisciplinarity and diversification* (ARU, 2020), began to resolve into four main sections:

- Design approaches
- Module content
- Activities and developing skills
- Assessment practice

For good accessibility and ease of use, we created separate colour-coded tables for each of the four sections. Each table included *Recommendations*, and *Examples and further ideas* provided substance alongside ideas, questions, and reflections. For example, recommendations for 'Module content' include topics such as ambiguity, (un)conventional reading lists, learning outcomes (LOs) as roadmaps, representation, global categorisations, and auditing out bias and stereotypes. In reference to global categorisations, *Examples and further ideas* cautions that 'Lazy categorisation supports inequalities of experience and supports myth-telling and stereotypes' (ARU, 2020, p. 5). Similarly, as part of the discussion of 'Team Formation' within 'Design Approaches', we recommended, 'Utilise or create personality tests or games in order to design diverse teams'. As we co-developed this tool, we understood the need for it to be shared and trialled to identify its strengths and weaknesses.

Learning and Teaching Conference

AL&T holds an annual learning and teaching conference each June to showcase and celebrate internal and external projects, trials, and research. The theme of the 2021 Conference (AL&T, 2021) was 'Maximising opportunities, minimising barriers', and Professor Jason Arday delivered the keynote speech, *Moving the Dial: Anti-Racism in Higher Education*. Presentation and workshop choices were guided by six golden threads, one of which, *Showcasing Interdisciplinarity and Diverse Representation*, provided an appropriate space for us to present *Fusion*.

The two RESAs and I presented our work, discussing the trajectory that led us to develop a basic tool. We explained the initial challenge we had set ourselves, 'to ponder and develop what it meant to diversify a breadth module' which resulted in *Fusion*. Our audience engaged strongly with the session, offering comments and insights about the power of interdisciplinarity in learning, the richness of cultural change, the scope for *Fusion* within RMs, and its power to support useful disruptions in learning.

Blazing Trails

Overlaid onto this part of the narrative sits the Coronavirus Pandemic. As it transpired, COVID-19 enabled a transformation in learning and teaching at ARU, an experience shared across the UK higher education sector. Relying on Microsoft Teams and our virtual learning environment (VLE), Canvas, we transitioned into an institution-wide provision of online teaching. The timing was fortuitous as an ambitious assumption had long been that online delivery would be required for the RMs. As a multi-campus institution, student choice would otherwise be determined and limited by where the teaching would take place. As such the acquiring, supporting, and improving of digital platforms and tools supported plans concerning RM learning and teaching. It also hugely supported the RM community of course leaders, project managers, and module leaders to manage the substantial new programme. Our Trailblazer community, as it came to be known, could also communicate and collaborate more flexibly and efficiently, and engage in development sessions, via online delivery.

The range of CPD covering the integration of the priority areas of sustainability, employability, and interdisciplinarity enabled Trailblazers to apply their learning through their curriculum design. Within this suite of development opportunities were the Ruskin Module Open Studios, designed and delivered by a colleague who was both an Academic Developer and Trailblazer. These welcoming and generous sessions pushed the community to prioritise, practise, and integrate creativity into our teaching and assessing processes. As a bonus, students were invited to take part in these RM developmental sessions. SU officers and RESAs attended when able and contributed generously to the activities, brainstorming, and discussions.

On a personal level, I had originally envisaged supporting RMs through my then role as an academic developer and had not intended to design and teach one. However, given the potential of the challenge as described above and generally in this book, the pull to do so strengthened. Additionally, my doctorate (undertaken in the United States) had been interdisciplinary. Consequently, I was fully cognisant of the practical and pedagogical challenges as well as the significant and complex benefits of interdisciplinary learning and research. As ideas churned in my mind regarding a theme which could create an interdisciplinary learning experience, while demonstrating diversification and inclusive learning, I took inspiration from multiple conversations with the RESAs.

The topic of hair as a cultural feature, priority, and symbol emerged as a theme in our formal and informal interactions. Inherent in our discussions were the politics and cultural significance of hairstyles (Mazrui & Anwar, 2014), haircare, and hair products.

As a challenge and thought experiment, I began to research the topic from a wide range of disciplines to gauge whether the topic could carry an entire module while fulfilling the RM brief of entrepreneurship, sustainability, and creativity. My investigation uncovered a vast world to explore and research further. Crucial for me as a practitioner and proponent of diversification, the larger aim included not only researching from a diverse range of authors and cultures but also actively incorporating a wide and diverse set of resources. Thus, in addition to book chapters and academic journal articles, I integrated blogs, videos, and artwork. Early on, a defining feature of the module was a rich, varied, and ever-evolving playlist of music tracks from a wide range of genres and artists.

Themes and Titles

After compiling the research and subject areas, I undertook a thematic exercise to meld relevant resources, voices, and research foci that aligned with the LOs. In the end, limited by the practicalities of a 15-credit module, which involved keeping an eye on independent study time and the number of themes we could reasonably cover, I had to cut several discipline/research areas, including maths, midwifery, and literature (i.e., novels/short stories).

Theme Weaving and Explorations

The final choice of six major themes represented those which could robustly demonstrate and capitalise on the richness of interdisciplinarity. They each carried diverse and heavy loads:

1 Locks, Lengths and Looks: culture and identity of Hair
2 Hairy Time Travel: forensics, drug-testing, genetics, and ageing
3 'Grasping her hair, he cut it off close': discipline, humiliation, control, and status
4 'Black is the colour of my true love's hair': symbolism, memory, authenticity, and pathos
5 'Cut your hair, boy!': a generation, its music, messages, and legacy
6 'Because I'm worth it?': consumerism, plastics, chemical and animal testing

The aim was for each theme to incorporate and overlay learning from multiple disciplines, facilitating discussions which drew on students' own discipline knowledge to encourage cross-fertilisation. Students' own lived experiences were equally relevant and would be crucial in contextualising each module theme.

Fusion offers a challenge to 'conventional truths' and expands upon this challenge by advocating for teachers to be creative in reading and resource lists through a diversity of reference types and media. Thus, *Theme 1: Locks, lengths & looks: The culture & identity of hair* provided space to explore both culture and identity both generally and individually. In addition to a guest lecture on *Black Women's Hair*, we read a book chapter, *The Gender and Sexual Politics of Hair* (Johnson, 2021), watched a Channel 4 documentary (2022), *Hair Power: Me and My Afro*, and Lady Gaga's (2011) music video for her song, *Hair*. This range of resources and areas for exploration, as specified in the LOs, linked strongly with students' personal experiences and subject-specific learning.

Fusion intentionally privileges the role of ambiguities and complexities in RMs. To probe unknowns, it singles out silenced voices and the 'other' in an appreciation of listening to multiple voices, including those traditionally unfamiliar, as well as seeking answers from other ways of living and thinking. This part of the guidance influenced Theme 3 regarding the power of hair to play a role in the conferring of status and the meting out of humiliation and punishment. This juxtaposition came alive through historical and contemporary illustrations which prompted questions surrounding powerholders using hair to honour or shame, the duties or actions meriting recognition or disgrace, and ways that these two extremes fitted within their economic histories. Resources exploring this set of contrasts included a reading (Choi, 2006), a video of *Japanese Hairstyles: Hein to Meiji period* (Nitta, 2021), archival records from the Bristol Workhouse in the nineteenth century (Bristol Archives, 2023), and current dress and hair codes in UK schools and workplaces.

One of the most challenging parts of designing and developing the RM was articulating the title. Early ideas focused almost exclusively on politics and culture and included, *How do we untangle the politics of hair?* and *How do we encounter the culture wars in our hair?* An early subtitle, *Get your hands off my plaits,* similarly expressed the module's political emphasis. But this interdisciplinary module was much broader and deeper in focus. The six themes, discussed above, all highlighted the centrality of hair in daily life and its role in a number of disciplines. This exercise led me to the only title I could articulate which captured the themes while retaining the political and cultural: my (overtly informal) title became, *Why all the fuss over hair?*

Exploiting the Learning Outcomes

To develop the themes within the taught curriculum and design creative assessments, the LOs had to be malleable and energetic. All RMs were furnished with a (fourth) LO regarding their *raison d'être* whereas the first three spoke to the trajectory of the module's main themes. My goal was for each LO verb to point decisively towards the action and activity of the learning and teaching process through interpretation, identification, and engagement. Their heavy lifting included charting the course for learning, teaching, assessment, and reflection (see Table 8.1).

Table 8.1 Learning outcomes: Why all the fuss over hair?

On successful completion of this module, the student will be expected to be able to:	
Knowledge and Understanding	1. Interpret the role of hair in past and modern-day power struggles, as portrayed in history, art, culture, and religion
Knowledge and Understanding	2. Identify ways that hair shapes, expresses, and transmits identity
Intellectual, practical, affective, and transferable skills	3. Engage in a collaborative project that responds to environmental, cultural, and/or political implications of hair
Intellectual, practical, affective, and transferable skills	4. Critically reflect on the limitations of a single discipline to solve wider societal concerns by applying knowledge created through the discovery and exploitation of connections across disciplines

Promoting Ruskin Modules

Communication within organisations often feels sluggish and ineffective. Messages frequently reach a significant minority but elude the majority, then run the risk of inciting debates and attracting naysayers after the fact. Surprisingly, these messages often sit unread on pinboards, in email in-boxes, and in social media posts, and communications about RMs suffered many of these perennial shortcomings. However, early efforts to attract staff interest led to institution-wide gatherings. To inform student engagement, the course leader collaborated with the AL&T Communications Manager to encourage RM Leaders (RMLs) to create 60-second videos promoting their RMs. These videos, sitting within the Student Life section of the ARU website, paved the way for Applicant Day online presentations for students to meet RMLs and engage with RM themes as they were choosing modules.

More than just showcasing *Why all the fuss over hair?*, I used the Applicant Day presentation on *Wicked Hair* in multiple learning opportunities. In addition to ensuring participants understood the technology of Microsoft Teams, the short sessions also discussed the purpose of RMs and the concept of a wicked problem. The presentation incorporated mini talks about *Hair in History* (e.g., the Irish cúlán for warriors), *Hair in Society* (discussing the Halo Collective (2020) perspective on black hair codes and discrimination), and *Hair Art* (showcasing Victorian mourning jewellery). Ending with a light-hearted quiz to identify celebrities by their 'hair-style', the session enabled me to visualise teaching the full online version during the following academic year. I enjoyed my 'fifteen minutes' with prospective students who were engaged and active. Both promotions (i.e., the video and the Applicant Day presentation) attracted the attention of colleagues who were not involved in RMs. This unforeseen benefit led to their inclusion within my RM as guest lecturers.

Actively Seeking Collaborations and Collaborators

In the wake of the Applicant Day sessions, two colleagues from different faculties contacted me. One, an expert in forensic science, offered to lecture on the forensic analysis of hair. While the module has a strong enrolment from forensics and criminology students, my colleague presented their topic and research so that it was accessible and meaningful to everyone, regardless of subject area. Another colleague from Education brought their research, *Considering Personal and Cultural Relationship with Hair*, about Black women and how their experience with their hair is affected by internal and external influences.

My attempts to enlist other colleagues resulted in a fascinating lecture from a colleague in psychology, which positioned hair loss in reference to trichotillomania, the overwhelming urge to pull out one's hair. This colleague situated the lecture within a larger discussion of alopecia. All these lecturers beautifully positioned their contributions within the theme into which their specialisation fitted.

Fusion and Wikis

Two of the most rewarding parts of developing and teaching this module combined my use of *Fusion* and the provision of spaces for students to contribute their ideas via Canvas. This VLE, like many, offers the easy creation of wiki pages which provide students with the opportunity to engage directly, share personal learning, and develop digital skills and confidence. Focused on the process of engaging in wiki development, Matthew et al. (2009) explain how, 'As they contribute to a wiki, students are creating course resources and building course content in a shared space where they can add, delete, and revise their writing' (2009, p. 54). Given the elasticity of the topic of hair as discussed in the themes, having a static, one-sided set of resources seemed short-sighted and limiting and against the spirit of *Fusion* and diversification in general. These shared spaces, 'The Music Room', 'In the News', and 'Our Language Glossary', reinforced the collaborative nature of the module learning.

The wikis did not exist simply for students to add content and suggestions. Instead, they were part of a more ambitious plan which required time, space, and encouragement to support us as a community of curious learners. They represented a discrete space for transforming the study of a quotidian entity into engaging with it through new and varied lenses. Building and fostering social learning through a community-based approach came with substantial challenges, however. The time-limited nature of building this shared experience with students from a wide spectrum of disciplines who did not know each, and who would separate when the RM ended, justified the need to be strategic and focused. If we view our community of learners as a community of practice in need of time and shared experience, we can more readily position these challenges: 'A community of practice is a sustained social network of individuals who share a common set of core values and knowledge, including a past history, grounded on common practices' (Hung et al., 2004).

To offer a special opportunity to reimagine our community in the waning stages of the lockdowns, I invited students to an event, with optional face-to-face attendance simultaneously complemented by an online presence. The event was a mini hackathon (DeFranco et al., 2021) that allowed the 20 or so students who could attend to develop their own RM curriculum (Bovill & Woolmer, 2019). I took us through the process of articulating a wicked problem, understanding the essential RM components, and discussing assessments. As a bonus, after we had completed the hackathon, those gathered were able to meet and collaborate with their teammates for their final assessment work. I provided food and drinks to reinforce the social side of the event.

Assessing Hair

In addition to the other examples discussed above, *Fusion* inspired the design of the module's assessments. The tool describes assessing interdisciplinarity using diverse methods, and to 'Question whether an interdisciplinary module should remain yoked to traditional assessment practice'. It sees RMs as an opportunity to scrutinise the hierarchy of conventional assessment practice alongside its rationale and processes. With these considerations in mind, I developed the first assessment with the objective of showcasing creativity and identity in line with LO1 and LO2. Two alternative formats offered students the choice either to *Represent* their own individual hair story or to *React* to an existing hair-related object.

Represent

Most students chose this option and produced interesting and strongly personal creative pieces. Students represented their hair story through a range of genres and types, including original artwork of various media (e.g., painting, graphic design, collage), song lyrics, written stories, a three-act play, and other forms of creative expression. Most of the pieces communicated individuality and emotion even as they connected clearly to module themes. Students' hair stories told their personal histories in unique ways. This creative work, however, was not marked.

Templates for students writing about representation included a description of their hair story, the rationale behind their choice, reflections on module learning and life experiences to decode symbols, language, and images, and connections to interdisciplinarity through the inclusion of two external resources. This reflective essay was marked. Clear marking criteria and rubrics supported the assessment processes alongside exemplars, a video of me explaining the assessment, and the opportunity to receive early feedback.

React

Closely related to *Represent*, the choice to *React* meant that students could choose to share their learning and reflections about pre-existing creations related to hair. As inspiration, I offered a range of ideas and resources, such as the Pre-Raphaelite painting by Rossetti (1874), *Proserpine*, Kenyon's (2003) poem, *Finding a long gray hair*, and the video, *The New Age of Trichology* (Visser, 2016). While some students used these resources, the majority found others which appealed more directly to them, including music videos, song lyrics, and other paintings and poems. A similar writing template and resources supported this choice of assessment.

Regardless of whether students chose to *Represent* their hair story or *React* to another, their reflections showed a strong identification with their object. The more challenging part of their writing came in discussing it through the lenses of interdisciplinarity. While some students were able to offer broad and connected analyses and discussions, others struggled to create and discuss relationships.

This part of the assessment clearly required stronger scaffolding and demonstrations from me. Similar challenges have been reported in other interdisciplinary programmes such as in a study by Self and Baek (2016), who concluded that interdisciplinary learning delivered by team teaching 'did not significantly benefit holistic learning experiences' (2016, p. 476). They hypothesised that the second-year undergraduates involved in their study lacked a strong grounding in one discipline, supporting the notion of 'Awareness of Disciplinarity as important to the success of interdisciplinary pedagogic strategies' (2016, p. 476). In the context of my RM, while some students displayed the appropriate depth of knowledge for a Level 5 undergraduate, others were unable to communicate, apply, and connect their learning in the context of interdisciplinary explorations.

Team Responses

The final assessment, in line with *LO3: engage in a collaborative project that responds to environmental, cultural and/or political implications of hair*, and *LO4: limitation of a single discipline to solve wider societal concerns*, was a team exercise to create a digital artefact. Resources for Theme 6 (i.e., 'Because I'm worth it?': consumerism, plastics, chemical, and animal testing) had particularly helped prepare and inspire planning for this assessment, including, for example, an online blog from National Geographic which explored tackling the 'plastic crisis' through the lens of collaborative, multipronged approaches (Borunda, 2019). Thus, the assessment had the trimester's resources, activities, and team-based work as the foundations for each team to develop their responses and deliver them via a digital presentation.

This team-based work involved enormous and challenging administrative work on my part. A significant reason for the challenges involved those students who were consistently not attending and/or engaging with the module.

I had designed a digital tool to aid me in forming interdisciplinary teams. Students responded to a range of preference-based questions (e.g., about food, sport, and travel preferences). Sorting the responses and selecting team members was time-consuming, but the tool worked well to form teams which represented good discipline and personal diversity. Problems arose, however, when students did not communicate with their teams, requiring additional administrative time. As teams began the process of coalescing, extra resources helped track and manage team member contributions and overall considerations. The assessment brief guided them through the activities and suggestions to collaboratively:

- Identify a question, problem, or issue to address
- Agree a project-based response to it (how can we address this issue?)
- Use the UN Sustainable Development Goals as a guide

- Manage team responsibilities using an action plan
- Track individual and team contributions

The (functioning) teams produced creative work which they presented to the entire class. Projects responded to a range of the environmental, cultural, and political implications of hair. Some teams explored and designed inclusive and sustainable hair product packaging, while others focused on cultural symbols, hair-coverings, and empathy.

Some of the individual written reflections regarding team project management, collaborative dynamics, and final output demonstrated a clear understanding of the project's rationale and integration of interdisciplinary design; a number of assessment reflections, however, fell short. Future decisions regarding this particular assessment need to gauge how to better scaffold the process for students, minimise tutor administrative and management duties, and provide stronger direction regarding the reflection itself.

Afterword

The RM community of Trailblazers continues to design, discuss, and collaborate. I have contributed to the ongoing programme of support by developing and presenting on *Fusion* and sharing my mini-hackathon resources. I have also presented on teamwork, discussing selection strategies using the tool I designed to build interdisciplinary teams, and lessons learned.

The tool, *Fusion*, encouraged me to design my RM with diversity and its many facets at its core. Fundamental to achieving diversification in learning and teaching is the collaborative process, and similarly building a curriculum which represents diverse perspectives, people, and positions requires a commitment to listening, reflecting, and evaluating preconceived and fixed notions of how things should be done. The inclusion of the wiki pages is one example of this design approach alongside the other examples described above.

Rarely a week goes by when I do not see or hear about hair in the mainstream media in reference to control, politics, and power. Co-designing *Fusion* and applying its guidance to *Why all the fuss over hair?* have enabled me to continue to contextualise hair in reference to race equality, identity, and aspiration. The future of hair is bright as problem-solving applications are underway in research and development labs across the globe. It is my hope that the students with whom I have shared this RM will carry this experience with them, influenced by the interdisciplinary learning that inspired the module to exist in the first place.

Points to Consider

Readers of this chapter may wish to consider:

- Co-developing a diversified and interdisciplinary curriculum with academic and non-academic peers

- Co-designing module content with students, particularly in reference to identity, culture, and subject knowledge
- Promoting wiki-pages for sharing a range of contemporary multi-media content

References

Anglia Learning & Teaching (AL&T) (2021). *Annual conference 2021.* Retrieved 5 July 2024, from https://www.aru.ac.uk/anglia-learning-and-teaching/cpd-opportunities/annual-conference/past-engage/annual-conference-2021

Anglia Ruskin University (ARU) (2020). Fusion: The interplay between interdisciplinarity and diversification. Anglia Ruskin University.

Anglia Ruskin University (ARU) (2018a). Active curriculum framework. Anglia Ruskin University. Retrieved 5 July 2024, from https://www.aru.ac.uk/-/media/Files/Anglia-learning-and-teaching/Strategy/Active-Curriculum-Framework.pdf

Anglia Ruskin University (ARU) (2018b). Education strategy 2018-2022. Anglia Ruskin University. Retrieved 5 July 2024, from https://www.aru.ac.uk/-/media/Files/about-us/corporate-documents/employability-strategy-2018-2023.pdf

Anglia Ruskin University (ARU) (2021a). Strategy for advancing race equality at ARU. Anglia Ruskin University. Retrieved 5 July 2024, from https://aru.ac.uk/-/media/Files/about-us/equality-diversity-and-inclusion/21-22–15981-Race-Equality-Strategy_SS_WEB.pdf

Anglia Ruskin University (ARU) (2021b). Race equality at ARU. Anglia Ruskin University. Retrieved 5 July 2024, from https://www.aru.ac.uk/about-us/equality-diversity-and-inclusion/race-equality

Anglia Ruskin University (ARU) (2022). Ruskin modules. Anglia Ruskin University. Retrieved 5 July 2024, from https://www.aru.ac.uk/student-life/support-and-facilities/careers-and-employability/innovative-curriculum/ruskin-modules

Borunda, A. (2019). The beauty industry generates a lot of plastic waste. Can it change? *National Geographic.* Retrieved 5 July 2024, from https://www.nationalgeographic.com/environment/article/beauty-personal-care-industry-plastic

Bovill, C., & Woolmer, C. (2019). How conceptualisations of curriculum in higher education influence student-staff co-creation in and of the curriculum. *Higher Education, 78*(3), 407–422. https://doi.org/10.1007/s10734-018-0349-8

Bristol Archives (2023). Records of the Clifton *Union* workhouse at 100 *Fishponds Road, Eastville,* 1847-1952. Bristol Archives catalogue. Retrieved 5 July 2024, from https://archives.bristol.gov.uk/records/30105

Brown, L., Potts, K., Pratt-Adams, S., & Priddle, J. (2018). *The ARU Inclusive Curriculum Framework: Underpinning principles for an active and inclusive curriculum.* Retrieved 5 July 2024, from https://www.aru.ac.uk/-/media/Files/Anglia-learning-and-teaching/Inclusive-learning-and-teaching/Inclusive-Curriculum-Framework.pdf

Channel 4 (2022). *Hair Power: Me and My Afro.* Channel 4. Retrieved 5 July 2024, from https://www.channel4.com/programmes/hair-power-me-and-my-afro

Choi, N.-Y. (2006). Symbolism of hairstyles in Korea and Japan. *Asian Folklore Studies, 65*(1), 69–86.

DeFranco, J. F., Eagle, C. S., Michael, J. B., Viega, J., & Voas, J. (2021). *Hackathons 101. Computer, 54*(5), 65–69. https://doi.org/10.1109/MC.2021.3064435

Gannon-Leary, P., Dordoy, A., McGlinn, S., Baldam, F., & Charlton, G. (2011). What would happen if we treated the student as someone whose opinion mattered?:

Student learning and teaching awards at Northumbria. In S. Little (Ed.), *Staff-student partnerships in higher education*. Continuum International.

Halo Collective (2020). *We're building a future without hair discrimination*. Retrieved 5 July 2024, from https://halocollective.co.uk/

Hung, D., Looi, C.-K., & Koh, T.-S. (2004). Situated cognition and communities of practice: First-person 'lived experiences' vs. third-person perspectives. *Journal of Educational Technology & Society*, *7*(4), 193–200. Retrieved 5 July 2024, from https://www.jstor.org/stable/pdf/jeductechsoci.7.4.193.pdf

Johnson, C. (2021). The gender and sexual politics of hair. In G. Biddle-Perry (Ed.), *A cultural history of hair in the modern age, Volume 6*. Bloomsbury Publishing Plc. https://doi.org/10.5040/9781474232104

Kenyon, J. (2003). Finding a long gray hair. Retrieved 5 July 2024, from https://allpoetry.com/Finding-A-Long-Gray-Hair

Lady Gaga (2011). *Hair* [video]. YouTube. Retrieved 5 July 2024, from https://www.youtube.com/watch?v=Okq8xHrIZ8I

Matthew, K. I., Felvegi, E., & Callaway, R. A. (2009). Wiki as a collaborative learning tool in a language arts methods class. *Journal of Research on Technology in Education*, *42*(1), 51–72. Retrieved 5 July 2024, from https://files.eric.ed.gov/fulltext/EJ856933.pdf

Mazrui, A. A., & Anwar, E. (2014). *The politics of gender and the culture of sexuality: Western, Islamic, and African perspectives*. University Press of America.

Nitta, F. (2021). *History of Japanese Hairstyles: Heian to Meiji Period* [Video]. Retrieved 5 July 2024, from https://www.youtube.com/watch?v=33TbFEPTemM&ab_channel=Q2Japan

Office for Students (OfS) (2022). *Securing student success: Regulatory framework for higher education in England*. Retrieved 5 July 2024, from https://www.officeforstudents.org.uk/media/1231efe3-e050-47b2-8e63-c6d99d95144f/regulatory_framework_2022.pdf

Rossetti, D. G. (1874). *Proserpine*. Tate Gallery. Retrieved 5 July 2024, from https://www.tate.org.uk/art/artworks/rossetti-proserpine-n05064

Self, J. A., & Baek, J. S. (2016). Interdisciplinarity in design education: Understanding the undergraduate student experience. *International Journal of Technology and Design Education*, *27*(3), 459–480. https://doi.org/10.1007/s10798-016-9355-2

Visser, S. (2016). The New Age of Trichology. Retrieved 5 July 2024, from https://sannevisser.com/The-New-Age-of-Trichology

Watkins, R. (2021). Race Equality Student Advocates. In *Race Equality at ARU*. Retrieved 5 July 2024, from https://www.aru.ac.uk/about-us/equality-diversity-and-inclusion/race-equality

Undergraduate Learners as Emerging Agents of Change for Sustainability and Environmental Justice

Roxana Anghel and Victoria Tait

The earth [is lent to us] for our life; it is a great entail. It belongs as much to those who come after us as to us; we have no right by anything that we do or neglect, to involve them in unnecessary penalties.

(John Ruskin, 1819–1900)

Introduction

The thinking about the interplay between the natural environment and intergenerational well-being by John Ruskin, the acclaimed art critic of the nineteenth century, was the inspiration for the Ruskin Modules (RMs) to:

> equip our students for the 21st century ... creatively develop students' capacity for critical reflection and reasoned argument, integrating the acquisition of graduate skills with wider societal concerns and challenges, bringing together students from different disciplines around key challenges.
>
> (Anglia Ruskin University (ARU), 2018, p. 8)

RM are an attempt to disrupt traditional education in favour of a transformative pedagogy based on several strategic approaches: experiential learning, interdisciplinarity, sustainability, creativity, and employability.

In this chapter, we discuss the first iteration of our RM, *Climate Justice and Social Inequality: Could you be an Agent for Change?* We focus on educating about sustainability through critical and social justice lenses, highlighting the inherent and only recently recognised (Dominelli, 2012) social and power dimensions to climate and environmental degradation and to a global transition to sustainability. The module responds to the pedagogical innovation expected of Higher Education Institutions (HEIs) to prepare skilled professionals for the challenges posed by climate change now and in the future, and for sustainability, its proposed solution (UNESCO, 2017).

DOI: 10.4324/9781003474593-11

Interdisciplinary Theoretical Foundations

For our RM, we focused on two complementary dimensions: understanding how sustainability can be achieved equitably, and the pedagogy needed to foster action in the real-world.

Much has been written about the need for sustainability to be incorporated into the HE curriculum and for pressing action in the face of challenges such as climate change and biodiversity loss (Holm et al., 2016; Stewart et al., 2022; UNESCO, 2014, 2017). However, debates on the definition of sustainability are widespread, with a frequent emphasis on degrowth narratives (Ruggerio, 2021). ARU's Global Sustainability Institute defines sustainability as 'envisaging a just society of innovation, opportunity and wellbeing which manages the full diversity of environmental risks' (ARU, 2022, para. 5). This definition highlights the complex interplay of socio-ecological systems and the need to ensure that justice is at the heart of transitions to sustainability.

Our RM emerged from a critical perspective inspired by the shared values, consciousness, and approaches characteristic of critical/green social work, education for sustainable development (ESD), and participatory research. Our starting points were social justice, democracy, respect for multiple epistemologies, equity, asset/strengths-based approaches, resistance, and praxis for social change (Banks & Brydon-Miller, 2019; Dominelli, 2013; Freire, 1970; Saleebey, 2009).

Social work practice, rooted in the 'person-in-(social) environment' concept (Germaine & Gitterman, 1980) and in resisting the injustice of socio-economic inequalities, has been called to expand, to include protection of the natural environment through community mobilisation (Dominelli, 2013; Shajahan & Sharma, 2018). Concern with the quality of the environment as a structural factor affecting the lives of low-income groups can be traced back to the social work of Jane Addams in the early twentieth century in the US who argued against 'biological' explanations of poverty, instead linking the origins of social problems to the poor living environment (Narhi & Matthies, 2016). Addams developed collective action to combat these structural injustices including establishing the first parks and recreation centres, and safer spaces for social gatherings.

In contemporary social work, a new global theoretical debate emerged in the 2010s, generating multiple nuances to the scope of social work in taking a position on environmental sustainability (Narhi & Matthies, 2016). Examples include 'deep ecological social work' which criticises the anthropocentric view of the human-nature relationship (Besthorn, 2011), 'eco-spiritual social work' which emphasises the spirituality and views of Indigenous people (Gray & Coates, 2013), 'eco-social work' which argues for environmental justice, the interdependence between humans and the non-human world, and for interdisciplinary research (Gray et al., 2012), and 'social and ecological social work' which promotes 'transformational social work' (Peeters, 2012).

In the UK, Dominelli (2012) conceptualised 'green social work' as holistic professional practice with a critical and political stance which critiques neoliberal modes of production and consumption as environmentally exploitative and as perpetuating social and environmental injustice. Dominelli (2013) advocates for supporting marginalised individuals and communities to mobilise in partnerships and alliances, affirm their rights, and take collective action to influence decision-makers towards environmental justice.

The impetus for a professional response to climate change and bringing sustainability to the forefront of social work consciousness is gaining momentum as sustainability is conceptualised as an ethical issue (Bowles et al., 2018). Agyeman (2005) found that less equitable societies have lower commitment to environmental quality, more environmental stress, and higher rates of premature deaths. However, Bowles et al. (2018), who researched the UK, US, and Australian national codes of social work practice, found that these concerns are not acknowledged despite an interest from practitioners to incorporate environmental issues in their practice and education. Given the slow response at the macro level, Mahees (2020) suggests that social workers must find ways to connect with other professionals who share this focus.

Social workers' concern with the nexus between social justice and environmental justice overlaps substantially with ESD, which seeks to develop the necessary knowledge, skills, values, and attributes *for* sustainability, rather than *about* sustainability (Shephard & Furnari, 2012). ESD, designated by the 1972 Stockholm Conference as essential to achieving sustainability (Holm et al., 2016), promotes the embedding of sustainable development principles into education (Laurie et al., 2016). Through pedagogies including peer-to-peer, interdisciplinary, and experiential learning, ESD aims for learners to have the skills and leadership to respond to the rapid environmental and social changes brought on by climate change (Thew et al., 2021). Nonetheless, ESD has faced challenges, including the unsustainability of the HE system itself (Cotton et al., 2009; Shephard, 2008; Sterling, 2021), and has been critiqued for deprioritising the critical deconstruction of 'development' (Misiaszek, 2020). However, Dominelli (2012, p. 29) observes that 'the realisation that poverty and the lack of environmental rights in disaster situations are intertwined is a relatively recent insight'. Indeed, alongside the skills mentioned above, it is vital that future professionals acknowledge the populations experiencing social inequality (e.g., low-income, Indigenous, Black, elderly, disabled), respect them and what is meaningful to them, and include them collaboratively in the sustainability process.

Both (critical) social work and ESD use participatory research to empower people whose lives are affected by oppression to influence social change (Banks & Brydon-Miller, 2019; Trott et al., 2019). Participatory research involves community stakeholders co-creating situated knowledge and change and values mutual respect, collaboration, equality, and knowledge democracy. Freire's (1970) concept of 'conscientisation' informs this approach. It stresses the importance of harnessing the critical and creative ability of those socially excluded to make decisions about their inclusion and so to liberate themselves (Bell et al., 2012). In this approach, people engage in critical analysis and reflective action through dialogue, enabling their otherwise silenced voices to actively reflect on the conditions producing their oppression and to develop bottom-up action.

Peeters (2012) argues that the transition to sustainability requires social and political action. At individual and community levels, this involves building social capital through the empowerment and cooperation of social actors. Peeters (2012) argues that this starts from the strengths and capacities of people which, when acknowledged and enabled, foster resilience and empowerment, essential conditions for bottom-up social change. Promoters of ecopedagogy (Misiaszek, 2021) argue that it is essential to analyse sustainability from the perspective of oppressed communities to understand the nexus between environmental and socio-historical oppressions and the continuous thick residue of coloniality.

To respond to these calls, the objectives of our module were for the students to:

1 Acquire critical literacy and consciousness about climate change and environmental degradation and its social and ecological causes and impacts, potentially initiating a transformation of their internal concepts towards cultural change
2 Enhance their sensitivity to social and climate justice and the imperative for the strengths and the voice of communities most affected to be recognised, acknowledged, respected, and engaged in co-producing sustainability and environmental justice
3 Acquire competencies and capitals to enhance their employability, and encourage leadership for sustainability in their employed roles

Matching Pedagogical Tools

Sustainability and environmental justice require societal transformation and competent citizens (Barth et al., 2007). Several sets of competencies have been proposed for dealing with the complexity of sustainability and other wicked problems (Rittel & Webber, 1973). Wiek et al. (2011) synthesised five competencies:

- *Systems thinking* (analyse complexity, cascading effects, and what transformation is needed)
- *Anticipatory* (future thinking, and understanding intergenerational equity)
- *Normative* (understand how complex social-ecological systems have evolved, and learn about justice and socio-ecological integrity)

- *Strategic* (understand real-world situations and collectively design trans-formative strategies with different societal actors, facilitating diverse per-spectives and 'getting things done')
- *Interpersonal* (requires stakeholder collaboration and interdisciplinarity via advanced communication skills, collaborating, leadership, trans-cultural thinking, and empathy)

Aligned with these overall considerations, we generated an 'enabling didactic' (Arnold & Lermen, 2005) to develop students' ethical and anticipatory skills, personality, and resilience. Our module was based on three pedagogical approaches: 'project-based experiential learning for co-productive change', 'interdisciplinarity', and 'distributed leadership'.

Project-Based Experiential Learning for Co-productive Change

The focus of this RM was on students emerging as agents of change *together with* not *on/for* communities (Agdal et al., 2019). Our work aligns with critical pedagogy which aims to make schools 'agents of change' in the belief that enlightened students and teachers can have an impact on and change society (Cho, 2013, p. 92). Critical pedagogy builds more egalitarian power relations, strengthens the learners' voices, inspires critical consciousness, constructs knowledge *with* students, and galvanises action for change. The aspiration is a blend of critical perception of reality which could lead to praxis (i.e., action taken based on critical dialogue and conscientisation of oppression). Misiaszek (2021) argues that successful ecopedagogical teaching increases the students' ability to read 'development' critically and gain insight into how globalisation from below can counter the dominant neoliberal discourse that sustainability via continuous growth is natural and inevitable. The aim is to empower the learner to take collective action and to understand the importance of this stance to equitable sustainability.

Students' learning towards becoming agents of change was assessed through collective (project proposal) and individual (reflective essay) assignments. For the proposal, we organised the students into ten teams of eight members and asked them to identify and research a community experiencing environmental risk and social inequality. Students' selections included diverse national and international examples such as the impact on vulnerable populations of local air pollution, the intergenerational impact of a chemical spill on a Native American community, and plastic pollution affecting the food, income, and health of a community in the Nile Delta. We asked students to analyse the complexity of the situation (*systems and normative competencies*), anticipate its consequences (*anticipatory competence*), and map the most affected community stakeholders and other actors with power to affect change (*strategic competence*). Finally, students proposed participatory methods that would enable these diverse stakeholders to access the conversation, voice their ideas, develop bottom-up and culturally sensitive action, and learn through reciprocity (SCIE, 2016) (*interpersonal competence*).

Overall, the task assisted students in acquiring skills, values, and knowledge to support disempowered groups to recognise their collective capacity for action (Arendt, 1972). We included learning opportunities that encouraged students to become sensitive to the strengths in a locality and to explore bottom-up routes to solutions. We drew on the *1991 Principles of Environmental Justice* developed by the *First National People of Color Environmental Leadership Summit* and on the *1997 Jemez Principles for Democratic Organising* (Energy Justice Network, 2023). Both documents argue for 'just sustainability' (Agyeman, 2005, p. 5) and highlight the central role that equity should play in sustainability discourses, making visible the environmental inequalities across race and class, and the rights of people of colour, their lands, and communities to freedom from ecological destruction.

Although students could not engage directly with real-world communities, they were able to engage in active and experiential learning (Thew et al., 2021) through researching, teamwork, sharing knowledge, managing the organisational and interpersonal aspects of the work, and reflecting together on their learning. In this mutual process, both students and lecturers learned from each other.

Finally, in their individual assignments, students critically reflected on whether they could be agents of change for climate and environmental justice. We used Rolfe et al.'s (2001) reflective model to guide them from observation and description (*what?*), through analysis (*so what?*), to critical thinking on implications and action (*now what?*). In the essay, students unpacked the skills, values, and knowledge acquired during the team project, the application of these skills in their future career, and the learning and/or action they might pursue.

Interdisciplinarity

Echoing ESD's aim to educate *for* sustainability, Morito (2002) calls for *thinking ecologically* using interdisciplinary knowledge production, practices, and engagements. This is a key principle of the United Nations (UN) Agenda for Sustainable Development Goals (SDGs) which encourage a move from ineffective silo approaches to multidisciplinary alliances (Stibbe et al., 2020). Consequently, a common RM learning outcome was for students to:

> Critically reflect on the limitations of a single discipline to solve wider societal concerns by applying knowledge created through the discovery and exploitation of connections across disciplines.
>
> (Baxter & Brown, 2018, p. 4)

There is no single standard for successful interdisciplinary module development (Graff, 2015). Our module included four sources:

- Lecturers
- Students' project teams
- Diverse stakeholders in the community selected by the students
- The (fictional) encounter between the student team and the community

Our module had 79 students from 41 courses on art, business, criminology, law, medicine, politics, education, psychology, sociology, sport and exercise science, and zoology. In creating the project teams, we aimed to ensure maximum diversity of knowledge domains and parity of viewpoints. The students' diverse disciplinary lenses were conceptualised as assets. We used an asset-based approach, which draws on pre-existing strengths in a community (Agdal et al., 2019), both in teaching community engagement and as a learning method on the module. We used students' disciplinary diversity to help them experience how multiple viewpoints can enhance understanding of a complex issue. Our aim was to facilitate dialogue among equals (Freire, 1970) to learn from each other's shared knowledge and experiences and achieve synergistic knowledge (Mu & Gnyawali, 2003). Similar to integrationist interdisciplinarity (Repko & Szostak, 2017), synergistic knowledge results when a group builds new learning from constructively integrating their diverse perspectives. During an in-class exercise, for example, we invited students to interpret an advertisement for a popular fast-food brand from their disciplinary perspectives. In the reflective essay, some students highlighted this as a particularly insightful moment when their perception widened. Another opportunity to appreciate interdisciplinary contributions was through the teams' concluding reflections on the value of their diverse viewpoints when researching and designing their proposal.

When teaching community engagement, we designed the asset-based approach to help students to understand the value of multiple epistemologies. This is important when working with communities whose knowledge may be typically marginalised due to discrimination and prejudice, but which have assets and wisdom outsiders do not possess. Students used stakeholder mapping because solutions to environmental risks require transcending the knowledge boundaries of diverse stakeholders (Columbie, 2021). They identified the community stakeholders most likely to be unheard and excluded from decision-making (e.g., the homeless population, children, and fishing families) and the organisational stakeholders who could become allies or who could resist change.

However, a tension emerged between the aim of the RMs to enable interdisciplinary learning for sustainability and the aim of this module for students to practice interdisciplinarity for environmental justice. The first emphasises the contribution that students could bring to solutions for sustainability, while the second encourages restraint from paternalistically imposing their own solutions on a community, instead learning to enable the participation and accessibility of the community to co-producing solutions. Therefore, the meaning of 'agent of change' here was not focused on their ideas about solutions needed by a community at risk, but on how to enable the contribution of disempowered communities to their own sustainability. Without this focus, environmental justice commentators anticipate that the transition to sustainability will maintain the existing social inequality gap and reduce the UN's 'leave no-one behind' ideals to mere rhetoric (Kharas et al., 2020). Thus, the purpose of the interdisciplinary in-class exercise was to help students experience the value of what others can bring to knowledge.

Interdisciplinarity also fosters insights into interdependence, which underpins our third pedagogical framework: distributed leadership.

Distributed Leadership

Exploring leadership in social work, MacAlister (2017, p. 2) highlights that leadership 'is not the responsibility of individuals acting alone … [it is] a social activity'. To help students cope with the complexity of the task and with the diversity between them, and be aware of the high risk of group conflict in team projects (Mu & Gnyawali, 2003), we used Astin and Astin's (1996) *Social Change Model of Leadership Development* for horizontal power sharing and equal learning opportunities.

Astin and Astin's (1996) model is action-oriented, designed to facilitate positive social change and to enhance development of qualities in all participants. For this, they need to practice eight individual and collective values which enhance self-knowledge and leadership competence. Individual values include 'self-consciousness', 'congruence', and 'commitment', while group values include 'collaboration', 'common purpose', and 'controversy with civility'. The latter enables negotiation and an environment of felt psychological safety (Holley & Steiner, 2005), which pre-empts the risk of toxic conflict (Tekleab et al., 2009). The values of 'change' and 'citizenship' connect the team to the community with whom they are working in their leadership activity. In our module, this approach aimed to give students skills and values supportive of their effort to facilitate co-production in their projects, and insights into democratic participation and not acting as the experts who should lead the change in a community.

Our strategy for facilitating distributed leadership included the teams: mapping their strengths and passions for the topic to facilitate consciousness of self and identification with teammates for a common purpose (Mu & Gnyawali, 2003); drafting a group agreement on values and actions they committed to share; meeting fortnightly in online team spaces to plan the aims and tasks of their project; and working in pairs on project tasks. Team health was monitored by a team-wellbeing liaison who would contact us if the team developed conflict and needed external facilitation.

We also used peer assessment, both midway through the module, when each team provided formative feedback on the draft project to another team, and at the end when teams wrote critical evaluations in support of the lecturers' assessment of each proposal. For both activities, we instructed the students to feedback intelligently and kindly, encouraging their critical analytical skills and collegiality.

Reflective Discussion

In this module we challenged the students to reflect on becoming agents of change for sustainability by considering inequitable sustainability, and how they could facilitate bottom-up co-production from within their discipline. However, we also challenged ourselves to be agents of change for the students' cultural transformation.

However, the literature warns of the difficulties of attempting this from within the internalised neoliberalism of contemporary HE education (Cho, 2013; Sterling, 2021) which limits the reach of critical pedagogy (Lopez-Lopez et al., 2021). This poses important questions for this module, including whether we have genuinely guided students towards transformation and emergent upskilling for action for social change.

In this section, we share our reflections on the enablers and constraining factors that interacted with our attempt to offer an interdisciplinary, experiential, and participatory form of learning, advocated as a pre-condition for understanding transformative change (Cho, 2013). Our critical reflections on the extent to which these ambitions were met are based on our observations and experiential reflections during and after the module delivery.

Structural Enabling and Constraining Factors

The ethos of the RM programme is to be transformative and disruptive. It aims to provide all students with a form of education that furnishes them with the capitals and employability skills needed to contribute meaningfully to today's world.

The programme engaged educators' energy in producing modules on topics they were passionate about and within new pedagogical frameworks such as sustainability, creativity, and interdisciplinarity. This brought together a diversity of topics, all aiming to challenge, stretch, and engage students in lateral critical thinking. This also gave the lecturers the opportunity to be current and to learn from each other. Unique within the programme, our module involved the collaboration of two lecturers from complementary fields.

In recognition of the complexity and trailblazing effort required to develop and deliver RMs, the central team created a CPD programme, a buddying scheme, and a virtual space for lecturers to form a community of practice. These were important developmental and pastoral resources helping the lecturers to share good practice and support. In our module, we benefited from a supportive working relationship with a teaching peer, which enabled us to exchange resources and expertise and to create debrief opportunities.

Alongside these opportunities, several factors also challenged the module. To achieve the aim of bringing transformative education to all Level 5 undergraduate students, the module was compulsory. Consequently, our module included students who had chosen it purposefully (83.5%) or who were randomly allocated (16.5%). This had implications for motivation, attendance, and teamwork, with some teams being affected by absent members. Students were also allowed to change RMs in the first teaching week. Although this was necessary for fairness, the instability of the cohort at a key moment in the transition to an unfamiliar topic and form of education impacted the foundations of a community of learning.

The wide scale of recruitment, covering two campuses and four faculties, together with the first delivery occurring at the tail end of the COVID-19 pandemic, took the module online. While this enabled better access to the module, it also allowed students to attend invisibly by switching off their cameras. This limited lecturers' ability to forge a relationship with the students and a dialogical approach to teaching, and reduced students' identification with the group, an important condition for psychological safety (Desivilya & Eizen, 2005). Consequently, some project teams experienced toxic conflict jeopardising their opportunities for synergistic learning.

The size of the cohort resulted in ten large project teams. Although we approached this challenge by pairing students per project tasks for manageability of load and responsibility, the number of teams proved too large to facilitate personalised learning. This reduced our opportunities to stimulate critical thinking and to attend to the detailed learning opportunities that would have emerged permanently in the teams.

Finally, although one of us was an experienced lecturer, neither of us had experience in working with a large cohort. To cope with the size of the group and to enable more space for interactive conversations during teaching, we split the cohort into two subgroups taught on alternating weeks. This, however, resulted in effort duplication, and a degree of confusion for the students.

Pedagogical Enabling and Constraining Factors

The RM provided two sources of experiential and active learning: the teaching method, and the student projects. Both formats provided us with ample, although not entirely new, learning as we each had expertise in at least one of these areas. However, the scale and intensity of module development, which continued into the delivery, involved substantial effort and stretch, which can cause lecturers intending to teach experientially to revert to more familiar formats. The advantage of working in a team, however, meant that students benefited from a mix of experiential and theoretical teaching formats, both necessary for a broad understanding of the topic.

The experiential project task was also challenging to the students, and a few struggled with the interaction in the teams and with conflict. The conflict was less about cross-disciplinary critical discussions (Mu & Gnyawali, 2003) and more about a lack of engagement, commitment, and effort from team-mates. Consequently, students who invested the effort perceived this as an unfair imbalance which could affect their results. This illustrates the tension highlighted by Cho (2013) between the aspirations of a transformative peda-gogy and the neoliberal thinking ingrained in education which encourages individualism and competition, causing stress and anxiety. If HEIs are to edu-cate for sustainability meaningfully, this struggle will be key to resolve. RMs are attempting to make these important first steps by focusing on developing interdisciplinary worldviews and the intellectual, practical, and emotional skills to develop them. In our module, many more students had a positive experi-ence, finding that the project task enabled their problem-solving, interpersonal communication, and research skills, and finding value in learning about real-world communities and from their diverse peers.

This brings us to the role of discipline diversity. The RMs philosophy con-tains the implicit assumption that cross fertilisation would occur from mixing multiple disciplines, synthesising across them. In application, however, this outcome needed a much more detailed and pre-emptive strategy.

We learned that the expectation that students would have developed a disci-plinary identity at Level 5 was unrealistic. In our module, students' reflections and critical contributions tended to be based mostly on their life experiences. Additionally, interdisciplinary teaching may have also taken students outside their educational comfort zones creating a reluctance to engage. Due to the structure of modern-day education, many students experience a mostly mono-disciplinary environment. Thus, students are variably prepared to cope with the challenges of an interdisciplinary setting (Strain & Potter, 2012) and this placed higher demands on the lecturers in relation to pastoral support.

Pastoral Enabling and Constraining Factors

We understood that facilitating distributed leadership would help to avoid group conflict. We thus blended teaching with compassion both by engaging the students' empathy with the challenges faced by communities disadvan-taged by social inequality and by historical insults to health and cultural iden-tity, and by taking a pastoral role accounting for the fragile balance between facilitation and the self-management of student teamwork. Attention to stu-dent wellbeing was particularly important following COVID-19, and we pro-vided immediate responses when wellbeing liaisons or other students sought support. For fairness, we adapted the assignment expectation for the engaging students who could not complete the work of absent peers.

A final learning point is that lecturers should also acknowledge their own frailties in challenging contexts, such as COVID-19, which made this a strenuous project and revealed a tension between achievement of scale and wellbeing.

Conclusions and Recommendations

While working on the societal transition to sustainability, the 2030 SDG Agenda urges the world to 'leave no-one behind' and to move towards multidisciplinary participatory alliances (Stibbe et al., 2020). In our RM, we intended to raise the awareness and critical literacy of students not only about the causes and history of current environmental crises but also about how climate change and sustainability have an embedded social dimension which needs to be addressed for a just future. Our work, therefore, extends Lopez-Lopez et al.'s (2021) 'pedagogy of care' by both bringing the intrinsic value of nature into students/citizens' consciousness and also by raising consciousness about the environmental discrimination of often unheard individuals and communities.

In this chapter, we have presented our experiences as pioneers of a RM in its first iteration. *Climate Justice and Social Inequality* is complex, a wicked problem, and so the module was a challenging attempt to educate students to be informed contributors, sensitised to the human dimension of this challenge. We have offered this not as experts but as educators who have started to grapple with the intricacies of the topic, and with the pedagogical approaches needed for climate justice.

Our analysis highlighted both the opportunities that such a module provides for the ambitions of education *for* sustainability and the interaction between structural and personal factors that can support or hinder its success. We therefore recommend the following:

- Although it is urgent that we educate ourselves and our students about sustainability and environmental justice, there is value in approaching innovation incrementally avoiding rapid over-scaling, to allow educators to pilot effective formats for maximum impact
- Reduce pressure and load-protect educators' wellbeing to release their imagination and ability to innovate, and to respond rapidly to students' learning needs
- Create genuine conditions for communities of learning by paying attention to scale and to opportunities for face-to-face learning
- Acknowledge student wellbeing as a critical condition for learning. Learning for sustainability needs to take place in groups, but the risk of group conflict is high – for critical thinking and interpersonal competence, groups need strong foundations and facilitated relationships throughout

- Scaffolding prior to the module would enable students to develop a disciplinary identity and prepare them for interdisciplinary learning at Level 5

Over a decade ago, Anderberg et al. (2009) found signs of irritation in the literature about universities appearing not to take seriously their responsibility for advancing theory, research, and pedagogy for sustainability and action. More recently, Sterling (2021) argued that universities are largely maladaptive and, with few exceptions, do not support the transformation needed for sustainability. Similarly, Misiaszek and Rodrigues (2023) question the capacity of the neoliberal higher education sector to educate students in another paradigm. However, Gardner et al. (2021) argue that advocacy and activism should be at the heart of the new academic purpose that is required for HE to contribute meaningfully to transformation. To an extent, RMs have opened the space for modules which problematise, take students out of their disciplinary silos, and encourage them to think actively about their role in the world as professionals and citizens.

Nevertheless, universities need to do more to become aware of the debate, engage with it, and embed transformative education. Through developing the module and writing this chapter, we have become sufficiently immersed in this debate to understand the tension between positions and paradigms and have begun to develop our own stance. This process, however, has shown us that transformational pedagogy takes time and can discourage previous certainties. For example, while still trusting that the SDGs could work as a galvanising tool, VT developed a more critical and nuanced understanding, and adopted a non-prescriptive pedagogical approach, enabling exploration of diverse perspectives and worldviews.

Ultimately, pedagogical impact takes time to metamorphose into transformative action. Our module has attempted to equip our students for it by initiating conscientisation about structures of power and the impact of environmental inequality on health, access, culture, and rights, and by encouraging them to include in their professional practice participatory approaches for community voice and influence in decision-making. We hope that the module presented and critiqued here offers an example and a degree of inspiration for educators who aim towards education that contributes to sustainability and to the common good (Sterling, 2021).

References

Agdal, R., Midtgård, I. H., & Russell, C. (2019). *Asset based community development: How to get started*. The Western Norway University of Applied Sciences.

Agyeman, J. (2005). *Sustainable communities and the challenge of environmental justice*. New York University Press.

Anderberg, E., Norden, B., & Hansson, B. (2009). Global learning for sustainable development in higher education: Recent trends and a critique. *International*

Journal of Sustainability in Higher Education, *10*(4), 368–378. https://doi.org/ 10.1108/14676370910990710

Anglia Ruskin University (ARU). (2018). Education strategy 2018-2022. Anglia Ruskin University.

Anglia Ruskin University (ARU) (2022). Global sustainability institute. Anglia Ruskin University. Retrieved 5 July 2024, from https://aru.ac.uk/global-sustainability-institute-gsi/about-us/mission-and-values

Arendt, H. (1972). *Crises of the Republic*. Harcourt Brace Jovanovich.

Arnold, R., & Lermen, M. (2005). Lernen, Bildung und Kompetenzentwicklung – neuere Entwicklungen in Erwachsenenbildung und Weiterbildung. In G. Wiesner & A. Wolter (Eds.), *Die lernende Gesellschaft. Lern kulturen und Kompetenzentwicklung in der Wissensgesellschaft*, pp. 45–60. MünchenWeinheim.

Astin, H. S., & Astin, A. W. (1996). *A social change model of leadership development. Guidebook version III*. Higher Education Research Institute, University of California. Retrieved 5 July 2024, from https://www.heri.ucla.edu/PDFs/pubs/ASocialChangeModelofLeadershipDevelopment.pdf

Banks, S., & Brydon-Miller, M. (2019). *Ethics in participatory research for health and social well-being: Cases and commentaries*. Routledge.

Barth, M., Godemann, J., Rieckmann, M., & Stoltenberg, U. (2007). Developing key competencies for sustainable development in higher education. *International Journal of Sustainability in Higher Education*, *8*(4), 416–430. https://doi.org/10.1108/14676370710823582

Baxter, P., & Brown, E. (2018). *Education strategy: Ruskin modules*. Anglia Ruskin University.

Bell, P., Addy, T., Madew, M., & Kainulainen, S. (2012). Universities as agents in the empowerment of local communities in Germany, Finland, and Russia. In L. Goodson, & J. Phillimore (Eds.), *Community research for participation: From theory to method*. Policy Press.

Besthorn, F. (2011). Deep ecology's contribution to social work: A ten-year retrospective. *International Journal of Social Welfare*, *21*(3), 230–238. https://doi.org/10.1111/j.1468-2397.2011.00851.x

Bowles, W., Boetto, H., Jones, P., & McKinnon, J. (2018). Is social work really greening? Exploring the place of sustainability and environment in social work codes of ethics. *International Social Work*, *61*(4), 503–517. https://doi.org/10.1177/0020872816651695

Cho, S. (2013). *Critical pedagogy and social change*. Routledge.

Columbie, J. Y. (2021). Adapting to climate change through disaster risk reduction in the Caribbean: Lessons from the Global South in tackling the Sustainable Development Goals. In S. Flood, Y. Z. Columbié, M. Le Tissier, & B. O'Dwyer (Eds.), *Creating resilient futures: Integrating disaster risk reduction, sustainable development goals and climate change adaptation agendas* (pp. 183–203). Palgrave Macmillan. https://doi.org/10.1007/978-3-030-80791-7_9

Cotton, D., Bailey, I., Warren, M., & Bissell, S. (2009). Revolutions and second-best solutions: Education for sustainable development in higher education. *Studies in Higher Education*, *34*(7), 719–733. https://doi.org/10.1080/03075070802641552

Desivilya, H. S., & Eizen, D. (2005). Conflict management in work teams: The role of social self-efficacy and group identification. *International Journal of Conflict Management*, *16*(2), 183–208. https://doi.org/10.1108/eb022928

Dominelli, L. (2012). *Green social work: From environmental crises to environmental justice*. Polity Press.

Dominelli, L. (2013). Environmental justice at the heart of social work practice: Greening the profession. *International Journal of Social Welfare*, *22*, 431–439. https://doi.org/10.1111/ijsw.12024

Energy Justice Network (2023). *Environmental Justice/Environmental Racism.* Retrieved 5 July 2024, from https://www.ejnet.org/ej/

Freire, P. (1970). *Pedagogy of the oppressed.* Penguin Books.

Gardner, C. J., Thierry, A., Rowlandson, W., & Steinberger, J. K. (2021). From publications to public actions: The role of universities in facilitating academic advocacy and activism in the climate and ecological emergency. *Frontiers in Sustainability, 2,* Article 679019. https://doi.org/10.3389/frsus.2021.679019

Germaine, C. B., & Gitterman, A. (1980). *The life model of social work practice.* Columbia University Press.

Graff, J. H. (2015). *Undisciplining knowledge: Interdisciplinarity in the twentieth century.* Johns Hopkins University Press.

Gray, M., & Coates, J. (2013). Changing values and valuing change: Towards an ecospiritual perspective in social work. *International Social Work, 56*(3), 356–368. https://doi.org/10.1177/0020872812474009

Gray, M., Coates, J., & Hetherington, T. (Eds.) (2012). *Environmental social work.* Routledge.

Holley, L. C., & Steiner, S. (2005). Safe space: Student perspectives on classroom environment. *Journal of Social Work Education, 41*(1), 49–64. https://doi.org/10.5175/JSWE.2005.200300343

Holm, T., Sammalisto, K., Caeiro, S., & Rieckmann, M. (2016). Developing sustainability into a golden thread throughout all levels of education. *Journal of Cleaner Production, 117*(3), 1–3. https://doi.org/10.1016/j.jclepro.2016.01.016

Kharas, H., McArthur, J. W., & Ohno, I. (2020). *Leave no one behind: Time for specifics on the Sustainable Development Goals.* The Brookings Institution.

Laurie, R., Nonoyama-Tarumi, Y., Mckeown, R., & Hopkins, C. (2016). Contributions of education for sustainable development (ESD) to quality education: A synthesis of research. *Journal of Education for Sustainable Development.* https://doi.org/10.1177/0973408216661442

Lopez-Lopez, M. C., Martínez-Rodríguez, F. M., & Fernández-Herrería, A. (2021). The university at the crossroads of eco-social challenges: Pedagogy of care and the community of life for a transformative learning. *Frontiers in Sustainability, 2.* https://doi.org/10.3389/frsus.2021.654769

MacAlister, J. (2017). *Leadership Statement for Frontline.* Retrieved 5 July 2024, from https://www.systemicleadershipinstitute.org/leadership-statement-for-frontline/

Mahees, M. T. M. (2020). Green social work: The role of social workers in ecological justice and collective environmental action. *E-Journal of Social Work, 4*(1), 15–23.

Misiaszek, G. W. (2020). Ecopedagogy: Teaching critical literacies of 'development', 'sustainability' and 'sustainable development. *Teaching in Higher Education, 25*(5), 615–632. https://doi.org/10.1080/13562517.2019.1586668

Misiaszek, G. W. (2021). An ecopedagogical, ecolinguistic reading of the Sustainable Development Goals (SDGs): What we have learned from Paulo Freire. *Educational Philosophy and Theory.* https://doi.org/10.1080/00131857.2021.2011208

Misiaszek, G. W., & Rodrigues, C. (2023). Teaching justice-based environmental sustainability in higher education: Generative dialogues. *Teaching in Higher Education, 28*(5), 903–917. https://doi.org/10.1080/13562517.2023.2214879

Morito, B. (2002). *Thinking ecologically: Environmental thought, values, and policy.* Fernwood.

Mu, S. C., & Gnyawali, D. R. (2003). Developing synergistic knowledge in student groups. *The Journal of Higher Education, 74*(6), 689–711. Retrieved 5 July 2024, from https://www.jstor.org/stable/3648235

Narhi, K., & Matthies, A.-L. (2016). Conceptual and historical analysis of ecological social work. In J. McKinnon, & M. Alston (Eds.), *Ecological social work: Towards sustainability*. Palgrave.

Peeters, J. (2012). Social work and sustainable development: Towards a socio-ecological practice model. *Journal of Social Intervention: Theory and Practice, 21*(3), 5–26.

Repko, A., & Szostak, R. (2017). *Interdisciplinary research: Process and theory* (3rd ed.). Sage.

Rittel, H. W., & Webber, M. M. (1973). Dilemmas in a general theory of planning. *Policy Sciences, 4*(2), 155–169. https://doi.org/10.1007/BF01405730

Rolfe, G., Freshwater, D., & Jasper, M. (2001). *Critical reflection in nursing and the helping professions: A user's guide*. Palgrave Macmillan.

Ruggerio, A. C. (2021). Sustainability and sustainable development: A review of principles and definitions, *Science of The Total Environment, 786*. https://doi.org/10.1016/j.scitotenv.2021.147481

Saleebey, D. (2009). *The strengths perspective in social work practice* (5th ed.). Pearson.

Shajahan, P. K., & Sharma, P. (2018). Environmental justice: A call for action for social workers. *International Social Work, 61*(4), 476–480. https://doi.org/10.1177%2F0020872818770585

Shephard, K. (2008). Higher education for sustainability: Seeking affective learning outcomes. *International Journal of Sustainability in Higher Education, 9*(1), 87–98. https://doi.org/10.1108/14676370810842201

Shephard, K., & Furnari, M. (2012). Exploring what university teachers think about education for sustainability. *Studies in Higher Education, 38*(10), 1–14. https://doi.org/10.1080/03075079.2011.644784

Social Care Institute of Excellence (SCIE) (2016). *Co-production: What it is and how to do it*. Social Care Institute of Excellence. Retrieved 5 July 2024, from https://www.scie.org.uk/publications/guides/guide51/what-is-coproduction/principles-of-coproduction.asp

Sterling, S. (2021). Concern, conception, and consequence: Re-thinking the paradigm of higher education in dangerous times. *Frontiers in Sustainability, 2*, 1–13. https://doi.org/10.3389/frsus.2021.743806

Stewart, I. S., Hurth, V., & Sterling, S. (2022). Editorial: Re-purposing universities for sustainable human progress. *Frontiers in Sustainability, 3*, Article 859393. https://doi.org/10.3389/frsus.2022.859393

Stibbe, D., & Prescott, D., The Partnering Initiative and UNDESA (2020). *The SDG Partnership Guidebook: A practical guide to building high impact multi-stakeholder partnerships for the Sustainable Development Goals*. Retrieved 5 July 2024, from https://sustainabledevelopment.un.org/content/documents/26627SDG_Partnership_Guidebook_0.95_web.pdf

Strain, M. M., & Potter, R. (2012). The twain shall meet: Rethinking the introduction to graduate studies course as interdisciplinary pedagogy. *Pedagogy, 12*(1), 139–160.

Tekleab, A. G., Quigley, N. R., & Tesluk, P. E. (2009). A longitudinal study of team conflict, conflict management, cohesion, and team effectiveness. *Group and Organisation Management, 34*(2), 170–205. https://doi.org/10.1177/1059601108331218

Thew, H., Graves, C., Reay, D., Smith, S., Petersen, K., Bomberg, E., Boxley, S., Causley, J., Congreve, A., Cross, I., Dunk, R., Dunlop, L., Facer, K., Gamage, K. A. A., Greenhalgh, C., Greig, A., Kiamba L., Kinakh, V., Kioupi, … Worsfold, N. (2021). Mainstreaming climate change education in UK higher education institutions. COP26 Universities Network Working Paper. Retrieved 5 July 2024, from https://www.gla.ac.uk/media/Media_814664_smxx.pdf

Trott, D. C., Sample, B. L., & Weinberg, E. A. (2019). Participatory action research experiences for undergraduates: Forging critical connections through community engagement. *Studies in Higher Education*, *45*(11), 2260–2273. https://doi.org/10.1080/03075079.2019.1602759

UNESCO (2014). *Roadmap for implementing the global action programme on education for sustainable development*. UNESCO. Retrieved 5 July 2024, from https://unesdoc.unesco.org/ark:/48223/pf0000230514

UNESCO (2017). *Education for sustainable development goals: Learning objectives*. UNESCO. Retrieved 5 July 2024, from https://unesdoc.unesco.org/ark:/48223/pf0000247444

Wiek, A., Withycombe, L., & Redman, C. L. (2011). Key competencies in sustainability: A reference framework for academic program development, *Sustainability Science*, *6*, pp. 203–218. https://doi.org/10.1007/s11625-011-0132-6

Chapter 10

Ruskin Module and Community Organising

Julia Carr and Jess Maddocks

Introduction

This reflection on the first delivery of the Ruskin Module (RM), *Who me? Make a difference in my community?*, is a piece of collaborative writing. It is entirely fitting that we wrote it in this way, as the module itself was a collaboration between Anglia Ruskin University (ARU) (Julia Carr) and Citizens UK (Jess Maddocks). Julia is a senior lecturer in Education at ARU and was involved in the initial stages of the RM development and approval. Jess is a Community Organiser with Citizens UK (Citizens UK, 2022a) and, at the time of the first delivery of the RM, worked for the Citizens Essex Chapter (Citizens Essex, 2022), of which ARU is an active member.

We designed the module using experiential pedagogy, to enable students to develop their understanding of how they can become changemakers through community organising. Experiential pedagogy is a style of teaching and learning that provides transformative learning opportunities. It is a process through which educators engage students in a cycle of direct experience, reflection, analysis, and experimentation (Independent Schools Experiential Education Network, 2019). Kolb and Kolb (2005) developed the pedagogical approach to experimental education which, they acknowledged, had been reflected in the work of many other theorists and pedagogues including John Dewey, Kurt Lewin, Jean Piaget, William James, Carl Jung, Paulo Freire, and Carl Rogers. Experiential pedagogy, they stated, was based on six assumptions: learning is a process and not an outcome; all of the learners are relearning; learning involves having resolutions to conflicts; learning is regarded as a holistic process; learning is a result of synergetic transactions that occur between each person and the environment; and learning involves creating knowledge.

This pedagogy dovetailed with the purpose of the RM, which was to enable the students to engage in a transformative experience that would empower them to start to become changemakers in their communities. While currently a single, definitive definition of changemaker appears not to exist, within a Higher Education context we identify with the University of

DOI: 10.4324/9781003474593-12

San Diego's Changemaker Hub (University of San Diego, 2022, para. 5) description:

Characteristics of a Changemaker:

- **Intentional about solving a social problem.** A changemaker has empathy for others and is driven by the genuine goal of making the world a better place.
- **Motivated to act.** A changemaker gives themselves the permission to do something about a social problem and keeps trying until they have made a difference.
- **Creative.** Changemakers are inquisitive, open-minded, and resourceful. They have the courage to see and do things differently.

Links to Literature

We designed this RM around three principles: community organising, sustainability, and experiential learning in an online environment. These principles were, to some degree, shaped by the overall concept of ARU's RMs which were all to be delivered online and were to include a focus on the United Nations (UN) Sustainable Development Goals (SDGs) (United Nations Department of Economic and Social Affairs (UN DESA), 2015). The content of the module focused on developing students' understanding of community organising and, by using experiential pedagogy, encouraging them to become changemakers in their communities. This short, and in no way comprehensive, review of literature focuses on these elements within a university setting.

RMs were designed to be delivered online, which offers both opportunities and challenges. Adkins et al. (2021), for example, reported that online education often takes place in relative isolation, with students having little exposure to a wider cohort of peers which they would experience in a face-to-face classroom. This contact with peers is important in building students' diversity awareness and cultural intelligence, which Roux et al. (2020) defined as the ability of an individual to effectively function in culturally diverse settings. They highlight that developing cultural intelligence does not depend on having an in-depth knowledge of all culturally diverse situations; rather, it is the ability to reflect on a culturally confusing situation and to make appropriate adjustments. Upton and Butters (2019) argue that it is imperative that universities develop both staff and students' cultural intelligence as part of cultivating the global mindset that is vital in response to the increasing globalisation of the markets in which they will work as graduates.

Adkins et al. (2021) discussed the ways in which an experiential learning approach can support diversity awareness and, therefore, increase cultural intelligence. Experiential learning provides not only relevant content for students but also a process and framework to facilitate learning through contact with a diverse community and interaction with authentic problems. A decade after producing his comprehensive and systematic book (Kolb, 1984) describing the process of experiential learning, Rainey and Kolb (1995) discussed the application of experiential learning to studying diversity.

Experiential learning aligns well with the development of cultural intelligence and understanding of diversity as it requires students to engage in a concrete experience and a reflection on that experience to develop a process of knowledge creation rather than simply acquiring information. This process of knowledge creation then develops students' capability of appropriately adjusting to culturally unfamiliar situations. Roux et al. (2020) confirmed that earlier research indicates that an experiential 'learning through doing' approach was an effective way of facilitating cross-cultural experiences which positively developed students' cultural intelligence.

Efthymiou et al. (2021) reported limited application of experiential learning approaches in online teaching and learning. However, they reflected that the recent move to an increasingly online environment in both education and work sectors has seen an increase in the available technology, and the necessary skills and familiarity with that technology, to enable the delivery of an experiential learning approach in a virtual classroom. This experiential learning approach, they posited, could enable students to test their previously developed understanding of concepts in a multicultural environment, learn from a diverse group of peers, and reflect on how they can apply this new knowledge.

The RM focus on community organising, and the development of the students' understanding of how this framework can be effective in empowering communities to make change for the better, was effective in showing students how they could apply their new knowledge. Beck and Purcell (2013) describe community organising as being about individuals and local communities taking responsibility for local issues and successfully solving these issues by building powerful autonomous local organisations. Citizens UK, who delivered the community organising training in the RM, believe that universities in the UK have a significant role to play in supporting the communities of which they are a part. The Assistant Director of Citizens UK, James Asfa (2022), stated that universities are powerful centres of knowledge and, while it is important to exchange that knowledge with communities, it is also vital that universities also engage in an exchange of power with potential community changemakers. This, he argues, is so important because, 'in terms of people, money and relationships, universities are by far the most powerful pillars of civil society' (Asfa, 2022, para. 8).

The experiential pedagogy used in this RM was facilitated through the focus on community organising, and asking the students to work together, in culturally diverse groups, on a real-life problem. Bhargava and Jerome (2020) reported that this approach has proved to be pedagogically effective. Using a 'learning through doing' approach to teaching students about community organising enables them to develop an understanding of community issues through engaging in cross-cultural dialogue to identify problems and viable solutions.

In addition, this design also enabled a focus on sustainability, and using the SDGs as a framework, students developed their understanding of how they can help overcome some sustainability issues as part of a diverse local, and global, community.

Browne et al. (2020) described how more traditional styles of teaching about sustainability issues led to a lack of integrated understanding in students. A diverse, experiential learning environment, they argued, can lead to transformative learning, resulting in students who are sensitive to the complex connections that characterise sustainability and who will act as agents of change in their communities. We hope, in a small way, that the outcome of this RM will be students who are culturally intelligent and ready to work in a diverse team to tackle the 'wicked problems' (Rittel & Webber, 1973) that affect their local and global communities.

Planning the Module

This module began life as a vehicle to enable students at ARU to have the opportunity of getting involved with community organising. Created by the political theorist Saul Alinsky in the 1930s' Chicago (Seal, 2008), community organising is a method of effecting social change. At its root is the idea that a powerful, organised civil society can work together to tackle local injustices and hold power holders accountable for the decisions that they make that affect our lives.

Citizens UK brought this method of making change to the UK in 1996 (Jameson, 2010) and it is in use in local alliances including faith institutions, schools, charities, trade union branches, and universities across the country. Central to the model is a programme of training for members of civil society institutions to teach them how to use five steps to social change: Organise, Listen, Plan, Act, and Negotiate to achieve change on local issues. Citizens UK have trained thousands of leaders in this method in institutions across the UK, including in schools, colleges, and universities.

Community organising is rooted in the local, and in the idea that teaching leaders to achieve change in local issues that they care about (e.g., a zebra crossing on a busy road outside a school). Training from Citizens UK can teach people how power structures work, how to effectively participate in public life, and, ultimately, how to make the change they want to see. By starting small and building leadership, these social justice 'wins' can scale up into national change, as seen with campaigns such as the *Real Living Wage* (Citizens UK, 2022b) and recording misogyny as a hate crime (Citizens UK, 2022c).

In the preliminary stages of the development of this RM, ARU had recently become a member of Citizens UK and we were discussing ways in which we could encourage students from across the university to work with the local community. The concept of community organising empowering local people to work together to make positive change in their community aligned with the stated values of ARU (ambition, innovation, courage, community, integrity, and responsibility) which sees the institution striving to develop collaborative working and supporting everyone to achieve their potential (Browne et al., 2020).

Community organising also aligns with the principle of RMs which sought to encourage students to work collaboratively on issues linked to the SDGs. The early planning stages of this module, therefore, saw us planning how we could embed community organising taster training into the module to, hopefully, spark the students' interest in working for change in their communities, and how we would assess their learning through the module.

A central challenge when we were writing the module was how to maintain a model of organising that is firmly rooted in geographical location when the students were not only studying at both the two core ARU campuses (i.e., Chelmsford and Cambridge) but were accessing the teaching and learning in an online environment, from wherever they were located.

We addressed this challenge by rooting the community organising training in the Essex Citizens Chapter (as a Cambridge Citizens Chapter did not exist at that time), using 'house meetings' to build links between students and members of other member institutions in Essex, such as faith organisations, charities, or not-for-profit organisations, but giving the students the freedom to link to issues in their communities. This proved to be enlightening as students spoke not only about the issues facing their communities wherever they were in the UK but also globally.

House meetings are not simply 'chats' but are meetings with a format that encourages the sharing of experiences and where communities can express their commitments to shared values and strategy (Leading Change Network, 2019). Our house meetings were themed around SDGs to show that, although global in scope, they were experienced in a very local way and that the way communities experienced them had distinct, and at times unexpected, similarities, despite being geographically remote. For example, worries about street safety and lighting were a common theme that cut across communities, and a house meeting framed around clean and affordable energy ended with an exciting consensus around the need for better cycling infrastructure around both the Chelmsford and Cambridge campuses, but also on a wider geographical sphere (the ultimate clean and sustainable energy being our own!)

We planned to train ARU students in relational techniques such as house meetings and 1-2-1s to develop listening campaigns. Where house meetings, as described previously, involve groups of people from local organisations coming together to share experiences, 1-2-1s are conversations between two people to understand shared interests, the issues affecting them, and those they care about. These two styles of meetings often take place as part of an organised listening campaign, which is a focused effort to develop the understanding of community concerns in a specific place, organisation, or community of interest. This training, we hoped, would enable students to further explore shared areas of concern they learnt, not only from recognising similarities in the things they cared about but also from understanding their differences.

The finished version of the first delivery of *Who me? Make a difference in my community?* consisted of four sessions of community organising training, focused on *Understanding Power and Self Interest*; *How to Listen for Issues*; *Strategising from Problem to Solution*; and *Power Analysis and Negotiation*.

Assessing the Learning in the Module

The form of assessment we chose for this module was based on several factors. The assessment had to align with the module learning outcomes, which required the students to show their understanding of both interdisciplinary working and sustainability issues in the local community, but it also needed to support the experiential pedagogy that underpinned the design of the module.

Consequently, we split the assessment into two assignments: a group presentation and an individual reflection. The group presentation required the students to show their understanding of how to link one of the SDGs to something affecting their communities as a local issue. We then asked students to apply their learning about community organising to explain how they would use this to respond to the local issue and help the community make the change they wanted to see. Students presented the group assignments during one of the module sessions so that they had the opportunity to respond to each other's ideas.

The second assignment was an individual reflection on their experience of taking part in the RM. This gave students the opportunity to reflect on the way in which the interdisciplinary nature of the group project had affected their experience and the effectiveness of their response to the community issue they had identified. This individual assignment was also designed to respond to a critique of experiential pedagogy that, while it has been shown to enhance students' learning, it values hands-on experiences above conceptual knowledge. The inclusion of reflective observation can be used to counter this critique by providing meaningful conceptual understanding and a rounded learning experience (Young, 2002).

Delivering the Module

In community organising, Citizens UK prioritise face-to-face interaction because at the heart of our method is building relational power between leaders in public life, and we believe that face-to-face 1-2-1s are the most effective tool to do this. At the start of the pandemic, Citizens UK had to radically change their method of working and switch to digital training and 1-2-1s. By the time we started delivering the ARU module, we had developed effective ways to deliver relational training online, but the module confronted us with a further challenge. Due to time constraints and digital exclusion, students were not always able to turn on their cameras, and those who could understandably did not want to be the only ones to do this. In a training environment that relies on gauging participants' reactions, this created some challenges, and we had to develop several ways of checking in with students and their learning that were not reliant on visual cues. While we encouraged students to speak during sessions and to use the online chat facility, we also used online tools such as *Jamboard* (a digital whiteboard) to allow students to work collaboratively to share ideas and feedback.

As the module progressed, and students started to use the relational tools we had taught them, it was clear that they were forming effective relationships and were more open to creating a space for shared vulnerability, which included turning their cameras on, even if they might be the only ones. By the time we came to the negotiation section of the training, and a session which included a negotiation role play between power holders and civil society leaders, students readily participated, with cameras on, and enthusiastically embraced their roles as local politicians, civil servants, or community leaders. They embraced the idea behind US Senator Elizabeth Warren's warning that 'if you don't have a seat at the table, you're probably on the menu!'

Learning about community organising is primarily experiential and comes from a long tradition of public political education delivered on factory floors, in people's homes, from the pulpit, and other collective spaces, and taught through action. It is in this environment of shared vulnerability, out of our comfort zone, that we learn most about our attitudes and experiences of power and our ability to negotiate pragmatically and achieve the change we want.

We knew that it was important that the module was a safe space for students to share their experiences and worries, so we needed to model this and be prepared to share our own experiences and vulnerabilities. We did this from the start of the module by telling stories about our own lived experiences, and many of the students soon overcame their initial reticence about talking to people they did not know, in an online environment, and readily shared their own experiences.

Evaluating the Module

Ultimately, the aim of this course was to develop students' desire to make societal change, to start by thinking about their own communities and the change they could accomplish there. It gave them the tools (i.e., 1-2-1s, house meetings, power analysis, negotiation, and problem to solution training) and experience of using these tools on issues that mattered to them. The group work showed that we had achieved this aim, with all groups incorporating their understanding of community organising into their presentations.

The students presented their ideas for the issues they would take forward and the people that they had identified as the power holders with whom they would need to negotiate. Many of these ideas showed potential as viable local campaigns which, if we had more time, we could have developed further. We could have organised a group of the most engaged students to form an action team and work together to create a 'real life' campaign from one of their proposals. In community organising we value democratic processes and recognise that they are effective tools for building engagement and buy-in for a campaign. When running this module again, we will ask students to take a final vote on the issue they want to take forward and continue to work on in 'real life'. This would help to capitalise effectively on their learning from the module and ensure continuity of the learning and action beyond the lifespan of the course. This will become easier to facilitate as community organising becomes further embedded at ARU.

The reflective assignments produced by the students were a good module evaluation tool and included some interesting reflections, providing clear feedback on the module itself as well as what they felt they had learned about themselves by taking part in it. One student reflected that they appreciated having team colleagues from a variety of academic and cultural backgrounds because it provided a better richness of ideas and originality of thoughts and opinions. Also appreciated was the way in which peers shared their personal experiences of different topics. However, they also reflected that the interdisciplinary nature of the group work leading to this richness of ideas meant that more time was needed to produce the presentation, and this resulted in a sense of discomfort. They reflected that interdisciplinary work seemed to take a lot of time and a lot of extra effort, certainly more than they had experienced in a single-discipline team, to develop the group's knowledge and ideas into a finished piece of work.

Many students wrote honestly about how the module had made them look at personal changes they would like to make. An example of this was a student who reflected that they had felt compelled to step back and examine their own personal values. They realised that they had never done anything for a charity or to make a positive change within their community. They resolved to do more for their community by helping to drive change for the better rather than just leaving it to others.

The reflection that had the most impact on us was from a student who, by halfway through the module, had already joined a protest movement in their home community. Having initially reflected that working with a diverse peer group had helped to develop new skills, such as learning to put into practice values such as respect, discipline, and productivity, they reflected that this would have been unlikely if they had worked alone, and that these new skills would be of use in the future, whether for studies or work. They went on to reflect that before the module, they had no understanding that people could make change in their community and felt that they had no influence over government decisions. When they realised that people like them could be influential in making a change, they joined a farmers' protest in their home country to demand a change in living conditions. The final reflection was on the personal change they had experienced saying that the module, and taking part in the protest, had helped them develop as a confident and independent individual who was keen to stay involved in helping to make change in communities.

Conclusion

Reflecting on the first delivery of this module, we believe that it was, overall, highly successful. We would have preferred some students to be much more involved during the sessions, but this is a perennial problem, often exasperated in an online teaching environment, and one for which educators are still searching for a comprehensive answer. There are some structural changes that we would like to make, including encouraging the students to become involved in community organising outside of the module, while the module is still running, and we have regular contact with them. However, as noted earlier, this will be easier as community organising becomes further embedded at ARU.

We both agree that this was an incredibly enjoyable teaching experience and one which had a positive impact on many students, as well as ourselves. It showed that it is possible to build relationships with students in an online environment and to positively affect both their learning and their development. While we realise that not many students will be so profoundly affected as to join a protest in their homeland while the module is still in progress, the students' reflections show that the module had an immediate impact by developing their cultural intelligence and showing them that they can act as agents of change in their communities. It would be amazing to talk to them in the future and to hear what the longer-term effects may be.

Points to Consider

Readers of this chapter may wish to consider:

- Collaborating with an external partner
- Using an experiential learning approach
- Developing students as agents of change

References

Adkins, D., Buchanan, S. A., Bossaller, J. S., Brendler, B. M., Alston, J. K., & Sandy, H. M. (2021). Assessing experiential learning to promote students' diversity engagement. *Journal of Education for Library and Information Science*, *62*(2), 201–219. https://doi.org/10.3138/jelis.2019-0061

Asfa, J. (2022). *Universities supporting community organising*. Retrieved 5 July 2024, from https://wonkhe.com/blogs/universities-supporting-community-organising/

Beck, D., & Purcell, R. (2013). *International community organising*. Policy Press.

Bhargava, M., & Jerome, L. (2020). Training teachers for and through citizenship: Learning from citizenship experiences. *Societies*, *10*(2), 36–48. https://doi.org/10.3390/soc10020036

Browne, G. R., Bender, H., Bradley, J., & Pang, A. (2020). Evaluation of a tertiary sustainability experiential learning program. *International Journal of Sustainability in Higher Education*, *21*(4), 699–715. https://doi.org/10.1108/IJSHE-08-2019-0241

Citizens Essex (2022). *Citizens Essex*. Retrieved 5 July 2024, from https://www.citizensuk.org/chapters/essex/

Citizens UK (2022a). *Citizens UK*. Retrieved 5 July 2024, from https://www.citizensuk.org/

Citizens UK (2022b). *The Campaign for a Real Living Wage*. Retrieved 5 July 2024, from https://www.citizensuk.org/campaigns/the-campaign-for-a-real-living-wage/

Citizens UK (2022c). *Make Misogyny a Hate Crime*. Retrieved 5 July 2024, from https://www.citizensuk.org/campaigns/make-misogyny-a-hate-crime/

Efthymiou, L., Ktoridou, D., & Epaminonda, E. (2021). A model for experiential learning by replicating a workplace environment in virtual classes. In *2021 IEEE Global Engineering Education Conference (EDUCON)* (pp. 1749–1753). https://doi.org/10.1109/EDUCON46332.2021.9453966

Independent Schools Experiential Education Network (ISEEN) (2022). *What is Experiential Education?* Retrieved 5 July 2024, from https://www.iseeninfo.com/what-is-experiential-education-

Jameson, N. (2010). People can play their part in the governance of the nation. *The Guardian*, 24 March. Retrieved 5 July 2024, from https://www.theguardian.com/society/2010/mar/24/communities-policy

Kolb, A. Y., & Kolb, D. A. (2005). Learning styles and learning spaces: Enhancing experiential learning in higher education. *Academy of Management Learning & Education*, *4*(2), 193–212. Retrieved 5 July 2024, from https://www.jstor.org/stable/40214287

Kolb, D. (1984). *Experiential learning: Experience as the source of learning and development*. Englewood Cliffs.

Leading Change Network (2019). *House Meeting Handbook: Harnessing the Power of Personal Networks and Storytelling to Build Leadership and Support for Your Campaign*. Retrieved 5 July 2024, from https://leadingchangenetwork.org/wp-content/uploads/2019/01/HouseMeetingGuide_011821.pdf

Rainey, M. A., & Kolb, D. A. (1995). Using experiential learning theory and learning styles in diversity education. In R. R. Sims, & S. J. Sims (Eds.), *The importance of learning styles: Understanding the implications for learning, course design, and education* (pp. 129–146). Greenwood Press.

Rittel, H. W., & Webber, M. M. (1973). Dilemmas in a general theory of planning. *Policy Sciences*, *4*(2), 155–169. https://doi.org/10.1007/BF01405730

Roux, P. W., Suzuki, K., Matsuba, R., & Goda, Y. (2020). Developing cultural intelligence (CQ) through experiential learning: Considering relevance and rationale in blended environments. *International Journal for Educational Media and Technology*, *14*(1), 29–37. Retrieved 5 July 2024, from https://jaems.jp/contents/icomej/vol14/03_Peter_W_Roux.pdf

Seal, M. (2008). *Saul Alinsky, community organizing and rules for radicals*. infed: The Encyclopaedia of Pedagogy and Informal Education. Retrieved 5 July 2024, from https://infed.org/mobi/saul-alinsky-community-organizing-and-rules-for-radicals/

United Nations Department of Economic and Social Affairs (UN DESA) (2015). *The 17 Goals*. Retrieved 5 July 2024, from https://sdgs.un.org/goals

University of San Diego (2022). *Changemaker Hub*. Retrieved 5 July 2024, from https://www.sandiego.edu/changemaker/about/mission-vision.php

Upton, S., & Butters, L. (2019). *The importance of developing cultural intelligence*. Retrieved 5 July 2024, from https://www.universityworldnews.com/post.php?story=20191017135800899

Young, M. (2002). Experiential Learning=Hands-On+Minds-On. *Marketing Education Review*, *12*(1), 43–51. https://doi.org/10.1080/10528008.2002.11488770

Chapter 11

Developing Professional Learning through an Interdisciplinary Community of Practice

John Parkin and Deborah Caws

Introduction

Ruskin Modules (RM) are an innovation in Anglia Ruskin University's (ARU) undergraduate curriculum providing students with opportunities to learn and develop the graduate skills of working collaboratively in interdisciplinary ways, thus preparing them for meeting the demands of the modern world.

In 2019, an open invitation encouraged and welcomed academics and Professional Services colleagues to propose and design a new type of interdisciplinary breadth module for undergraduate students working at Level 5 (Year 2) in any discipline across the University. This formed a creative, iterative process in which participation in creating these new modules was voluntary, and colleagues, who became ARU's first RM leaders, were called Trailblazers. Trailblazers came from different subject disciplines with varying levels of experience in teaching and module leadership, ranging from highly experienced lecturers and module leaders to those new to teaching in Higher Education (HE), hence the challenge of building a community of members from different backgrounds. RMs account for one 15-credit module in the second year of undergraduate courses, thus occupying a small, but important part of a degree programme.

RMs now form an integral component of students' undergraduate degree courses at ARU. Students choose one RM from those available, undertaken over one trimester, as part of their course. To anchor modules to a central purpose, each RM focuses on one or more of the United Nations (UN) Sustainable Development Goals (SDG) (UN, 2015), which provides context for real-world issues and a basis for interdisciplinary working. RMs engage students in interdisciplinary activities, drawing on disciplinary knowledge, skills, and theory from several fields to address and seek innovative solutions for 'wicked problems' (Rittel & Webber, 1973). Although each RM varies in subject matter, content, assessment activities, and learning experiences, they all offer students opportunities to take different perspectives on, and develop problem-solving skills, for real-world problems, along with skills in reflection and critical thinking.

DOI: 10.4324/9781003474593-13

ARU delivered the first tranche of compulsory RMs online in the 2021/22 academic year to Level 5 students at ARU's two core campuses and across all four Faculties, which signalled a substantial change in the ways students learn as well as the curricula of their degrees. It was also a significant undertaking for the Trailblazers who faced challenges relating to their pedagogic practices. Module leaders often taught large student cohorts, with up to 132 students enrolled in a module, who were coming together for the first time from different disciplines and with diverse learning experiences.

To support module leaders to design and deliver their modules, the Institutional Lead for Ruskin Modules (ILRM) organised formal and informal professional development workshops and meetings throughout the planning stages and during the first delivery of the modules, which were facilitated online via video conferencing and messaging tools in Microsoft Teams. A central feature of support for RM leaders was a weekly voluntary, unstructured, hour-long online forum, known as 'T-Time' (i.e., Trailblazer Time), for module leaders to engage in an informal discussion about how they were 'getting on' with designing and delivering their RMs. Between meetings, Trailblazers used Teams to communicate and share resources and ideas. Over time, module leaders engaged in meaningful professional learning, shaping the direction and identity of the Trailblazer group, and their individual practices.

In this chapter, we explore and explain how an opportunity to take part in a university-wide curriculum innovation led to the formation of a multidisciplinary group of academics and professionals who became a Community of Practice (CoP) (Wenger, 1998). Using semi-structured focus-groups with module leaders, we sought to determine how an interdisciplinary community can support professional learning relating to teaching and module leadership.

Literature Review

The Case for Interdisciplinary Higher Education

In HE, one discipline alone may not be sufficient to support students to develop the skills necessary for addressing global issues (Jacob, 2015). Interdisciplinary studies have emerged as a significant strategy to support students to develop these skills in response to a need for universities to serve a modern, knowledge-based world economy and to address complex world issues (Davies & Devlin, 2010). Davies and Devlin explain how interdisciplinarity offers students opportunities to 'experience "different ways of knowing" from students' core or preferred disciplines' (2010, p. 3). Gombrich (2018, pp. 43–44) offers a clear rationale for implementing an interdisciplinary curriculum in HE:

- No specific discipline is necessary for most graduate jobs, except for those which are explicitly linked to professional training (e.g., nursing or law).

- The internet is changing the way we learn, forcing us to reconsider how knowledge is structured. Interdisciplinary models may 'fit' better than information that is siloed into individual discipline areas.
- Academic research in several key areas requires interdisciplinary training to address complex real-world problems.

Preparing to Teach Interdisciplinary Higher Education

The Trailblazers designed RMs to provide students with opportunities to view the world through different perspectives while developing important graduate skills. Nevertheless, to implement an interdisciplinary curriculum in an institution, particularly one fostering a monodisciplinary structure, there were epistemological issues to be addressed (Davies & Devlin, 2010). For example, interdisciplinary programmes may conflict with faculty expectations and cause lecturers to re-examine their own disciplinary comprehension (Bryant et al., 2014). Further, Braßler (2020) notes that lecturers must resolve conflicts originating in discipline-based differences in teaching and knowledge traditions and overcome discipline-based prejudices as well as professional centricity. Stepping outside discipline-specific paradigms also requires academics to re-examine their views and understandings of discipline-specific language to consider how to support students to bridge gaps between any discipline-specific cognitive models, and new ways of 'seeing' the world (Davies & Devlin, 2010).

Ashby and Exter (2019) explain that discipline-specific scholarship in HE arose during the industrial era when specialisation among professionals developed in discrete work domains. They argue that although disciplines have evolved over time, the discipline-specific institutional structures and pedagogies have remained unchanged (Ashby & Exter, 2019).

In addition, Davies and Devlin (2010) explain that compulsory interdisciplinary study may disadvantage students without broader interests outside their chosen discipline-specific courses. Therefore, a significant challenge for the academics designing and delivering RMs was to consider and explore how best to develop their practice as teachers in HE to deliver innovative, interdisciplinary modules within a monodisciplinary institution.

Interdisciplinary HE lacks a clearly defined pedagogy, which instructors and curriculum designers working in traditional institutional structures find challenging (Ashby & Exter, 2019). To 'de-silo' academics from these discipline-specific structures, academics and faculty leaders need to create opportunities to loosen discipline boundaries and foster 'ground up' curriculum design through cross-disciplinary, collaborative approaches that forge connections across discipline boundaries (Hannon et al., 2018). This approach requires significant consideration for academics' professional development and acknowledgement of new, interdisciplinary pedagogic approaches (Lyall et al., 2015). Traditional 'top down' professional development activities, such as training and staff conferences, are insufficient in supporting academics to develop effective interdisciplinary teaching practice (de Laat et al., 2017).

Although lecturers often assume that learning to teach is principally achieved through 'on the job' experiences of academic staff in universities (Warnes, 2008), many institutions now offer teacher development programmes and qualifications such as the Postgraduate Certificate in Higher Education (PGCert HE), often aligned to the UK Professional Standards Framework for Teaching and Supporting Learning in Higher Education (UKPSF) (HEA/Advance HE, 2011). These standards promote values such as inclusive practice, and the use of evidence-informed teaching approaches. However, professional development in teaching may depend on individual lecturers' commitment to examining and evaluating their own practice (Bright et al., 2021). Typically, this takes the form of coaching, mentoring, peer-reviews of teaching materials, and observations of teaching between more and less experienced lecturers (Bright et al., 2021). Implicit in these strategies is that lecturers' understanding of pedagogy is still largely the product of trial and error (Harland, 2012). Mercieca (2017) explains that academics are often isolated within their own practice, which usually results from the solitary nature of teaching (Vrieling et al., 2019).

Lindvig et al. (2019) bemoan the paucity of literature concerning creating interdisciplinary curricula and activities within monodisciplinary universities. They argue it is impossible to alter the strong framing of discipline-specific educational structures within institutions, which should not view interdisciplinarity as opposing a monodisciplinary paradigm. Lindvig et al. (2019), for example, explain that gaps can exist at the boundaries and spaces between individual disciplines, where opportunities can be fostered for developing interdisciplinary curricular innovations, and that the skills needed in seeking and acting on these opportunities require 'the art of interstitiality' (2019, p. 358) to take advantage of a full landscape of disciplines within an institution. Lyall et al. (2015) note that even within very traditional monodisciplinary universities, opportunities for interdisciplinary education do exist. Yet, they argue, fully embracing an interdisciplinary curriculum innovation, such as RMs, requires a specific, interdisciplinary pedagogical approach.

Problem-Based Learning (PBL), which helps to move learning from teacher-centred to student-centred, which has benefits for both students and lecturers, is an effective pedagogic strategy for interdisciplinary learning (Braßler, 2020). As PBL fosters a 'ground up' approach to designing curricula around a problem, it emphasises the development of generic skills such as creativity and problem-solving. However, Stentoft (2017) explains that interdisciplinary learning does not occur simply when lecturers use PBL and calls for greater consideration and enquiry into how students may overcome epistemological differences between disciplines and the related emotional discomfort. Hannon et al. (2018) assert that this is best achieved in interdisciplinary teams, where academics from two or more disciplines work to synthesise disciplinary knowledge around a problem for students to solve. This approach requires commitment from individuals to ensure that one disciplinary pedagogy is not marginalised, and an understanding that students with prior monodisciplinary learning will need guidance and support to develop new skills in interdisciplinary inquiry (Lyall et al., 2015).

Braßler (2020) explains that when lecturers from two or more disciplines work collaboratively to co-create curricula, they may explore alternative values and perspectives enabling them to develop more realistic interdisciplinary problems to solve. This, in turn, forms a model of the nature of interdisciplinary cooperation for students. For Braßler (2020), lecturers who implement interdisciplinary PBL strategies may become key 'institutional entrepreneurs', and the driving force for increasing interdisciplinarity across institutions. This supports Lyall et al.'s (2015) findings that successful interdisciplinary provision needs committed academics who are enthusiastic about developing such opportunities, and who may form multidisciplinary teaching teams.

Potential for Professional Learning within a Community of Practice

Lave and Wenger (1991) introduced the concept of Communities of Practice (CoP) as a model to describe learning occurring within a group of practitioners. Central to this concept, practitioners engage in 'legitimate peripheral participation', meaning that engagement in the social practice itself entails practice-based learning as an integral constituent (Lave & Wenger, 1991). Wenger (1998) later developed the concept, emphasising the potential benefits of learning that are not the direct product of formal teaching or training. The basic premise is that CoPs are 'groups of people who share a concern or a passion for something they do and learn how to do it better as they interact regularly' (Wenger, 2010, p. 1). An intention to collaborate and engage in learning may drive these groups, or they may develop through a social learning experience. Wenger (2010) outlines three central characteristics: firstly, members of a CoP share a *domain* of interest within which they form their identity. Secondly, the *community* engages in shared activities and discussions where information is shared, and, crucially, it is the regular interaction which facilitates learning. Finally, the *practice* is what members do. With time and sustained interaction, members develop a shared repertoire of resources, experiences, tools, and ways to address common issues arising in practice (Wenger, 2011). Brown (2010) explains that a CoP has the potential to bring several disciplines together to address wicked problems. However, tensions may arise between the community's continued openness and mutual learning while also needing to codify their practices for public consumption.

Wenger (1998) explains that CoPs are everywhere, and it is likely we belong to several CoPs in both our personal and professional lives. Membership is voluntary and non-hierarchical, and members' knowledge and expertise may vary, and all members take collective responsibility for managing their knowledge and learning (Wenger, 1998). Mercieca (2017) explains that the concept of a CoP fits well with the growing trend towards developing teaching practice in HE. For example, one advantage is that an academic can access a community at the level that best fits their own 'Zone of Proximal Development' (ZPD). They may collect ideas for practice from the group, trial these in their own teaching, and then reflect on this within the CoP to seek feedback (Mercieca, 2017).

Vygotsky (1978) described a unique distance between what a learner knows and can do and what they have the potential to know or do as the ZPD. In this zone, potential learning is achieved with guidance from, or in collaboration with, more capable peers. The emphasis on the role of social interaction between individuals and their environment, alongside an acknowledgement that instruction can move ahead of development, are important characteristics of learning that occurs within a CoP (Mercieca, 2017).

Diverging from Wenger's original ideas, Fenton-O'Creevy et al. (2015) suggest intentional cultivation of a CoP acts as a mechanism for supporting learning, though this does not imply that a CoP should have an instructional role. The process of reifying the community's practices forms the repertoire associated with participants' practice developed in a CoP, and this has the potential to be shared outside of the CoP (Tummons, 2018). When applied to academics' professional learning, this has the significant potential to add to and strengthen the Trailblazers' knowledge and skills relating to interdisciplinary education.

Mercieca (2017) explains that the social dimension of learning underpins the concept of a CoP. Eun (2019) makes the case for sociocultural and social cognitive theories associated with human development in understanding the process of professional development and its implementation for teachers. Bandura (1977a), for example, highlighted the social aspects of learning through which learners engage in observation and imitation of models found in social contexts, which Mercieca (2017) finds useful in understanding the social nature of learning through a CoP. Bandura (1977b) also contributes to the notion of self-efficacy as a driver of greater self-development. Eun (2019) emphasises that teachers with greater self-efficacy are more likely to be effective in implementing new, innovative teaching methods.

McDonald and Star (2008) found that a CoP acts as a safe space for reflection on practice and for collaboratively addressing common issues, and CoPs have become fora for members to share and evaluate strategies as they respond to student needs. For McDonald and Star (2008), the investment of staff time to engage in community activities yielded significant returns: staff valued practical outcomes as the CoP had created a bank of useful tools ranging from assessment and marking templates to exemplars of good practice. Crucially, McDonald and Star (2008) reported that group members had changed their pedagogic practice and had increased their pedagogic understanding of scaffolding students' learning.

Similarly, Terry et al. (2018) used a CoP approach with a multidisciplinary Professional Learning Community (PLC) to explore strategies for piloting blended learning classes. Group members came together from various disciplines to meet informally and voluntarily as colleagues. Terry et al. (2018) concluded that when implementing a new pedagogic approach, the PLC offered opportunities to share and discuss teaching strategies supporting participants to explore their practice. This, they argue, differs from the traditional 'top down' mechanism for professional development, such as taught training (Terry et al., 2018).

Furthermore, the use of technology may enhance the way academics work together within a CoP to share examples of best practices and resources. For example, Sherer et al. (2003) found that developing an online portal through which members communicate and share media and other resources via digital platforms supports professional learning communities by adding capacity for greater breadth and depth to group members' learning.

Fenton-O'Creevy et al. (2015) highlighted the need to consider the potential gains from developing learning partnerships based on the CoP model to increase learning capacity both for staff professional development and more broadly by including students and other partners. Therefore, a CoP has the potential to support staff to engage in significant professional learning and development.

Research Methods

We adopted a qualitative approach to explore Trailblazers' experiences of taking part in the CoP, including the impact they felt this participation had on their own professional learning as teachers in HE. This was both in relation to delivering the RMs and more broadly within their wider roles at the University. Having gained ethical approval prior to the start of the study from ARU's Ethics panel, we invited Trailblazers to participate in semi-structured focus groups via Teams video conferencing.

We contacted all 20 Trailblazers via a group email and placed an open invitation in the Trailblazer community Teams channel. The inclusion criteria for participants were that they had been involved in the teaching or leadership of a RM during the 2021/22 academic year and that they may, or may not, have taken part in the T-Time forums. The exclusion criterion was that participants could not take part in this research if they were involved in the strategic leadership of the RMs. We obtained participants' informed consent before the start of the focus groups and provided them with a Participant Information Sheet, which included information about anonymity and confidentiality, and how they could withdraw their data within the two weeks following the focus groups.

We ran two semi-structured focus groups in January 2022 via Teams, with three Trailblazers in the first group and two in the second. We recorded the focus-groups and used the live transcriptions automatically generated by Teams. We reviewed the recordings and edited the transcribed text for accuracy. We used a question schedule for top-level questions in the focus groups to enhance the reliability of the study by ensuring consistency in the data collection process (LeCompte & Goez, 1982), while also enabling us to explore ancillary issues as they arose (Newby, 2010). These steps were important in ensuring the interpretive validity of the research (Maxwell, 2002).

Findings and Discussion

We analysed the focus group data using Thematic Analysis (Braun & Clarke, 2006). We first coded the data separately and then met to discuss and agree on the themes to increase inter-rater reliability. The four interconnected themes which emerged from the data were Building the Community, Towards Developing an Interdisciplinary Pedagogy, Emotional and Practical Support, and Innovations Beyond the Community, which fed into the overarching concept of Professional Learning for Teaching Interdisciplinary Higher Education (see Figure 11.1).

Building the Community

The ILRM provided CPD workshops to support Trailblazers to plan, develop, and deliver RMs, and these focused on discussing concepts relating to interdisciplinarity, and addressing the SDGs, through building students' awareness of sustainability. The T-Time meetings ran in conjunction with these workshops and continued throughout the first module delivery.

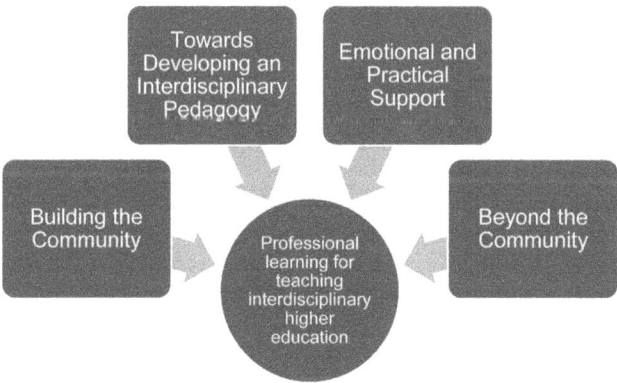

Figure 11.1 The four themes affecting the creation of a T-Time Community of Practice

Wenger (2010) explains that CoP members come together to share a domain of interest, thereby forming a group identity, and our focus group participants discussed the group's sense of identity and how they had defined themselves. For example, group members commented on having multiple identities aligned to their roles in the University, subject disciplines, and as Trailblazers. Participant P1, an academic developer and experienced lecturer, commented on the use of the term 'Trailblazers' as a collective identity: "I just enjoyed coming to a collection of like-minded individuals". P1 also explained that some group members were academics not attached to a faculty, meaning that access to teaching and learning information outside the Trailblazer group was more difficult. This suggests that the weekly T-Time forum was essential as individuals from different faculties and Professional Services formed the Trailblazer group. P1 wondered if, "There might not have been the same need if we'd all been faculty-based".

A sense of shared experience outside group members' usual working practices added to the domain of interest that united the Trailblazers through the CoP. This point resonates with Hannon et al.'s (2018) findings that in developing interdisciplinary provision, academics from different disciplines (and faculties) need opportunities to collaborate, de-siloing them from discipline-specific structures. The CoP approach provided this opportunity for Trailblazers, allowing space for them to explore innovative ideas for practice.

Participants in both focus groups valued the T-Time forums as a useful support mechanism. For example, P1 noted how, "I would clear my diary to make sure I could come". P1 also explained that some CPD meetings they had attended in the past were "not as useful... [but] I never, ever, felt that about T-Times, so for me, they were so valuable that I would [continue attending them]".

The ILRM coordinated T-Time forums by setting up calendar invites with links to Teams meetings. However, the RM strategic lead did not impose a structure on the T-Time forums, and participation was voluntary and led by attendees. P1 described T-Time sessions as, "very organic: they just happened ... they didn't need leading ... we just started talking and it would just happen, and I think that only evolved over time, so I think in some ways they're always useful".

This resonates with Wenger's (1998) description of a CoP in which there is no hierarchy, and members' knowledge and experiences are varied, and all members take collective responsibility for managing the learning they need. Furthermore, the Trailblazers valued each other's personal disciplinary knowledge and experiences equally while taking part in the CoP. This reduced the risk of one pedagogy or disciplinary body of knowledge from being marginalised in favour of another, which Lyall et al. (2015) found to be important in developing multidisciplinary teams who are dedicated and passionate about interdisciplinary education.

Lave and Wenger's (1991) notion of legitimate peripheral participation is useful as Trailblazers initially felt isolated from other colleagues developing RMs before teaching began. As teaching commenced, Trailblazers felt more like part of a RM community, and as P2, an experienced lecturer and course leader, commented,

> I didn't feel as if there was a community, at least before term started. I, kind of, get the sense of everybody was working on a Ruskin Module, so we all were facing similar challenges. So, in that sense, I felt there was a community which built up once the Ruskin Modules got started, but perhaps not before.

Our findings mirror those found by McDonald and Star (2008), whose participants valued opportunities to share their experiences and collect useful ideas and resources to use in their teaching. Participants explained how they synchronously shared ideas in Teams sessions relating to delivering the module online, including setting up and organising virtual learning platforms. P1 noted that,

> It [allowed Trailblazers to] bounce those ideas off people in T-Times, so I found that really useful ... it's not just learning from what other people were doing and telling me, it was thinking, 'I think ... that I want to try this', and it was somebody to run those ideas past.

Online asynchronous group members' contributions supported and extended participation in the CoP beyond T-Time forums. For example, Trailblazers created a shared area in Teams, where members uploaded resources and engaged in professional dialogue. This added to the sense of a shared repertoire (Wenger, 2011) of resources, experiences, tools, and ways to address common issues arising from practice. Trailblazers' access to the community for their own individual professional learning needs reflects Mercieca's (2017) notion that a CoP fits well with the trend towards increasing professional development for teaching in HE. For example, we found that Trailblazers both contributed to and learned from the CoP according to their professional expertise and learning needs. For example, P3, an experienced lecturer and course leader who had worked in the university for over a decade, said:

> I don't think we ever specifically met. It was ... at meetings or sending messages on Teams, or calling people on Teams, and there wasn't anything official that we set up ... We're just always there for anybody that's got questions ... and we're always chatting and talking to each other about different ideas and whatever.

Towards Developing an Interdisciplinary Pedagogy

A challenge for Trailblazers was adapting their teaching to meet diverse students' distinct needs, which was vital since students were accustomed to discipline-specific teaching. Shulman (2013), for example, explains that over time, teachers develop a specific type of knowledge for teaching their subject, and this pedagogic-content-knowledge enables teachers to know best how to teach their subject matter. Consequently, teaching a module specifically designed to draw on several disciplines, modelling interdisciplinary working, to student groups formed from several disciplines, challenged Trailblazers to adapt their teaching to meet a broader range of students' learning needs. Most Trailblazers prepared for this by fostering a problem-based pedagogic approach, using active learning strategies (Pratt-Adams et al., 2020). These strategies required Trailblazers to consider assessment methods and setting assignments which enabled students to demonstrate their learning creatively. All participants discussed assessment practices, with P1 saying,

> I didn't use learning outcomes, but I used [a colleague]'s assessment criteria as a framework to start writing my own … I've never had to write one … I'm passionate about the idea that a student doesn't know what outstanding [is] … so how do you write them so [that] the students understand what you're looking for and that's really hard with reflection.

Davies and Devlin (2010) emphasise the importance of addressing epistemological issues arising from differences within disciplinary structures and teaching methods, which the Trailblazers experienced. For example, the focus groups discussed the challenge of designing assignments and this illuminated the complexity of resolving the conflicts between discipline-specific and interdisciplinary pedagogic approaches that the Trailblazers encountered. P3, for example, commented that it was surprising that RM students appeared to respond differently from those in the discipline-specific modules they usually taught, noting that,

> there was a time where I was thinking … 'what am I doing wrong? Because they're not responding in the same way that the [discipline] students responded online', so that was reassuring to know that, actually, everybody [Trailblazers] did seem to have this divide.

P1, P3, P4, and P5 discussed the value of sharing ideas and learning from each other within the Trailblazer CoP. This was one central strategy for developing ideas and approaches to a pedagogic practice appropriate for interdisciplinary content. Topics ranged from practical ideas related to online delivery to developing a conceptual understanding of interdisciplinarity. P4, an associate lecturer new to teaching, explained,

> I could gain good insights about how to deliver some of the sessions … because we had the different topics such as interdisciplinarity, sustainability or employability, [and] I would say I've got more experience in the

sustainability part, and in the employability, but don't in the interdisciplinary, so I could see what other colleagues were doing.

In addition to sharing experiences and pedagogic ideas, P4 explained that by meeting weekly, Trailblazers were engaged in a period of continuous professional development:

we were students somehow because we had the opportunity to open our mind and see how other people were doing the same task, so basically ... the task was how to get students solving wicked problems, but we approached it from our own areas of expertise ... Listening [to] the experience of others is helping me to expand my way of approaching my own sessions.

An interesting observation offered by P3 was that engagement in the Trailblazer community resulted in a model for interdisciplinary working that could be offered as an example for students:

I just got to talk to people from different disciplines that I would never normally interact with, and I think it helped me talk to the students as well because to try and explain the interdisciplinary side to them, I used my experience of the [T-Time] meetings to say to them, 'it isn't just about students'.

This echoes Braßler's (2020) finding that when academics from different disciplines work together to develop interdisciplinary provision, this can model interdisciplinarity for students. T-Time discussions relating to how best to support students to understand the concept of interdisciplinarity served as an ongoing mechanism for Trailblazers to reflect on and refine their own understanding of interdisciplinarity. The opportunity to collaborate within the CoP as a multidisciplinary team also promoted engagement in crossing disciplinary boundaries in their own practice, which reflects Hannon et al.'s (2018) findings. Reflecting on the process, P3 reported, "It made me want to expand out of my silo ... and it's really made me want to push that interdisciplinary interprofessional a lot more ... it's probably changed where I see myself, the trajectory that I want to be on".

Emotional and Practical Support

Focus group participants appreciated the emotional support they received from other Trailblazers. Vrieling et al. (2019) noted how teaching can be a solitary experience, a view which P3 supported, who said, "For me it was that emotional support, and just having a lovely group of people to share that experience with was brilliant". P5, who had only recently started lecturing, agreed stating, "what was nice about it was that you just kind of realized that you're not alone".

As noted above, McDonald and Star (2008) described how PLCs provide opportunities to share teaching strategies to support student learning. As well as receiving emotional support, participants discussed the practical support they received from others in their PLC. Demonstrating this point about the impact on professional development, P1 explained how it was beneficial to explore colleagues' Canvas (i.e., the Virtual Learning Environment at ARU) sites, noting "You know where we got to see other people's Canvas sites and I thought, 'oh yeah … that looks good', and [that] gave me ideas that way. So, some of it is just sparking an idea through sharing stuff that way".

P1, reflecting how the CoP also supplied practical support in an empowering way, noted that, "It was just so supportive; you know, nobody said, 'That's rubbish'". Overall, this supported Trailblazers to develop self-efficacy in their practice, leading to increased confidence in leading their modules.

Innovations beyond the Community

As noted above, Lyall et al. (2015) and Hannon et al. (2018) both explained how working across disciplines requires communication, collaboration, critical and analytic thinking, and multidisciplinary working. This supported the Trailblazers to develop their ideas relating to interdisciplinary education through synthesising and integrating their individual discipline-specific knowledge and pedagogy with others in the community, opening further opportunities for interdisciplinary innovation outside the RMs.

Thus, while T-Time forums led to professional learning of individual members, the interdisciplinary nature of the group also facilitated innovations beyond the community. P2 and P5, who work in different faculties at ARU and taught different RMs, experienced this: after developing a relationship through the T-Time sessions, P5 explained, "[we] ran a series of three workshops … I don't think that would ever have happened if we hadn't gotten to know each other through the Ruskin Module group … I think it's helped to make those connections across the university". P2 agreed, saying, "It has made me think about a few more things which I would like to do, so, in some sense, it's emboldened me".

Summary of Findings

In Table 11.1, we summarise the key findings from this small-scale research based on the four themes we drew from the analysis.

Conclusion and Implications

In this study, we have explored how an informal interdisciplinary CoP was established to support RM tutors. As the CoP was developing, members built up a sense of community not only by being called Trailblazers but also by

Table 11.1 The impact on professional learning for interdisciplinary higher education of four themes affecting the creation of a T-Time Community of Practice

Building the Community	The 'T-Times' provided unique opportunities for Trailblazers to 'come together' as a multidisciplinary team. After some initial facilitation, for example, from the ILRM in setting up the meetings, the open agenda enabled the CoP to form
Towards Developing an Interdisciplinary Pedagogy	The non-hierarchical nature of a CoP meant that each academic's disciplinary knowledge and experience was valued equally, allowing for successful synthesis and integration of Trailblazers' individual disciplinary perspectives both epistemologically and in terms of pedagogy. This allowed academics to begin to develop a shared understanding and approach to interdisciplinary pedagogy
Emotional and Practical Support	The social learning nature of the CoP enabled Trailblazers to gain what they each needed from the community in terms of their own emerging and developing understanding of interdisciplinary pedagogy and practice. This included opportunities to trial and reflect on teaching ideas within the group leading to increased confidence and an emerging sense of self-efficacy for delivering the RMs
Beyond the Community	While the focus of the CoP was on the design and delivery of the Ruskin Modules, it served as a useful form of professional development in teaching in HE. This was shown by Trailblazers' engagement in other cross-disciplinary and interdisciplinary innovations outside of RMs

controlling the T-Time sessions and the issues and topics they wanted to discuss.

Our research has shown that those who took part in the interdisciplinary CoP felt that the T-Time forums had a positive impact on their teaching practice as they developed new skills. Furthermore, participants felt they received emotional and practical support from other members of the community who were sharing a common experience. While some participants learnt more about interdisciplinarity as a concept through the RMs and their teaching, others developed interdisciplinary skills in work and endeavours beyond the T-Time sessions.

This study has implications for future research and practice. Focus group participants were Trailblazers who engaged in T-Time sessions but did not include those who did not. Consequently, it would be valuable to explore why non-participating Trailblazers did not attend the sessions and why they chose not to be part of the CoP. A further natural progression of this work is to analyse how the T-Time CoP develops in subsequent iterations of the RM initiative, and the extent to which new RM team members join the group. Additionally, the effectiveness of the T-Time structure could also be explored in a face-to-face setting.

The findings of this study also have practical implications, as other universities could implement the CoP described here to support informal professional learning. In addition to creating a CoP exploring interdisciplinarity, the model could be used to explore other institution-wide initiatives such as sustainability and general improvements to academics' own teaching practices.

Points to Consider

Readers of this chapter may wish to consider:

- Using a CoP approach
- Collaboratively supporting development of pedagogic innovations
- Co-creating ongoing support for CoP members

References

Advance HE/HEA (2011). *The UK Professional Standards Framework for teaching and supporting learning in higher education.* Retrieved 5 July 2024, from https://s3.eu-west-2.amazonaws.com/assets.creode.advancehe-document-manager/documents/advance-he/UK%20Professional%20Standards%20Framework_1570613241.pdf

Ashby, I., & Exter, M. (2019). Designing for interdisciplinarity in higher education: Considerations for instructional designers. *TechTrends, 63*(2), 202–208. https://doi.org/10.1007/s11528-018-0352-z

Bandura, A. (1977a). *Social learning theory.* Prentice Hall.

Bandura, A. (1977b). Self-efficacy: Toward a unifying theory of behavioral change. *Psychological Review, 84*(2), 191–215. https://doi.org/10.1037/0033-295X.84.2.191

Braßler, M. (2020). The role of interdisciplinarity in bringing PBL to traditional universities: Opportunities and challenges on the organizational, team and individual level. *Interdisciplinary Journal of Problem-Based Learning, 14*(2), Article 4. https://doi.org/10.14434/ijpbl.v14i2.28799

Braun, V., & Clarke, V. (2006). Using thematic analysis in psychology. *Qualitative Research in Psychology, 3*(2), 77–101. https://doi.org/10.1191/1478088706qp063oa

Bright, J., Eliahoo, R., & Pokorny, H. (2021). Professional development. In H. Pokorny, & D. Warren (Eds.), *Enhancing teaching practice in higher education* (2nd ed.). SAGE.

Brown, V. A. (2010). Can there be a community of practice? In V. A. Brown, J. A. Harris, & J. Y. Russell (Eds.), *Tackling wicked problems through the transdisciplinary imagination.* Routledge.

Bryant, L. H., Niewolny, K., Clark, S., & Watson, C. E. (2014). *Complicated* spaces: Negotiating collaborative teaching and interdisciplinarity in higher education. *Journal of Effective Teaching, 14*(2), 83–101. Retrieved 5 July 2024, from https://files.eric.ed.gov/fulltext/EJ1060430.pdf

Davies, M., & Devlin, M. (2010). Interdisciplinary higher education. In M. Davies, M. Devlin, & M. Tight (Eds.), *Interdisciplinary higher education: Perspectives and practicalities.* Emerald Group Publishing Limited.

de Laat, M., Vrieling, E., & van den Beemt, A. (2017). Facilitation of social learning in teacher education: The 'Dimensions of Social Learning Framework'. In J. McDonald, & A. Cater-Steel (Eds.), *Communities of practice facilitating social learning in higher education*. Springer.

Eun, B. (2019). Adopting a stance: Bandura and Vygotsky on professional development. *Research in Education*, *105*(1), 74–88. https://doi.org/10.1177/0034523718793431

Fenton-O'Creevy, M., Hutchinson, S., Kubiak, C., Wenger-Trayner, B., & Wenger-Trayner, E. (2015). Challenges for practice-based education. In E. Wenger-Trayner, M. Fenton-O'Creevy, S. Hutchinson, C. Kubiak, & B. Wenger-Trayner (Eds.), *Learning in landscapes of practice boundaries, identity, and knowledgeability in practice-based learning*. Routledge.

Gombrich, C. (2018). Implementing interdisciplinary curricula: Some philosophical and practical remarks. *European Review*, *26*(S2), S41–S54. https://doi.org/10.1017/S1062798718000315

Hannon, J., Hocking, C., Legge, K., & Lugg, A. (2018). Sustaining interdisciplinary education: Developing boundary crossing governance. *Higher Education Research & Development*, *37*(7), 1424–1438. https://doi.org/10.1080/07294360.2018.1484706

Harland, T. (2012). *University teaching: An introductory guide*. Routledge. https://doi.org/10.4324/9780203120606

Jacob, J. W. (2015). Interdisciplinary trends in higher education. *Palgrave Communications*, *1*(1), 1–5. https://doi.org/10.1057/palcomms.2015.1

Lave, J., & Wenger, E. (1991). *Situated learning: Legitimate peripheral participation*. Cambridge University Press.

LeCompte, M. D., & Goez, J. P. (1982). Problems of reliability and validity in ethnographic research. *Review of Educational Research*, *52*, 31–60. https://doi.org/10.3102/00346543052001031

Lindvig, K., Lyall, C., & Meagher, L. R. (2019). Creating interdisciplinary education within monodisciplinary structures: The art of managing interstitiality. *Studies in Higher Education*, *44*(2), 347–360. https://doi.org/10.1080/03075079.2017.1365358

Lyall, C., Meagher, L., Bandola, J., & Kettle, A. (2015). *Interdisciplinary provision in higher education*. Retrieved 5 July 2024, from https://s3.eu-west-2.amazonaws.com/assets.creode.advancehe-document-manager/documents/hea/private/interdisciplinary_provision_in_he_1568037335.pdf

Maxwell, J. (2002). Understanding and validity in qualitative research. In A. M. Huberman, & M. B. Miles (Eds.), *The qualitative researcher's companion*. SAGE Publications.

McDonald, J., & Star, C. (2008). The challenges of building an academic community of practice: An Australian case study. *In Engaging Communities, Proceedings of the 31st HERDSA Annual Conference, Rotorua, 1-4 July 2008*, pp. 230–240. Retrieved 5 July 2024, from https://fac.flinders.edu.au/dspace/api/core/bitstreams/f35ab9b9-ab20-472d-904a-faa3edaabfae/content

Mercieca, B. (2017). What is a community of practice? In J. McDonald, & A. Cater-Steel (Eds.), *Communities of practice facilitating social learning in higher education*. Springer.

Newby, P. (2010). *Research methods for education* (2nd ed.). Routledge.

Pratt-Adams, S., Richter, U., & Warnes, M. (2020). *Innovations in active learning in higher education*. University of Sussex/Fulcrum. https://doi.org/10.20919/9781912319961

Rittel, H. W., & Webber, M. M. (1973). Dilemmas in a general theory of planning. *Policy Sciences*, *4*(2), 155–169. https://doi.org/10.1007/BF01405730

Sherer, P. D., Shea, T. P., & Kristensen, E. (2003). Online communities of practice: A catalyst for faculty development. *Innovative Higher Education*, *27*(3), 183–194. https://doi.org/10.1023/A:1022355226924

Shulman, L. S. (2013). Those who understand: Knowledge growth in teaching. *Journal of Education*, *193*(3), 1–11. https://doi.org/10.1177/002205741319300302

Stentoft, D. (2017). From saying to doing interdisciplinary learning: Is problem-based learning the answer? *Active Learning in Higher Education*, *18*(1), 51–61. https://doi.org/10.1177/1469787417693510

Terry, L., Zafonte, M., & Elliott, S. (2018). Interdisciplinary professional learning communities: Support for faculty teaching blended learning. *International Journal of Teaching and Learning in Higher Education*, *30*(3), 402–411. Retrieved 5 July 2024, from https://files.eric.ed.gov/fulltext/EJ1199424.pdf

Tummons, J. (2018). *Learning architectures in higher education: Beyond communities of practice*. Bloomsbury Publishing.

United Nations (UN) (2015). *Do you know all 17 SDGs?* Retrieved 5 July 2024, from https://sdgs.un.org/goals

Vrieling, E., Van Den Beemt, A., & de Laat, M. F. (2019). Facilitating social learning in teacher education: A case study. *Studies in Continuing Education*, *41*, 1–18. Retrieved 28 November 2024, from https://ro.uow.edu.au/asdpapers/703

Vygotsky, L. S. (1978). *Mind in society: The development of higher psychological processes*. Harvard University Press.

Warnes, M. (2008). The Effects of Postgraduate Certificates: A report on the second phase, *Networks*. (Special Issue) 10. Retrieved 5 July 2024, from https://aru.figshare.com/articles/journal_contribution/The_Effects_of_Postgraduate_Certificates_A_report_on_the_second_phase/23781750?file=41715414

Wenger, E. (1998). *Communities of practice: Learning, meaning and identity*. Cambridge University Press.

Wenger, E. (2010). Communities of practice and social learning systems: The career of a concept. In C. Blackmore (Ed.), *Social learning systems and communities of practice*. Springer.

Wenger, E. (2011). *Communities of practice: A brief introduction*. Retrieved 5 July 2024, from https://scholarsbank.uoregon.edu/xmlui/bitstream/handle/1794/11736/A%20brief%20introduction%20to%20CoP.pdf

Chapter 12

The Humanistic Temperament

Reflections on the Ruskin Module, *AI and the Future*

Michael Wilby

Introduction

Six decades ago, CP Snow (1959) argued that modern 'intellectual life' consisted of two competing cultures: the arts and humanities on the one hand, and the natural sciences on the other. The latter he thought of as a sometimes shallow but mainly energetic culture whose practitioners had 'the future in their bones'; the former he thought of as a reflective but often recalcitrant culture whose practitioners 'wished the future didn't exist'. Between the two cultures, he said, lay 'a gulf of mutual incomprehension' (Snow, 1959, p. 12). For all the heated controversy it generated (for which, see especially Leavis, 1963), the point of Snow's distinction was not so much to pit the two cultures against each other, as to argue for the 'creative chances' that might arise when they are brought together. The 'menaces' of modern society ('H-bomb war, overpopulation, the gap between the rich and the poor') required, Snow (1959, p. 49) argued, a response from a *third* culture of those 'trained not only in scientific but [also] in human terms'.

Although Snow's lecture is in many ways dated, the underlying point (i.e., that hyper-specialisation in academia and higher education can leave us, as individuals and as a society, ill-equipped to deal with some of the most pressing large-scale global issues) seems to me sound and to encapsulate at least one major aspect of the motivation behind 'breadth modules' such as the Ruskin Modules (RMs). There are extremely pressing issues, relating, among other things, to genuine existential threats to the planet and to our species, wide-scale injustice, and crises in mental health that are best understood and tackled from an interdisciplinary or multidisciplinary perspective that is flexible and adept at talking across disciplinary boundaries.

The purpose of this chapter is to reflect on the role that the humanities, and philosophy in particular, can perform in orchestrating disparate cross-disciplinary ideas and findings and assembling them in a common, natural language idiom, and how this envisaged role helped shape and structure the way in which I designed the content, assessment, and weekly delivery of my module. I begin by outlining the underlying rationale behind RMs; I then

DOI: 10.4324/9781003474593-14

discuss how the humanities (and philosophy in particular) are well-placed (although not uniquely so) to fulfil that rationale; finally, I discuss how this informed the design of my module, *AI and the Future: A Threat to Humanity?*

To give the reader a brief sense of this module and its content, here is the introduction which the students could access when they arrived at the home page of their online learning environment:

> This module will introduce you to the key issues surrounding Artificial Intelligence (AI) and machine technology. What is it? How does it work? On what ethical principles will it run? How will it change our lives? How will it change our societies? Is AI a new life form? And, if so, are we ready to grant it the rights and responsibilities that come with that? These questions are likely to be asked increasingly over the coming years, and this module aims to make you well equipped to understand, contribute, and help shape the debates to come. *AI and the Future* is a multidisciplinary module that looks to apply ideas that you are studying elsewhere on your course to the questions of the future: ethics, political thought, law, history, computing, psychology, business, creativity, and the nature of humanity all come to bear on this important topic.

As one can see from this, *AI and the Future* was self-consciously very wide in scope. The aim of the module was not so much to provide the students with a definitive set of threats and benefits that AI might bring, but to provide a space for students to consider and discuss the potential ramifications of the development of machine technology across our lives, including work, commerce, art, law, interpersonal relations, and even our sense of self. By providing the students with key theoretical concepts from a range of disciplines, as well as knowledge of some of the latest developments in AI, the students could bring their own backgrounds to bear on how to 'make sense' of the brave new world of artificial intelligence (AI) and human-machine interactions that we are bringing into being.

The challenges that arise with AI bring with them a set of interconnected issues that cut across the social, cultural, political, psychological, and even biological aspects of our lives (Bostrom, 2014; Chalmers, 2022; Mitchell, 2019; Russell, 2019). The purpose of this chapter is to reflect on what is involved in tackling such interconnected 'wicked problems' within the context of interdisciplinary breadth modules in Higher Education, why the Humanities are well placed to 'make sense' of such problems, and how this influenced the design and delivery of *AI and the Future*.

Wicked Problems: Ruskin Modules within the Context of HE

RMs provide two main families of benefit: first, they provide a *personal benefit* for individual students, by way of widening their perspective and improving their employability; second, they provide a *civic benefit*, by shining light on psychological, societal, or global issues that might not be visible from the perspective of individual disciplines. The two benefits dovetail: in tackling the problems, students gain both employable skills and enlarged perspectives; while the problems are tackled more effectively by way of the variety of skills and perspectives that students from different disciplines bring.

One of the personal benefits for students mentioned above (i.e., an enlarged mentality) fits with some of the most well-known invocations of what the purpose of a university education is (or should be). In his hugely influential collection, *The Idea of a University* (based on lectures originally delivered in 1852), Newman (1852 [1947], p. 391) argued for the value of a 'liberal education' which involved a form of integrated learning, rather than 'a sort of bazaar, or pantechnicon' of individual disciplines and subjects 'in which wares of all kinds are heaped together for sale in stalls independent of each other'. For Newman (1852 [1947], p. 46), a university education should include 'the comprehension of the bearings of one science on another, and the use of each to each, and the location and limitation and adjustment and due appreciation of them all, one with another'.

Similarly, Collini (2012, p. 56) states that,

A university ... is a protected space in which various forms of useful preparation for life are undertaken in a setting and manner which encourages the students to understand the contingency of any particular packet of knowledge, and its interrelations with other, different forms of knowledge.

While Newman directly contrasts the intrinsic value of education with its economic utility, regarding the latter as having no part to play in a university education, Collini (2012, p. 91) takes a more nuanced view (see also McCowan, 2015) where the aim of employability is embedded within a wider remit in which students are expected to:

extend and deepen their understanding of themselves and the world, acquiring, in the course of this form of growing up, kinds of knowledge and skill which will be useful in their eventual employment, but which will no more be the sum of their education than that employment will be the sum of their lives.

This, then, is one of the central personal benefits a university education provides for students: to extend and deepen their understanding of themselves, others, and the world; a benefit which includes, but is not limited to or by, acquiring knowledge and skills that would be useful in employment. The 'enlarged mentality' that comes with thinking outside of narrow disciplinary silos is how RMs can contribute to that mission.

With regard to the *civic benefit* of a university education, Calhoun (2006, p. 10) mentions five key roles:

1 Equip citizens for occupations needed by the public for economic development or other purposes.
2 Advance social mobility.
3 Produce new technologies and other innovations.
4 Contribute to both the continuity and creativity of culture.
5 Directly inform the public sphere and prepare citizens to participate in it.

It is in this fifth role that RMs have the potential to be especially helpful. The 'public sphere' (Habermas, 1962 [1989]), whose relative demise in recent decades has been well documented (Marquand, 2004; Putnam, 2000), can be defined as 'the social space in which different opinions are expressed, problems of general concern are discussed, and collective solutions are developed communicatively' (Wessler & Freudenthaler, 2018, para. 1). The rationale of the RMs seems very much of a piece with this conception of the public sphere and of its importance. The RMs were presented as engaged with 'wicked problems', which are 'seemingly intractable problems ... composed of interrelated dilemmas, issues, and other problems at multiple levels of society, economy, and governance' (Horn & Weber, 2007) and so require collaborative resolutions that are generated discursively and openly. As one recent major work in the philosophy of education puts it: 'if democracy is to be a way of life, shot through and through with occasions of joint deliberation, future citizens must learn how to be adept discussants. They must be good listeners, able to enter and understand others' perspectives, skilled at mutual engagement' (Kitcher, 2022, p. 301; see also Nussbaum, 2010).

The concept of a 'wicked problem' originated in a paper by Rittel and Webber (1973) which dealt with wide-scale social planning problems. Such problems, the authors thought, are elusively defined and their resolutions require educated 'judgement' rather than a clearly defined metricised solution. Judgements are required because the problems that wicked problems generate are holistically integrated with many other aspects of public life, meaning that any resolutions resist a definitive separation into 'true-or-false', but should rather be thought of as temporarily 'good-or-bad' or 'better-or-worse' to a certain degree and in certain respects. They require multiple perspectives and an open-ended enquiry which does not necessarily have a clear ending point. Wicked problems were contrasted with 'tame' or 'benign' problems 'which are definable and separable and may have solutions that are findable' (Rittel & Webber, 1973, p. 160). The trio of problems mentioned by Snow in the introduction to this chapter would be examples of wicked problems (other examples mentioned by Horn and Weber (2007) include climate change, pandemic responses, international drug trafficking, and terrorism).

RMs, then, are explicitly designed to engage with wicked problems, and the open discussion of wicked problems helps fulfil the civic benefit of 'directly informing the public sphere and preparing citizens to participate in it' (Calhoun, 2006, p. 10). The issues generated by the advent of AI and machine technology, as discussed above, are an integral part of any such discussions and clearly meet the criterion of a wicked problem.

The Humanities as Magpie Disciplines

This brings us to the role of the humanities. Although seemingly perpetually in crisis (Reitter & Wellmon, 2021), the humanities are well-placed to contribute to the resolution of wicked problems and hence are well-placed to fulfil at least one key purpose of a RM. The humanities are distinct in two ways: a distinctive *subject matter*, or a distinctive *methodological style* or process. Collini (2012, p. 64), for example, characterises the humanities as,

> that collection of disciplines which attempt to understand, across barriers of time and culture, the actions and creations of other human beings considered as bearers of meaning, where the emphasis tends to fall on matters to do with individual or cultural distinctiveness and not on matters which are primarily susceptible to characterisation in purely statistical or biological terms.

For the purposes of this chapter, I want to focus more on the methodological aspect of the humanities, rather than on the claim that they are distinctively concerned with a particular subject matter (viz, 'human beings'). This is not to deny that the humanities are in most cases centrally concerned with the human being, but the issue is certainly more complex than simply stating that the humanities take human beings as their subject matter, since the direct subject matter of large swathes of, say, metaphysical, or even ethical, philosophy do not concern themselves directly with humans, while large swathes of the natural sciences (e.g., psychology, neuroscience, neurobiology, biology), not to mention the social sciences, do (see Ruse (2020) for discussion).

From a methodological perspective, we might say this: what humanities subjects have in common is that their enquiries are *indexed* from a human perspective. The type of questions asked and the type of answers that are accepted are framed with regard to, and evaluated in terms of, their relevance to human beings. For instance, while the natural and social sciences typically take an approach which is self-consciously *objective* (what the philosopher Nagel (1986) calls the 'view from nowhere'), the humanities typically take an approach that (explicitly or implicitly) regards the enquiry as indexed from a potential multiplicity of humanistic perspectives, whether that is individual, cultural, or species-wide. In a deliberate echo of Nagel, this is what Wallace (2013) calls 'the view from here', a humanistic conception that deals with 'concepts and explanations which are rooted in our more local practices, our culture, and our history' (Williams, 2000, p. 482), an approach that can be contrasted with a scientistic conception which aims at an 'absolute conception of the world' which 'might describe the world "as it is in itself", that is to say, give a representation of it which is to the largest possible extent independent of the local perspectives or idiosyncrasies of enquirers' (Williams, 2000, p. 481).

It is perhaps an exaggeration to call this a 'methodology' at all. It is more of a temperament. If the aim of research in the humanities is a form of understanding of a subject matter indexed to human concerns, then any particular methodology towards that end is in principle dispensable. With reference to literature studies, for instance, Carter says that it is 'acceptable in this field to find something interesting, swoop down on some bit of useful theory or other and add that to the research construction with the goal of better understanding' (Carter, 2013, p. 131). Carter calls this kind of approach 'magpieism': a 'honing in on what seems important, then using a range of approaches and theories as they seem helpful' (Carter, 2013, p. 131).

This magpie approach was first articulated as such by the medievalist scholar Martin (1992, pp. 236–237; in Carter, 2013, p. 128) in the following passage:

> those who spoke in favour of magpies suggested that they had found methods and terminology derived from a variety of complete intellectual systems illuminating in particular cases. Such systems, one might argue, are not necessarily incompatible with each other... one need not be a doctrinaire Marxist or Freudian to find aspects of their thought relevant to works of art .... Since we live in, and have to negotiate a world of plural discourses, what can be the objections to critical pluralism?

Although he is suspicious of the term itself, Collini (2012, p. 75) likewise regards 'magpieism' as part of the humanistic temperament, but cautions against thinking of it as an 'anything goes' methodology or a 'showy light-footedness', stating, rather, that it requires honed skills of 'noticing and characterising' and powers of 'illuminating and persuading':

> any particular methodology or theoretical vocabulary only furnishes a set of tools or, at most, a set of lenses; it still takes particular users to make use of them, and they can be made use of more or less skilfully ... the activity of "characterising" ... requires that we become as dextrous as possible in deploying, and in reflecting upon our deployment of, the widest possible range of vocabularies.

This is not to say that humanities subjects *need* to take the magpie approach. It surely is the case that for some topics a particular methodology or theoretical framework is exclusively well fitted to making insightful progress on an issue. For instance, progress might be made on certain aspects of linguistic meaning by way of the methodological tools of logical analysis (Soames, 2003), or certain underlying features of conscious experience by way of the methodological tools of phenomenology (Smith, 2016): for some questions, it might well be that too many recipes spoil the broth.

However, when it comes to wicked problems, it is, as we have seen, part of their nature that there is no neat way to either formulate or answer them. They need to be prodded and poked from a variety of angles using a variety of intellectual tools, methods, and outlooks. What the humanist temperament can add to this is not an overarching methodology or subject-matter (although perhaps these too can contribute) but an organising or orchestrating role that frames the enquiry within what I have been calling 'the human-indexed perspective'.

Philosophical Sense-Making

The humanist temperament, as I have been describing it, is a tendency to frame questions, and evaluate their answers and resolutions, in terms of their impact on the lives of human beings. And this tendency, I have argued, is important for approaching 'wicked problems' and hence for RMs. For some questions, this invites the 'magpie approach' as described by Martin and Carter and encourages what Nussbaum (2010, p. 7) calls the 'spirit of the humanities': 'searching critical thought, daring imagination, empathetic understanding of human experiences of many different kinds, and understanding of the complexity of the world we live in'.

I want now to discuss this more firmly with relation to my home discipline of philosophy. There is, as one might expect, no accepted definition or characterisation among philosophers of what philosophy is. Plato's Socrates, in Book V of *The Republic*, says 'we shall rightly call a philosopher the man [*sic*] who is easily willing to learn every kind of knowledge', but for our purposes this seems too vague, even though it does incorporate the kind of magpieism we have been discussing.

A more recent and widely cited characterisation of philosophy comes from the 20th century American philosopher, Sellars (1962 [1963], p. 35):

The aim of philosophy, abstractly formulated, is to understand how things in the broadest possible sense of the term hang together in the broadest possible sense of the term … To achieve success in philosophy would be … to 'know one's way around' with respect to all these things, not in that unreflective way in which the centipede of the story knew its way around before it faced the question, 'how do I walk?', but in that reflective way which means that no intellectual holds are barred.

Again, this is very broad, but it does give us a sense of one articulation of the aim of philosophy: to achieve a reflective and systematic understanding of the world, in its fullest generality, by whatever means necessary (magpieism again, which, in this context, one might argue is a form of intellectual pragmatism). Drawing partly on Sellars' definition, Moore (2012) describes this simply as 'making sense of things', where the 'sense' that is made is 'the meaning of something, the purpose of something, or the explanation for something' (Moore, 2012, p. 5) and what it is to make sense of that something is 'a matter of rendering intelligible, with all the associations with productivity that that has' (Moore, 2012, p. 6).

This last point is, I think, quite important when thinking about wicked problems, as well as the role of RMs. The idea that we need to 'render intelligible', in a human-indexed way, the value/meaning/purpose/explanation of something seems to be exactly what is going on when we, say, ask about the effects of the fashion industry, or the role of work in our lives, or what place one has in the city (to take some examples from recent RMs). This 'rendering intelligible' is not just to passively understand and learn about an inert body of knowledge that is already out there but is also to actively *create* an understanding of, and perhaps bring resolutions to, a messy, complex reality that we live within and are in the process of sustaining or bringing into being. Philosophical sense-making, in this sense, is a matter of actively digesting, absorbing, and shaping facts, data, and ideas, using whatever methodological means necessary, to make them intelligible, both to ourselves and to others.

AI and the Future: A Threat to Humanity

With this in mind, I now turn to a short discussion of the RM that I led, *AI and the Future: A Threat to Humanity?* The topic was chosen because it will affect numerous areas of our lives in various ways. The question of how we should evaluate and weigh the competing pros and cons of incorporating AI into our lives is certainly a wicked problem. It does not admit of a straightforward formulation, nor a straightforward true/false answer. There are respects in which AI will likely improve our lives (especially medical care), respects in which it might well create havoc with our lives (the automation of work), and other respects in which its effects are as yet unknown and perhaps as yet unthought of. The topic is unavoidable, and, if we are not to just succumb to a form of fatalism about the advent of technology, students (i.e., future citizens) need to be aware of what AI is, what it could become, the myriad effects it is likely to have across all aspects of life, and how to evaluate, and render intelligible, all this, via discursive, informed, and open discussion.

To enable this, the course outline included ten weeks of content (together with one week of assessment preparation and one week of review). The early weeks of the module (Weeks 1–3) were more descriptive and prescribed. Taken alone these early weeks focused more on what Rittel and Webber called 'tame' or 'benign' problems 'which are definable and separable and may have solutions that are findable' (1973, p. 155). Week 1 discussed the historical background to AI (the scientific revolution, the early proto-computers designed by two of the pioneers of modern computing: Charles Babbage and Ada Lovelace, as well as the role Alan Turing played in the development of digital computing during the inter-war period). Week 2 discussed the 'architectures of AI' (i.e., the different logical structures by which AI can run, and the different capacities that AI exhibits as a result of these structures). Week 3 looked at the concept of 'intelligence' and the different forms it can take, including 'superintelligence' (Bostrom, 2014). Students were encouraged in these early weeks to discuss and understand the issues (e.g., to provide their own 'recipe' for a symbolic processing machine; or to create their own version of the 'Turing Test': a test devised by Turing (1950), in which any computer that manages to fool a human being into thinking, from its answers, that it was itself a human being should be deemed 'intelligent') but the main purpose of these early weeks was to provide some of the core facts about the nature of AI upon which future weeks would build.

From Week 4 onwards, the topics became less prescribed and more open to interpretation: the current effects of AI including concerns about online *filter bubbles* (i.e., 'a social epistemic structure in which other relevant voices have been left out, perhaps accidentally' (Nguyen, 2020, p. 141)) and *echo chambers* (i.e., a social epistemic structure from which other relevant voices are actively excluded and discredited (Nguyen, 2020, p. 141)); the likely effects of AI on the workplace, and what it means for the meaning of work; the problem of value alignment (Russell, 2019) and how we can ensure that AI systems can stay in step with our values; the nature of creativity, AI artworks, and whether AI can ever be truly creative; the desirability of 'post-human' machine-human amalgamations, to take some of the issues discussed. For each of these later topics, the questions and answers can be formulated from many different perspectives and whether AI is 'good' or 'bad' becomes difficult to definitively answer. They are wicked problems, requiring judgement, open-ended enquiry, and intermeshing viewpoints. The art student might take a wholly different perspective from the computer studies student on what counts as art, on what makes an artwork valuable, and on whether AI-art in some sense diminishes human art. Indeed, the discussion of the 'posthuman' proved to be unexpectedly (for me, at least) provocative, with some students excited by the prospect and others likening it to eugenics. Even the question of whether it was appropriate to discuss the topic openly (given the arguable parallel with eugenics) was brought up and challenged.

In all this, open, respectful dialogue was key. Because of the large classes, students were regularly placed in small 'breakout rooms' and were asked to report back after ten minutes. In addition, regular polls (using Microsoft Teams) were used to generate interim reports on what the class as a whole felt about a particular issue. In this respect, students recognised that there was, to use

Rittel and Webber's (1973) phrase, a no 'stopping rule' (i.e., no way of saying whether you had come to a definitive final answer to the question). Finally, students were regularly asked during the class to do their own on-the-spot 'research' on a topic, to (in the magpie-like fashion mentioned earlier) find information online relevant to the topic at hand and bring it back to the class to feed into the discussion.

Finally, the assessment was a 3,000-word patchwork text, chosen partly to reflect the patchwork nature of the wicked problems of AI. The patchwork text had five parts: Parts 1–3 were mini-essays of 500 words each on topics covered in the module and represented by a list of 23 questions, from which the students could choose three. Part 4 was a 500-word reflective mini-essay that related aspects of the module back to either the students' own course or to the United Nations (UN) Sustainable Development Goals (SDGs) (UN, 2015), which formed a key plank of the brief across all RMs. Part 5 was a 1000-word essay in which students were asked to design their own AI system (and the principles on which it would run) for a particular task (e.g., an AI teacher, or an AI police officer); for this task, students were asked to consider both the pros and cons and to try to include potential 'fixes' for the cons.

Concluding Remarks

The general gist of this chapter has been to outline the distinctive way in which the humanities can be used to tackle problems that are large-scale and open-ended (i.e., wicked problems). The RM that I ran, *AI and the Future: A Threat to Humanity?*, was a useful testing ground for this kind of approach. The humanities provide skilled and reflective ways of thinking about large-scale problems from human-indexed perspectives, and one means by which they can do this is via the multi-perspectival, amethodological temperament of magpieism.

However, the point of this is not to say that the humanistic temperament is the *only* way to address wicked problems. Both the *artistic temperament* and the *scientific temperament* can do so too. For instance, whereas the humanities look to render sense-making into a natural language idiom, art can make use of *visual methodologies* that capture 'more detail and a different kind of data than verbal and written methods' (Glaw et al., 2017, p. 1; see also Vince & Warren, 2012). Similarly, the scientific drive towards unbiased objectification and quantitative analysis has been given new impetus by the advent of 'big data' which might yet find ways of uncovering wide-scale societal or historical patterns relevant to answering wicked problems that would have been invisible to the 'naked brain', so to speak (Kelleher & Tierney, 2018). The humanistic temperament, like these other temperaments, is a central tool in understanding the world and the critical tasks that we face. As Collini (2012, p. 85) puts it, '[t]he kinds of understanding and judgement exercised in the humanities are of a piece with the kinds of understanding and judgement involved in living a life'.

Points to Consider

Readers of this chapter may wish to consider:

- Stressing the enhancements to student employability offered by interdisciplinary breadth modules
- Exploring the interconnectedness of wicked problems
- Using a 'Magpie Approach' to explore complex topics

References

Bostrom, N. (2014). *Superintelligence: Paths, dangers, strategies*. Oxford University Press.

Calhoun, C. (2006). The university and the public good. *Thesis Eleven*, *83*, 7–43. https://doi.org/10.1177/0725513606060516

Carter, S. (2013). The methodology of magpies. *International Journal of Research & Method in Education*, *37*(2), 125–136. https://doi.org/10.1080/1743727X.2013.843074

Chalmers, D. (2022). *Reality+: Virtual worlds and the problems of philosophy*. Allen Lane.

Collini, S. (2012). *What are universities for?* Penguin Books.

Glaw, X., Inder, K., Kable, A., & Hazleton, M. (2017). Visual methodologies in qualitative research: Autophotography and photo elicitation applied to mental health research. *International Journal of Qualitative Methods*, *16*(1), 8. https://doi.org/10.1177/1609406917748215 https://doi.org/10.1177%2F1609406917748215

Habermas, J. (1962 [1989]). *The structural transformation of the public sphere*. MIT Press.

Horn, R. E., & Weber, R. P. (2007). *New Tools for Resolving Wicked Problems: Mess Mapping and Resolution Mapping Processes*. Retrieved 5 July 2024, from https://www.strategykinetics.com//New_Tools_For_Resolving_Wicked_Problems.pdf

Kelleher, J. D., & Tierney, B. (2018). *Data science*. MIT Press.

Kitcher, P. (2022). *The main enterprise of the world: Rethinking education*. Oxford University Press.

Leavis, F. R. (1963). *Two cultures?: The significance of C.P. Snow*. Chatto & Windus.

Marquand, D. (2004). *Decline of the public*. Polity Press.

Martin, P. (1992) Chaucer and feminism: A magpie view. In J. Dor (Ed.), *A Wyf ther was: Essays in honour of Paule Mertens-Fronk* (pp. 235–246). University of Liege Press.

McCowan, T. (2015). Should universities promote employability? *Theory and Research in Education*, *13*(3), 267–285. https://doi.org/10.1177%2F1477878515598060

Mitchell, M. (2019). *Artificial intelligence: A guide for thinking humans*. Penguin Random House.

Moore, A. W. (2012). *The evolution of modern metaphysics: Making sense of things*. Cambridge University Press.

Nagel, T. (1986). *The view from nowhere*. Oxford University Press.

Newman, J. H. (1852 [1947]). *The idea of a university*. Longmans, Green, and Co. Retrieved 5 July 2024, from https://www.gutenberg.org/files/24526/24526-pdf.pdf

Nguyen, C. T. (2020). Echo chambers and epistemic bubbles. *Episteme*, *17*(2), 141–161. https://doi.org/10.1017/epi.2018.32

Nussbaum, M. (2010). *Not for profit: Why democracy needs the humanities*. Princeton University Press.

Putnam, R. D. (2000). *Bowling alone: The collapse and revival of American community*. Simon & Schuster.

Reitter, P., & Wellmon, C. (2021). *Permanent crisis: The humanities in a disenchanted age*. The University of Chicago Press.

Rittel, H. W., & Webber, M. M. (1973). Dilemmas in a general theory of planning. *Policy Sciences, 4*(2), 155–169. https://doi.org/10.1007/BF01405730

Ruse, M. (2020). Willem Drees on the humanities. *Zygon: Journal of Religion and Science, 56*(3), 691–703. https://doi.org/10.1111/zygo.12727

Russell, S. (2019). *Human compatible: Artificial intelligence and the problem of control*. Allen Lane.

Sellars, W. (1962 [1963]). Philosophy and the scientific image of man. In R. Colodny (Ed.), *Science, perception, and reality* (pp. 35–78). Humanities Press/Ridgeview. Retrieved 5 July 2024, from http://www.ditext.com/sellars/psim.html

Smith, J. (2016). *Experiencing phenomenology: An introduction*. Routledge.

Snow, C. P. (1959). *The two cultures and the scientific revolution*. Cambridge University Press. Retrieved 5 July 2024, from https://apps.weber.edu/wsuimages/michaelwutz/6510.Trio/Rede-lecture-2-cultures.pdf

Soames, S. (2003). *Philosophical analysis in the twentieth century* (Vols 1 & 2). Princeton University Press.

Turing, A. (1950). Computing machinery and intelligence. *Mind, LIX*(236), 433–460. https://doi.org/10.1093%2Fmind%2FLIX.236.433

United Nations (UN) (2015). *Transforming Our World: The 2030 Agenda for Sustainable Development*. Retrieved 5 July 2024, from https://sdgs.un.org/

Vince, R., & Warren, S. (2012). Participatory visual methods. In C. Cassell, & G. Symon (Eds.), *The practice of qualitative organisational research: Core methods and current challenges*. Sage. Retrieved 5 July 2024, from http://repository.essex.ac.uk/1169/1/Vince_%26_Warren_Final_Version.pdf

Wallace, R. J. (2013). *The view from here: On affirmation, attachment, and the limits of regret*. Oxford University Press. https://doi.org/10.1111/ejop.12231

Wessler, H., & Freudenthaler, R. (2018). *Public sphere. Oxford Bibliographies*. https://doi.org/10.1093/obo/9780199756841-0030

Williams, B. (2000). Philosophy as a humanistic discipline. *Philosophy, 75*(4), 477–496. https://doi.org/10.1017/S0031819100000632

Chapter 13

Interdisciplinary Learning Design

George Evangelinos, Neil Dixon, and Himara Govinnage

Introduction

Ruskin Modules (RMs) aim to develop critical thinking, creativity, and reasoned arguments by integrating knowledge across disciplines to explore societal issues through bringing together students from different disciplines (ARU, 2018). Our RM, *Is Technology Changing Us?*, focuses on how to future gaze and anticipate potential, unintended consequences of introducing new technologies.

In this chapter we examine how interdisciplinary thinking is conceptualised through learning-design by examining the vision, teaching, and support of our module offering (van den Akker, 2003). We give an overview of interdisciplinary learning, describe the design and development of the module, and use our own model of interdisciplinary thinking to explore how the student assessments demonstrated interdisciplinarity through constructively aligning the learning design and assessment metrics.

Interdisciplinary Thinking, Metacognition, and 'Wicked Problems'

Interdisciplinary thinking can be characterised as the metacognitive ability of utilising multiple domains of knowledge, understanding, and skills to solve problems. Building on the heuristic framework of Lakatos (1970), Khagram et al. (2010) describe interdisciplinary research in terms of scholarship when integrating different knowledge domains. Reaffirming Menken et al.'s (2016) view, Klaassen (2021) defines interdisciplinary education as 'the integration of different disciplinary knowledge fields, which are used to solve societal challenges' (2021, p. 228)'. With Klaassen (2021, p. 228) defines interdisciplinary education as 'the integration of different disciplinary knowledge fields, which are used to solve societal challenges'.

According to Cambridge Assessment (2015), metacognition can be broadly interpreted as the approaches that learners take when monitoring and evaluating their learning behaviours and planning their own development. An important element of metacognition, alongside *metacognitive knowledge*, is critical self-reflection, or *metacognitive regulation*, in the context of learning and self-

DOI: 10.4324/9781003474593-15

development. When these concepts are combined, they can be used to semantically define interdisciplinarity and set a conceptual framework to explore it further.

Reality and societal transformation are ontologically complex, multidimensional concepts that inherently benefit from interdisciplinary study. This apparent complexity of reality constitutes an intrinsic reason for the emergence of interdisciplinary approaches to learning (Darbellay, 2019). Thus, the notion of interdisciplinarity involves exploration of real, open-ended, ill-defined, 'wicked problems' in nature and/or society (Gómez Puente et al., 2015).

Wicked problems vary in their complexity and context and as such the exploration of potential solutions requires an individualised approach (Neubert et al., 2017). Importantly, wicked problems are further characterised by the uncertainty of a resolution, and the resulting risks and learning opportunities the potential resolution affords, in addition to the different perspectives and views on the solution (Veltman et al., 2020).

We designed our module to explore the wicked problem of 'how to anticipate the potential, unintended consequences of introducing new technologies on different groups or individuals'. This problem can be characterised as wicked because 21st century technology systems integrate an array of technologies to perform increasingly complex tasks in a multitude of evolving environments (Lattuca et al., 2004).

Work on this wicked problem, or others, requires studying the interrelationships of multiple points of view that have traditionally been considered to belong to distinct disciplines, to disentangle the complexity and make progress towards solutions (Klein, 1990). Thus, interdisciplinarity can be conceptualised as the ability to integrate multiple knowledge domains, contexts, and approaches to problem-solving from different disciplines. Common ground is using communicative approaches to bring awareness to conflicting insights or assumptions among disciplines (Repko, 2007). The notion of integrating knowledge is complementary to the idea of establishing common ground across disciplines.

Both integration of knowledge and common ground are integral to developing interdisciplinarity (Newell, 2001). In particular, the concept of integration is a cognitive ability which is necessary for students to develop interdisciplinary thinking and, as such, should be assessed as a learning outcome (Boix Mansilla & Duraisingh, 2007). Therefore, we further elaborate these notions in this chapter in terms of the skills, competences, and capabilities needed to communicate, collaborate, and problem-solve in an increasingly complex array of culturally and scientifically diverse environments.

Technological Transformation and Interdisciplinary Thinking

Our module's wicked problem, 'How to anticipate the potential, unintended consequences of introducing new technologies on different groups or individuals', was explored through the lens of human/machine interfacing in the context of technological transformation, and the implications to society more generally. Technological transformation can be interpreted as the evolution of interactive, dynamic systems of components that arise in multiple disciplinary domains (Gero, 2014). Interdisciplinary approaches are fundamental to the facilitation and acceleration of innovation and the emergence of new technology applications (Darbellay, 2019). This kind of technology-system sophistication requires the capacity to integrate knowledge and understanding across multiple domains (Czerniak, 2007), especially when operating within dynamic environments and with consideration of evolving social factors (Lattuca et al., 2013). As such, technological transformation can be characterised as an intrinsically interdisciplinary concept that cannot be confined within traditional disciplinary boundaries.

We developed learning activities and assessments that conceptualise practice and explicitly establish links between learning outcomes, disciplinary approaches, and student performance as illustrated by the student assessment artefacts (Gütl & Chang, 2008). To ensure interdisciplinary integration was evidenced through the student experience, Khagram et al.'s (2010) three core elements of interdisciplinary research were applied when developing the assessments. The main elements of our approach can be characterised as 'a) forms and functions of theories … b) the underlying philosophies of knowledge … [and] c) the combination of enquiry approaches' (Khagram et al., 2010, p. 89). This approach facilitated the exploration of interdisciplinary integration through analysis of the learning activity and by examining the assessment artefacts of the students for evidence of technological transformation knowledge and understanding and the ability to predict the likely impact of emerging technologies to society.

Interdisciplinary Learning Design

The overarching aim of our RM, *Is Technology Changing Us?*, was to assess knowledge and understanding of the societal implications of technological transformation. To model interdisciplinary learning, the module developed interdisciplinary thinking by applying two distinct, seemingly disparate, disciplinary approaches to learning. We designed the module to engage students in interdisciplinary, metacognitive learning, using constructively aligned learning outcomes, activities, and assessment artefacts. Specifically, the learning outcomes listed in Table 13.1 guided the learning design, teaching delivery, and module assessment.

The first learning outcome is common to all RMs and was designed so students can demonstrate their interdisciplinary learning (Baxter & Brown, 2018, p. 4). We formulated the remaining learning outcomes around the knowledge and problem-solving methods used in the module, which students demonstrated by completing the assessments. It was important that we carefully designed assessments to develop and assess interdisciplinary learning in

Table 13.1 Learning outcomes: Is technology changing us?

No.	Learning outcome
1	Critically reflect on the limitations of a single discipline to solve wider societal concerns by applying knowledge created through the discovery and exploitation of connections across disciplines
2	Understand and explain the key principles behind evidenced-based enquiry methodologies, such as speculative design and design fiction
3	Apply these principles to generate research-informed, imaginative insights around technological innovations that address a variety of current and emerging scenarios
4	Explore possible futures by communicating through written and multimedia messages to an audience in a way that stimulates debate
5	Apply critical thinking and academic skills to communicate solutions to problems in future scenarios

a way that students could experience unfamiliar approaches and develop their own thinking around the module context in relation to the intended learning outcomes. Students learned how to apply a variety of approaches, holistically and complimentary to each other, by completing three assignments: (a) a technology assessment group report, (b) a fiction narrative, and (c) a critical self-reflection on their understanding of interdisciplinary thinking.

Having established a working definition of interdisciplinary thinking, and briefly explored the potential of utilising Learning Design principles in interdisciplinary module development, we give an account of the learning, teaching and assessment methods used, and the student experience.

Vision: Modelling Interdisciplinary Learning

The learning, teaching, and assessment approaches explain how we facilitated student interdisciplinary learning. Evidence of student performance and understanding of interdisciplinarity was explored through the constructively aligned assessment artefacts. To highlight the student experience, we have incorporated a reflection by a former student on the module acting as a co-researcher, written six months after completing the module.

To frame our exploration of the assessments, we propose a model of interdisciplinary metacognitive thinking (IMT) (see Figure 13.1).

The purpose of the IMT model was to define interdisciplinarity in terms of our practice, and to explore and further conceptualise the notions of metacognitive interdisciplinarity, in the context of an exploration of how technology is transforming our society. Specifically, the assessment artefacts were used as evidence and analysed and categorised in the areas of the model to formulate our understanding of how interdisciplinary learning could be elucidated further.

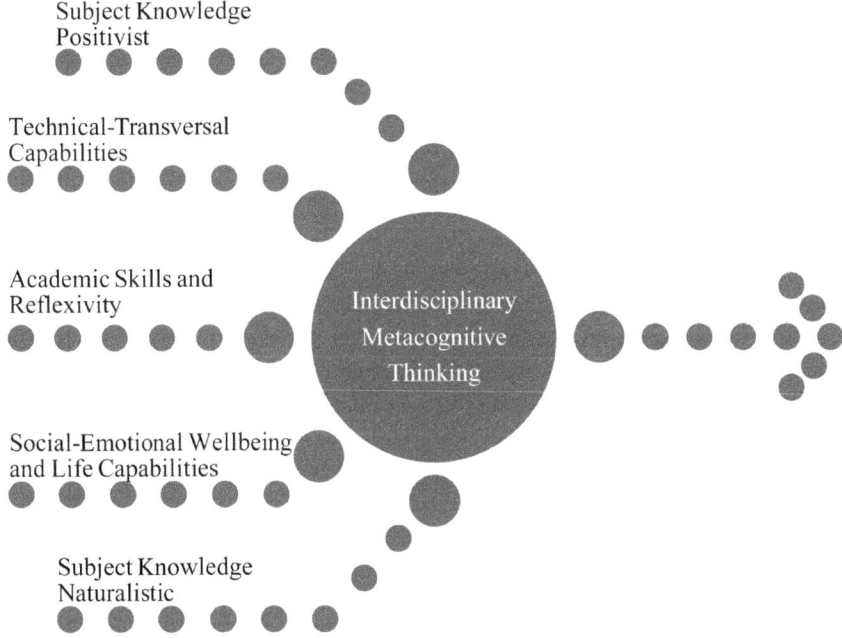

Figure 13.1 Interdisciplinary metacognitive thinking

This proposed model for characterising IMT includes the following areas:

- *Subject Knowledge Domain(s)* are the disciplinary grounded knowledge fields, which encompass theories, methods, and models that explain within a discipline what is known about a phenomenon. As evidenced etymologically, interdisciplinarity naturally arises from the intermixing of at least two different disciplines, or the interplay of the different subject knowledge domains and the disciplinary approaches. In our model, these are considered in the epistemological context of a continuum across the disciplinary paradigms of post-positivist and naturalistic methods.
- *Academic Skills and Reflexivity* is metacognition and metacognitive regulation, defined as the students' ability to evaluate learning behaviours and plan the next actions.
- *Digital Capabilities (Technical-transversal Capabilities)* are the skills and knowledge needed to operate in the digital world.
- *Social-emotional Wellbeing and Life Capabilities* are students' connection to social groups, such as individual students, the university community, family, or work.

Teaching: Engaging Students with Interdisciplinary Learning

We used pedagogic methods to facilitate students' learning to synthesise knowledge, establish and evaluate methods, and explore different perspectives (Scott, 2015). Specific pedagogies can be applied to many different disciplines, so there is not always one best way to teach Subject Knowledge. Learning is an interaction between the teacher and students, so students equally need to develop reflexivity, critical thinking (Ashby & Exter, 2019), and problem-solving skills to gain an understanding of Subject Knowledge. In terms of reflexivity, we designed the module assessment to collect both students' current perceptions of emerging technology in society and challenge prior assumptions.

In the weekly lectures, we asked students to answer a variety of discussion questions via an online audience response tool. We used student responses as a basis of discussion during the lectures and gave them the chance to examine different perspectives, find common ground, and potentially change their own points of view. Following the lectures, students worked in seminar groups, for which we provided them with structured discussion questions and exercises, with the aim of further examining their own experience in more detail.

The first half of the module's taught curriculum was focused on orientating students towards the practical applications and risks of emerging technologies, which helped them to develop critical thinking and problem-solving skills. We used examples and case studies to illustrate and familiarise students with various technology concepts such as Artificial Intelligence (AI), Robotics, and Blockchain, to name a few. For example, students applied Amazon's *Just Walk Out* technology (Amazon, 2022), a cashier-less facial recognition system, to the University's café and library to investigate the implications of such technologies to society. By using existing technology applications, we intended to orientate students and prompt them to connect emerging technologies to familiar contexts (Lattuca et al., 2004). Each seminar consisted of a practical exercise during which students acted as technology managers investigating the ethical barriers and risks of their chosen technology. This practical approach encouraged the development of students' problem-solving skills. We structured the module teaching progressively so that each session built on knowledge gained in the previous week.

Support: Facilitating Interdisciplinary Learning

We administered and delivered this module using Microsoft Teams including private channels that we created to facilitate group work for the technology assessment. However, these channels required significant maintenance. For example, student registration information was only finalised in the second half of the module delivery. As a result, constant monitoring and updating of the student groups was required to add any newcomers and to formulate functioning groups into which students were engaged and equally distributed whenever possible. Furthermore, due to a significant minority of students who were either not attending or not engaging in group work, we received persistent requests for group changes. This posed a question of how to best ensure parity, as some students were asking to be put into friendship groups with other students. However, other students had legitimate concerns as they were in inactive groups with only one or two other students engaging in their group. Each request had to be considered individually as some students had already begun working.

During the lectures and seminars, we were aided by designated Student Associate Learning and Teaching (SALT) students, who were employed to help with the module delivery due to the large number of students. SALTs helped to facilitate the synchronous and asynchronous aspects of the delivery, including monitoring the discussion boards on the Learning Management System (LMS) and specifically a generic frequently asked questions (FAQ) discussion topic that students were invited to post their questions on. SALTs were trained to either answer some questions or escalate them to the teaching team. Another responsibility of SALTs was to monitor the Teams channels during the timetabled seminar sessions to check that the students had understood the task, and to provide support to simple technical difficulties. SALTs also supported the delivery of the synchronous expert lecturers by monitoring the Teams chat window, identifying relevant questions and comments of interest, and bringing them to the attention of the lecturers as appropriate. If there were any questions which they, themselves, could respond to, they replied to them directly during the chat and they brought to the attention of the module tutors the ones they could not reply to so that these could be addressed individually, or as a group, in the forthcoming session.

Demonstrating Interdisciplinary Metacognitive Thinking: Exploration of the Assessments

Our teaching emphasised problem-solving and critical thinking as evidenced by the learning content, active teaching methods, and student assessment outcomes. These learning approaches are necessary elements for developing interdisciplinary thinking and, although often native to disciplinary teaching, they are normally considered in isolation. However, it remains a challenge to encourage students to learn outside their own disciplinary area of expertise (Golding & Baik, 2013). Nevertheless, assessment is the most practical way students can highlight their learning (Butler et al., 2005) in a structured approach, as dictated by the requirements of the disciplines. For these reasons, the assessment for this module included a team technology assessment, an individual work of fiction, and a personal reflection. What follows is a description of how the assessments worked in practice, and an exploration of effectiveness of the assessments for interdisciplinary learning in relation to the IMT model, corroborated by the student case study.

Narrated Media and Personal Reflections

For their personal reflections, students produced a video recording created as a narrated PowerPoint slideshow, or by using any screen capture software. The goal of this assignment was for students to recognise their own learning in the module with a focus on interdisciplinarity. The reflection was guided by providing the students with a PowerPoint template built using Gibb's (1988) reflection cycle that was further elaborated in terms of the impact of technology on society. First, students were asked to describe their technology application of choice establishing the pertinent disciplines or points of view and reflecting on their feelings and thoughts on the likely impact to society. We then asked them to identify the advantages and disadvantages of the technology application and establish the context and boundaries of the situation. Finally, they had to discuss critically what they had learned with reference to interdisciplinary approaches, and what they could take forward and apply to their future studies.

Although some students found this assignment challenging, overall, they performed as expected, with most students achieving the minimum requirements of the learning outcomes and a good percentage performing exceptionally as evidenced by the overall grade distribution. However, it was noticeable that even high-performing students found it hard to overtly associate their reflections with interdisciplinary learning. Students generally struggled to articulate how different disciplines may contribute to explore the implications of their technology application of choice to society.

The following extract from the student self-reflection case study shows how they integrated their own *Subject Knowledge* to form a notion of interdisciplinarity, which they used to inform their own disciplinary area of Civil Engineering. The case study shows how reflection may be used to facilitate understanding of wicked problems in Engineering, which fundamentally require multi-disciplinary and cross-disciplinary approaches. The case study, *Academic Skills and Reflexivity*, shows that reflection helped the student to see solutions to Civil Engineering problems in new ways. The case study provides useful questions to include in our reflective template for students to use as a guide. This gives a practical illustration of Gibbs' (1988) model, which when viewed in isolation is an abstract concept. More specifically, the questions we will use in the future to guide student reflection will include *What problem did you solve?* and *What are the perspectives of different stakeholders on this problem?* These questions will help students see the complexity of technological transformation and the benefits of these approaches to their own discipline.

The module allowed me to develop my interdisciplinary skills in engineering disciplines to explore the challenges within sustainability, politics, economy, technology, and the environment, which evoke contrast with stakeholders from different disciplines working together. For example, integrating parking for electric vehicles (EV) in public car parks saves funds for local authorities, and fosters public acceptance of the technology.

From an educational perspective, the consensus is that technology generally tends to cross many traditional borders, including social sciences, politics, engineering, and e-commerce. For example, statistical inference algorithms allow businesses to predict market trends and consumer purchasing habits by revealing patterns and correlations in increasing business revenue, market position, and growth to distinguish a reasonably limited form of interdisciplinary practice.

Having considered these developments, I decided to use a new approach where I cross-integrated, seemingly, unrelated disciplinary knowledge such as product design. For example, lamppost integrated electric charging stations that allowed me to integrate disciplinary approaches to one another. I demonstrated how innovations among disciplines could be explained through interdisciplinarity, through a fused process that is redefining the traditional understanding of each discipline.

Technology Assessment and Group Work

The technology assessment was based on positivist scientific methods such as evidence-based risk analysis to identify the risks of the students' chosen technology, both ethical and legal, and the implications to the wider societal wellbeing. This assessment was designed to give students an insight into one way of exploring the wicked problem in a practical way, by illustrating the important and critical issues around technological solutions and explaining ways of how the undesired implications, or risks, could be eliminated or mitigated.

Students were given the opportunity to select an emerging technology and to apply it to the context or situation of choice. This allowed them to explore their own interests and created an opportunity to seek out and explore real-world problems (Ashby & Exter, 2019). The learning outcomes of the technology assessment were designed to assess students' critical thinking skills by requiring them to identify the potential advantages/disadvantages of an emerging technology and the likely impact on society. Students were also required to rate the disadvantages they had identified and explain how these could be managed or mitigated by undertaking a simplified risk analysis. By the time students had successfully completed the technology assessment, using the template provided, they had developed the necessary knowledge to evaluate the socio-economic and ethical-legal impact on society in the context of the situation, and in relation to the wider societal wellbeing.

The student reflection shows the extent of research conducted by the student to learn the *Subject Knowledge* to inform their technology assessment, which helped them see different perspectives and point of view about how to practically define one solution for the wicked problem. In future, we need to set the expectation to students that they will come to an understanding of the *Subject Knowledge* only by conducting some of their own research, and using a problem that is related to their own disciplinary area of expertise means they will already have a starting point for their research.

> I learned to critically evaluate research from both academic articles on technology and reports from international organisations, such as the United Nations. I found out that governments worldwide work together under the Paris Agreement (United Nations, 2016) to meet their global climate change agendas. Of particular interest were public transport interventions that reduced carbon emissions and more specifically by using big data to optimise service delivery. After considering the literature I realised that tensions exist among critical stakeholders due to lack of identified outcomes for relevant policies to promote energy-saving transport services.

> Reflecting on my technology report, I could have improved by considering the perspective of these critical global stakeholders who organise closely and widely the sustainable infrastructure and critically analyse their aims and objectives in more depth. Organisations such as network operators, regulatory organisations, innovative organisations, International Road Transport Union (IRTU) led by the United Nations Economic Commission for Europe (ECE/UNECE) can work together to contribute towards achieving the UN Sustainable Development Goals.

Fiction Writing and Creativity

For the fiction assessment, students drafted a story set in a near-future world to illustrate insight into a human perspective of technology and explore its impact on behaviour, emotions, and beliefs. Students were expected to apply the same technology application to both the fiction and technology assessments. By successfully integrating knowledge, students appreciated how the seemingly disparate approaches of evidence-based risk analysis and fiction writing could be combined to communicate the risks of their technology application to an individual or society in general.

Students were encouraged to see fiction writing as a tool to help them reflect on individual attitudes, multiple perspectives, and beliefs about technology and challenge prior assumptions (Jarvis, 2019) with the main objective being to create empathy for a specific character and bring feelings about the technology into consciousness through imagination (Dirkx, 2001). By evaluating the general risks of technology and exploring their impact on fictional characters, students viewed the complex issue through different lenses. Our aim was to enhance students' understanding of issues around technology and have a transformational impact on their learning (Martin, 2008). The fiction assignment was designed to assess the creativity learning outcome by nurturing students' imagination of how and why new technologies may form a part of, and change, peoples' lives, and communicate their findings through fiction in an accessible way that could stimulate further discussion and debate.

Nurturing creativity requires a degree of freedom and flexibility to allow students to express their thinking in innovative ways. However, as their contributions had to be assessed against the learning outcomes, clear descriptions of the marking standards (Dunne et al., 2005) were provided in the form of a qualitative rubric. This marking scheme was designed to be universally applicable but also flexible enough to reward original thinking and individual expression when evaluated against a set of common criteria. Assessment criteria were provided from the outset so that students could review their own work and develop it further when needed (Stevens & Levi, 2013). As students were new to interdisciplinary methods, it was important to guide them through the process by implementing good assessment practices (Dunne et al., 2005). We implemented this by detailing the assignment aims and expectations, how the taught theory could be applied to practice, and by providing exemplars of good practice highlighting the type of work expected to meet the learning outcomes.

The student reflection below shows that *Subject Knowledge* was necessary to use in fiction as an effective problem-solving method, further helped by the degree of empathy with the specific character used in their work. We will incorporate these findings into the assignment description for future deliveries of the module, to emphasise the process of using *Subject Knowledge* to inform the creative process.

I explored situations where interdisciplinary studies developed limits and resistances, in my case, allowing critical stakeholders a position of policy influence. Design fiction allows us to act out a potential/plausible scenario where the story shows limits in power and influence between interdisciplinarity and alternative approaches to innovate new disciplines.

My character, the 'actor' or 'conservator', holds an influential position that is willing to adapt for interdisciplinary legal enforcement towards sustainable EV transport by enabling new approaches and strategies to integrate law and policy enforcement. I used the concept of AI optimisation in public transport, allowing me to factor in personal knowledge from project-based modules, which allowed further insights and ideas for research into the discipline of Civil Engineering.

The frame of reference used was based on related papers that represented a form of literature mapping of specific identifiable researched works previously and presently within a segmentation or key term topics. The review of the literature enabled me to reference original work in support of interdisciplinary studies based on evidence of published academic work.

Conclusion and Recommendations

As this was the first iteration of the module delivery, further analysis is required to extrapolate evidence for ongoing improvement. An initial analysis of the student assessment artefacts, the module evaluation survey, and student feedback has identified areas in need of further investigation. These initial findings have already instigated changes in our practice and identified areas for further research and development. The findings are summarised below under the headings of our IMT model:

- In general, and in various degrees, students found it hard to identify and associate with alternative *Subject Knowledge Domain (s)* although they were mostly comfortable with their own. This indicated that further targeted work is needed for students to appreciate the nature, and necessity, of interdisciplinary approaches.
- Students exhibited various degrees of competency in *Academic Skills and Reflexivity,* but this was not deemed to be related to the interdisciplinary nature of the module and was attributed to the variability of the academic potential of the cohort.
- We found the *Digital Capabilities* of students to be adequate in relation to the requirements of this module, as most of them were able to produce an audio-visual asset to communicate their work. In some limited circumstances, students reported problems with the use of technology, but on further investigation we attributed these to limitations or malfunctions of the technology, rather than student competency.
- A wide variety of interpretations and student behaviours was evidenced in the assessment artefacts and was identified as *Social-emotional Wellbeing and Life Capabilities,* an area of significant importance that merits further investigation to uncover any latent socio-emotional factors.

In conclusion, this work on Interdisciplinary Learning Design uncovered areas for further research and improvement. Students do not seem to readily understand interdisciplinary concepts and further work is needed to optimise and improve learning, teaching, and assessment practices. However, there is ample evidence that students have much to gain by experiencing and developing interdisciplinary thinking.

Points to Consider

Readers of this chapter may wish to consider:

- Using interdisciplinary metacognitive thinking
- Including a range of assessment formats
- Using fiction writing to assess creativity

References

Amazon (2022). *Just Walk Out*. Retrieved 5 July 2024, from https://justwalkout.com/

Anglia Ruskin University (ARU) (2018). Education Strategy 2018–2022. Anglia Ruskin University.

Ashby, I., & Exter, M. (2019). Designing for interdisciplinarity in higher education: Considerations for instructional designers. *TechTrends*, *63*(2), 202–208. https://doi.org/10.1007/s11528-018-0352-z

Baxter, P., & Brown, E. (2018). *Education strategy: Ruskin modules*. Anglia Ruskin University.

Boix Mansilla, V., & Duraisingh, E. D. (2007). Targeted assessment of students' interdisciplinary work: An empirically grounded framework proposed. *The Journal of Higher Education*, *78*(2), 215–237. https://doi.org/10.1080/00221546.2007.11780874

Butler, S., Stonewater, J., & Kinney, J. (2005). The application of an assessment model to a costume history course: A case study. *Clothing and Textiles Research Journal*, *23*(4), 333–349. https://doi.org/10.1177/0887302X0502300413

Cambridge Assessment (2015). *Getting started with metacognition*. Cambridge International Examinations. Retrieved 5 July 2024, from https://cambridge-community.org.uk/professional-development/gswmeta/index.html

Czerniak, C. M. (2007). Interdisciplinary science teaching. In S. K. Abell, & L.G. Norman (Eds.), *Handbook of research on science education* (pp. 537–560). Routledge. Retrieved 5 July 2024, from https://www.routledge.com/Handbook-of-Research-on-Science-Education/Abell-Lederman/p/book/9780805847147

Darbellay, F. (2019). From interdisciplinarity to postdisciplinarity: Extending Klein's thinking into the future of the university. *Issues in Interdisciplinary Studies*, *37*(2), 90–109. Retrieved 5 July 2024, from https://files.eric.ed.gov/fulltext/EJ1248672.pdf

Dirkx, J. M. (2001). The power of feelings: Emotion, imagination, and the construction of meaning in adult learning. *New Directions for Adult and Continuing Education*, *89*, 63–72. https://doi.org/10.1002/ace.9

Dunne, L., Morgan, C., O'Reilly, M., & Parry, S. (2005). *Student assessment handbook: New directions in traditional and online assessment*. Routledge.

Gero, A. (2014). Enhancing systems thinking skills of sophomore students: An introductory project in electrical engineering. *International Journal of Engineering Education*, *30*(3), 738–745.

Gibbs, G. (1988). *Learning by doing: A guide to teaching and learning methods*. FEU. Retrieved 5 July 2024, from https://thoughtsmostlyaboutlearning.files.wordpress.com/2015/12/learning-by-doing-graham-gibbs.pdf

Golding, C., & Baik, C. (2013). Interdisciplinary assessment: The challenge of interdisciplinary learning and teaching. In L. Clouder, C. Broughan, S. Jewell, & G. Steventon (Eds.), *Improving student engagement and development through assessment: Theory and practice in higher education* (pp. 138–149). Routledge. https://doi.org/10.4324/9780203817520

Gómez Puente, S. M., van Eijck, M., & Jochems, W. (2015). Professional development for design-based learning in engineering education: A case study. *European Journal of Engineering Education*, *40*(1), 14–31. https://doi.org/10.1080/03043797.2014.903228

Gütl, C., & Chang, V. (2008). Ecosystem-based theoretical models for learning in environments of the 21st century. *International Journal of Emerging Technologies in Learning (iJET)*, *3*(1), 50–60. Retrieved 16 January 2025 from https://www.learntechlib.org/p/45192/

Jarvis, C. (2019). The educational power of fiction: An interdisciplinary exploration. In C. Jarvis, & P. Gouthro (Eds.), *Professional education with fiction media* (pp. 1–26). Springer International Publishing. https://doi.org/10.1007/978-3-030-17693-8_1

Khagram, S., Nicholas, K. A., Bever, D. M., Warren, J., Richards, E. H., Oleson, K., Kitzes, J., Katz, R., Hwang, R., Goldman, R., Funk, J., & Brauman, K. A. (2010). Thinking about knowing: Conceptual foundations for interdisciplinary environmental research. *Environmental Conservation, 37*(4), 388–397. https://doi.org/10.1017/S0376892910000809

Klaassen, R. G. (2021). Pedagogies of integration in challenge based or interdisciplinary education. In H.-U. Heiss, H.-M. Jarvinen, A. Mayer, & A. Schulz (Eds.), *Blended learning in engineering education: Challenging, enlightening – and lasting?: SEFI 2021* Conference TU Berlin, 13–16 September 2021. SEFI. Retrieved 5 July 2024, from https://pure.tudelft.nl/ws/portalfiles/portal/103000439/Pedagogies_of_integration_in_challenge_based_or_interdisciplinary_education.pdf

Klein, J. T. (1990). *Interdisciplinarity: History, theory, and practice.* Wayne State University Press.

Lakatos, I. (1970). Falsification and the methodology of scientific research programmes. In I. Lakatos, & A. Musgrave (Eds.), *Criticism and the growth of knowledge* (pp. 91–195). Cambridge University Press.

Lattuca, L., Knight, D., & Bergom, I. (2013). Developing a Measure of Interdisciplinary Competence for Engineers. In *2012 ASEE Annual Conference & Exposition Proceedings*. Retrieved 5 July 2024, from http://peer.asee.org/21173

Lattuca, L. R., Voigt, L. J., & Fath, K. Q. (2004). Does interdisciplinarity promote learning? Theoretical support and researchable questions. *The Review of Higher Education, 28*(1), 23–48. https://doi.org/10.1353/rhe.2004.0028

Martin, A. (2008). Digital literacy and the 'Digital society'. In C. Lankshear, M. Knobel, & M. Peters (Eds.), *Digital literacies: Concepts, policies and practices* (Vol. 30, pp. 151–176). Peter Lang Publishing Inc.

Menken, S., Keestra, M., Rutting, L., Post, G., de Roo, M., Blad, S., & de Greef, L. (2016). *An introduction to interdisciplinary research: Theory and practice.* https://doi.org/10.1515/9789048531615

Neubert, J., Lans, T., Mustafic, M., Greiff, S., & Ederer, P. (2017). Complex problem solving in a changing world: Bridging domain-specific and transversal competence demands in vocational education. In M. Mulder (Ed.), *Competence-based vocational education and professional education: Issues, concerns and prospects* (Vol. 23, pp. 953–969). Springer. https://doi.org/10.1007/978-3-319-41713-4_44

Newell, W. H. (2001). A theory of interdisciplinary studies. *Issues in Integrative Studies, 19*(1), 1–25. Retrieved 5 July 2024, from http://hdl.handle.net/10323/4378

Repko, A. F. (2007). Integrating interdisciplinarity: How the theories of common ground and cognitive interdisciplinary are informing the debate on interdisciplinary integration. *Issues in Integrative Studies, 25*, 1–31. Retrieved 5 July 2024, from https://interdisciplinarystudies.org/wp-content/issues/vol25_2007/03_Vol_25_pp_1_31.pdf

Scott, C. L. (2015). The futures of learning 3: What kind of pedagogies for the 21st century? In *Education research and foresight: Working papers*. United Nations Educational, Scientific and Cultural Organization (UNESCO). Retrieved 5 July 2024, from http://unesdoc.unesco.org/images/0024/002431/243126e.pdf

Stevens, D. D., & Levi, A. J. (2013). *Introduction to rubrics* (2nd ed.). Stylus Publications.

United Nations (UN) (2016). *The Paris Agreement: What is the Paris Agreement?*. Retrieved 5 July 2024, from https://unfccc.int/process-and-meetings/the-paris-agreement/the-paris-agreement

van den Akker, J. (2003). Curriculum perspectives: An introduction. In J. Akker, W. Kuiper, & U. Hameyer (Eds.), *Curriculum landscapes and trends.* Springer Netherlands. https://dx.doi.org/10.1007/978-94-017-1205-7_1

Veltman, M. E., van Keulen, J., & Voogt, J. M. (2020). Using problems with wicked tendencies as vehicles for learning in higher professional education: Towards coherent curriculum design. *The Curriculum Journal, 32,* pp. 559–583. https://doi.org/10.1002/curj.100

Chapter 14

Conclusion

Mark Warnes, Uwe Richter, Simon Pratt-Adams, and Elaine Brown

Introduction

The purpose of writing this book was to collect the contributors' experiences of developing and delivering interdisciplinary breadth 'Ruskin' modules at ARU. Some elements of Ruskin Modules (RM) are unique, especially the decision to make them compulsory for all Level 5 (i.e., second year) undergraduates, deliver them online, and position them alongside course curricula rather than integrated within. Most interdisciplinary programmes in the UK make use of elective modules in different courses which can be chosen by students from other courses (Hallett, 2024). Some of these options can form thematic clusters or pathways, such as modules on similar topics over three years. ARU, however, offers few electives, making this approach unavailable. Furthermore, as ARU is a regional university with (then) two main campuses, online delivery was logistically the best option.

Other instances of interdisciplinary courses often involve the rebranding of joint or combined honours degrees, such as the *Interdisciplinary Programmes* course at the University of Bristol (2024), the *Interdisciplinary Course* at the University of Durham (2024), and *Interdisciplinary Studies* at the University of St Andrews (2024). However, in these examples, it is unclear how much synergy exists between the combined disciplines to make the courses interdisciplinary. The nearest resemblance to the approach taken by ARU is at the London School of Economics and Political Science (LSE), where the *LSE100* is 'an interdisciplinary course taken by all first-year undergraduate students as part of [their] degree programme' (LSE, 2024a, para. 1). *LSE100* consists of assessed 'half units' (LSE, 2024b) integrated into undergraduate programmes.

RM philosophy rests on three pillars of interdisciplinarity, sustainability, and employability, and while each RM contains variations on these themes, the ethos is maintained throughout. Part 1 of the book sets the scene by introducing the central concepts of disciplinarities (i.e., mono-, cross-, multi-, inter-, and trans-disciplinarity) and transformative education, a history of the RM scheme from inception to deployment, and an exploration of a core element

DOI: 10.4324/9781003474593-16

of RM CPD, the *Ruskin Module Open Studios.* The case studies in Part 2 comprise a collection of eight sample modules representing the diverse range of RMs devised and delivered by passionate Trailblazers. In this final chapter, we bring together the issues that framed discussions and debates about the value of interdisciplinary breadth modules presented in this book.

Lessons Learnt

Reflecting on the process to design and introduce RMs at ARU, several aspects stand out as working well, yet other parts of the process are subject to continuous improvements.

After introducing interdisciplinary breadth modules at the policy level, the university community was engaged at the grassroots level by inviting colleagues to express their interest in designing and facilitating a RM. This led to proposals from enthusiastic and motivated colleagues who inspired students through these new modules. Many of these inspired students experienced transformative learning which led to new reflections on themselves and their futures. Many students also saw the benefit of skills learned in their RM that they could take back to their courses, future employment, and personal life.

However, the intention of fostering interdisciplinary teams of tutors to facilitate RMs and model interdisciplinary interactions has faced challenges in gaining widespread acceptance, despite our efforts to engage interested volunteers and seek direct support from faculties. Similarly, there has been limited uptake in the implementation of RMs that engage with real stakeholders, such as employers, councils, and other organisations, to address real-life complex 'wicked' problems. Overcoming the logistical hurdles of organising interdisciplinary teaching teams and collaborating with external stakeholders remains a key area for development.

Naming the RM Leaders as 'Trailblazers' established them (both between themselves and within ARU) as a community of innovators. As explored in Chapter 11, regular meetings of this community led to strong peer-to-peer support and sharing of resources, such as contracts for teamwork and marking rubrics.

However, as a new initiative it has taken time to bed RMs into the fabric of the university and to address resistance from staff who have found it difficult to buy into the rationale behind RMs and how student outcomes connect with their course modules. Similarly, despite offering students the opportunity to share and apply their disciplinary knowledge and skills in new ways, some still do not understand how RMs relate to their courses. It is, therefore, part of an ongoing strategic plan, continuous professional development, and sharing of innovative practices evolving from RMs, to further embed the competencies related to interdisciplinarity, sustainability, and employability as relevant throughout all course curricula rather than just covered by RMs. Echoing findings by Lyall et al. (2015), recent research (Richter & Warnes, 2024) into the interdisciplinary nature of RMs confirms that active collaborative learning and teaching approaches and authentic activities and assessments are prerequisites for embedding interdisciplinarity into the wider curriculum. However, online delivery has been identified as a challenging environment for active collaborative, interdisciplinary learning, and ARU is exploring other delivery forms such as blended learning.

Current Developments

The relevance of interdisciplinarity in Higher Education, especially in research, is growing. The London Interdisciplinary School (LIS) was set up in 2017 and received degree awarding powers in 2021 based on 'a core belief: [that] the 21st-century leader requires a broad set of interdisciplinary approaches and methods to tackle the world's most complex problems' (LIS, 2024, section 6 para. 3). While an innovative higher education concept, the LIS faced challenges including regulation 'geared towards single-discipline approaches' (Rowsell, 2024, para. 3), the lack of interdisciplinary learning outcomes, and 'winning recognition and status in the conservative and hierarchical UK higher education system' (Rowsell, 2024, para. 5). Nevertheless, the rationale for LIS highlights the deficit of higher education, which does not necessarily focus on equipping students for a complex world which requires thinking beyond disciplinary boundaries.

While the COVID-19 pandemic accentuated the need for interdisciplinary research to solve complex and urgent global problems (Eng-Chye, 2020; Thain, 2021), a recent Times Higher Education (THE) research project in partnership with Schmidt Science Fellows (Daley & Hantrais, 2024; Morgan, 2023) found 'that universities are not walking the talk on interdisciplinary science, with about a third of participating global universities failing to reward staff for cross-disciplinary research or to measure the success of such work' (Bothwell, 2023, para. 1). Other substantial obstacles include the lack of reward and promotion for interdisciplinary researchers, discipline-focused academic regulations, and the logistics of creating and delivering interdisciplinary curricula (Brown, 2024; Goodman, 2023; Marshall, 2022; Upton, 2023).

Interdisciplinary learning and teaching is promoted, both nationally and globally, via networks such as Interdisciplinary Learning and Teaching UK (2024) and the Interdisciplinary Learning Network (2024). Similarly, the University College for Interdisciplinary Learning at the University of Manchester (2024), ARU's Interdisciplinary Education Network (ARU, 2023a), and LSE's (2024b) interdisciplinary student research conference, *Knowledge Beyond Boundaries*, are university-level initiatives to develop interdisciplinary teaching and research.

Looking Ahead

The primary purpose of this book is to demonstrate how interdisciplinary breadth modules were implemented in one university and how they may be adapted to other higher education settings. As a result, each case study includes practical ideas to assist readers in considering the option of adopting and adapting our approaches to suit their own context.

The next steps for RMs are to increase the number of modules from which students can choose, increase interdisciplinary team teaching to widen the number of disciplinary perspectives covered, and model disciplinary integration. RMs are based on complex social challenges and work has commenced to source these challenges from ARU's Research Institutes and external organisations.

More broadly, ARU has welcomed the transformative learning experienced by RM students and wants to expand this transformative approach across the curriculum, including an exploration of the feasibility of interdisciplinary undergraduate major projects. Research into the characteristics and components of this transformative approach is underway with initial findings presented by students in their keynote address at the Interdisciplinary Learning and Teaching (UK) Conference in April 2023 at ARU (ARU, 2023b).

The case studies in this book are based on the authors' experiences of delivering the first iteration of RMs in the 2021 academic year. In September 2024, ARU began delivering the fourth iteration, and RMs are well on the way to becoming an established stage in the undergraduate learning journey at ARU. The range of RMs from which students can choose has changed over the years with some originals continuing, some ending, and new modules introduced.

We hope this book sparks your imagination and motivates and inspires you to design and develop your own interdisciplinary breadth modules with the potential to significantly transform and improve the educational journeys and future prospects of students.

References

Anglia Ruskin University (ARU) (2023a). *Interdisciplinary Education Network*. Retrieved June 11, 2024, from https://www.aru.ac.uk/anglia-learning-and-teaching/interdisciplinary-education

Anglia Ruskin University (ARU) (2023b). *Interdisciplinary Learning and Teaching (UK) Conference 2023*. Retrieved 23 July 2024, from https://www.aru.ac.uk/anglia-learning-and-teaching/interdisciplinary-conference

Bothwell, E. (2023). Universities 'paying lip service' to interdisciplinary research. *Times Higher Education*, 18 October. Retrieved 23 July 2024, from https://www.timeshighereducation.com/depth/universities-paying-lip-service-interdisciplinary-research

Brown, R. A. (2024). University hiring must be centrally organised around interdisciplinarity. *Times Higher Education*, 30 January. Retrieved 23 July 2024, from https://www.timeshighereducation.com/opinion/university-hiring-must-be-centrally-organised-around-interdisciplinarity

Daley, C., & Hantrais, L. (2024). A ranking for interdisciplinarity is a poor measure for the quality of research and teaching in universities. *LSE Impact blog*, 17 January. Retrieved 23 July 2024, from https://blogs.lse.ac.uk/impactofsocialsciences/2024/01/17/a-ranking-for-interdisciplinarity-is-a-poor-measure-for-the-quality-of-research-and-teaching-in-universities/

Eng-Chye, T. (2020). It's time to rebuild the university on a foundation of interdisciplinarity. *Times Higher Education*, 28 June. Retrieved 23 July 2024, from https://www.timeshighereducation.com/blog/its-time-rebuild-university-foundation-interdisciplinarity

Goodman, J. R. (2023). Real interdisciplinarity would bridge the quantitative-qualitative divide. *Times Higher Education*, 18 June. Retrieved 23 July 2024, from https://www.timeshighereducation.com/blog/real-interdisciplinarity-would-bridge-quantitative-qualitative-divide

Hallett, R. (2024). Designing Challenge-based Interdisciplinary Education: Curriculum Structures and Hybrid Expertise (Keynote). *Interdisciplinary Learning and Teaching Conference 2024*, University of Manchester, 21 March. Retrieved 23 July 2024, from https://stories.manchester.ac.uk/interdisciplinaryconference/index.html

Interdisciplinary Learning Network (2024). *The Interdisciplinary Learning Network*. Retrieved 23 July 2024, from https://idlnetwork.substack.com/

Interdisciplinary Learning and Teaching UK (2024). *Interdisciplinary Learning and Teaching UK*. Retrieved 23 July 2024, from https://interdisciplinaryuk.net

London Interdisciplinary School (LIS) (2024). *Why We Are Here*. Retrieved 23 July 2024, from https://www.lis.ac.uk/about

London School of Economics and Political Science, The (LSE) (2024a). *About LSE100: The LSE Course*. The London School of Economics and Political Science. Retrieved 23 July 2024, from https://info.lse.ac.uk/current-students/lse100/about-lse-100

London School of Economics and Political Science, The (LSE) (2024b). *Knowledge beyond boundaries. LSE's interdisciplinary student research conference*. The London School of Economics and Political Science. Retrieved 23 July 2024, from https://info.lse.ac.uk/current-students/lse100/events/Knowledge-Beyond-Boundaries

Lyall, C., Meagher, L., Bandola Gill, J., & Kettle, A. (2015). *Interdisciplinary provision in higher education: Current context and future challenges*. University of Edinburgh. Retrieved 23 July 2024, from https://www.research.ed.ac.uk/files/23462207/Lyall_et_al_2015.pdf

Marshall, S. (2022). Interdisciplinary research should be central to student experience. *Times Higher Education*, 27 August. Retrieved 23 July 2024, from https://www.timeshighereducation.com/blog/interdisciplinary-research-should-be-central-student-experience

Morgan, J. (2023). 'Jealousy' and 'lack of community' hit interdisciplinary research. *Times Higher Education*, 26 September. Retrieved 23 July 2024, from https://www.timeshighereducation.com/news/jealousy-and-lack-community-block-multidisciplinary-research

Richter, U., & Warnes, M. (2024). Embedding interdisciplinarity into the curriculum: Findings from Ruskin modules. ARU Education Committee (Internal Report).

Rowsell, J. (2024). Interdisciplinary campus battles UK sector status quo. *Times Higher Education*, 28 June. Retrieved 23 July 2024, from https://www.timeshighereducation.com/news/interdisciplinary-campus-battles-uk-sector-status-quo

Thain, M. (2021). Post-pandemic recovery requires radical interdisciplinarity. *Times Higher Education*, 18 July. Retrieved 23 July 2024, from https://www.

timeshighereducation.com/blog/post-pandemic-recovery-requires-radical-interdisciplinarity

University of Bristol (2024). Interdisciplinary Programmes (Joint Honours). University of Bristol. Retrieved 23 July 2024, from https://www.bristol.ac.uk/academic-quality/approve/interdisciplinary-programmes/

University of Durham (2024). Interdisciplinary Courses (Combined Honours). University of Durham. Retrieved 23 July 2024, from https://www.durham.ac.uk/study/undergraduate/interdisciplinary-courses/

University of Manchester (2024). University College for Interdisciplinary Learning. University of Manchester. Retrieved 23 July 2024, from https://www.college.manchester.ac.uk/

University of St Andrews (2024). Interdisciplinary studies. University of St Andrews. Retrieved 23 July 2024, from https://www.st-andrews.ac.uk/subjects/interdisciplinary/

Upton, B. (2023). Interdisciplinarity lacks clout to keep its cash. *Times Higher Education*, 05 April. Retrieved 23 July 2024, from https://www.timeshighereducation.com/news/interdisciplinarity-lacks-clout-keep-its-cash

Index

For Product Safety Concerns and Information please contact our EU representative GPSR@taylorandfrancis.com
Taylor & Francis Verlag GmbH, Kaufingerstraße 24, 80331 München, Germany